Unbreakable

Unbreakable

50 Goals in 39 Games

Wayne Gretzky and the Story of

Hockey's Greatest Record

Mike Brophy & Todd Denault

McCLELLAND & STEWART

Library and Archives Canada Cataloguing in Publication is available upon request

ISBN: 978-0-7710-1755-1
ebook ISBN: 978-0-7710-1756-8

Published simultaneously in the United States of America by
McClelland & Stewart, a division of Penguin Random House Canada Limited,
a Penguin Random House Company

Library of Congress Control Number is available upon request

Cover photograph © Doug Griffin / Toronto Star / Getty Images
Caption: December 31, 1981: He did it!: Wayne Gretzky of Edmonton Oilers celebrates one of five goals he scored last night against Philadelphia; giving him a record of 50 in 39 games; a new National Hockey League standard.

Typeset in Bembo by M&S, Toronto

Printed and bound in the USA

McClelland & Stewart,
a division of Penguin Random House Canada Limited,
a Penguin Random House Company

www.penguinrandomhouse.ca

1   2   3   4   5   20   19   18   17   16

Penguin
Random
House

I dedicate this book to the most amazing sisters a brother could ask for, Lori Brophy and Denise Smith. Your love and support are appreciated and overwhelming!

— MB

I dedicate this book to my brother, Kent,
who was one of Wayne Gretzky's earliest supporters, and whose admiration of all things 99 has never wavered. Luv Ya, Bro!

— TCD

Contents

1   **Introduction**

20   **Game 1 | October 7, 1981**
Vs. Colorado Rockies

29   **Game 2 | October 9, 1981**
Vs. Vancouver Canucks

34   **Game 3 | October 10, 1981**
Vs. Los Angeles Kings

42   **Game 4 | October 14, 1981**
Vs. Winnipeg Jets

48   **Game 5 | October 16, 1981**
Vs. Calgary Flames

52   **Game 6 | October 18, 1981**
Vs. Chicago Black Hawks

57   **Game 7 | October 20, 1981**
Vs. Calgary Flames

62   **Game 8 | October 21, 1981**
Vs. Hartford Whalers

67   **Game 9 | October 23, 1981**
Vs. Pittsburgh Penguins

72   **Game 10 | October 24, 1981**
Vs. Colorado Rockies

78   **Game 11 | October 27, 1981**
Vs. New York Islanders

84   **Game 12 | October 28, 1981**
Vs. New York Rangers

89   **Game 13 | October 31, 1981**
Vs. Quebec Nordiques

95   **Game 14 | November 4, 1981**
Vs. Toronto Maple Leafs

100   **Game 15 | November 7, 1981**
Vs. Colorado Rockies

105   **Game 16 | November 11, 1981**
Vs. Hartford Whalers

109   **Game 17 | November 12, 1981**
Vs. Boston Bruins

114   **Game 18 | November 14, 1981**
Vs. New York Islanders

120   **Game 19 | November 15, 1981**
Vs. New York Rangers

125   **Game 20 | November 17, 1981**
Vs. St. Louis Blues

129   **Game 21 | November 19, 1981**
Vs. Minnesota North Stars

133   **Game 22 | November 21, 1981**
Vs. Vancouver Canucks

138   **Game 23 | November 23, 1981**
Vs. Detroit Red Wings

145   **Game 24 | November 25, 1981**
Vs. Los Angeles Kings

151   **Game 25 | November 27, 1981**
Vs. Chicago Black Hawks

155   **Game 26 | November 29, 1981**
Vs. Winnipeg Jets

161   **Game 27 | December 1, 1981**
Vs. Montreal Canadiens

167   **Game 28 | December 2, 1981**
Vs. Quebec Nordiques

173   **Game 29 | December 4, 1981**
Vs. Vancouver Canucks

177   **Game 30 | December 5, 1981**
Vs. Vancouver Canucks

182   **Game 31 | December 9, 1981**
Vs. Los Angeles Kings

187   **Game 32 | December 13, 1981**
Vs. New York Islanders

193   **Game 33 | December 16, 1981**
Vs. Colorado Rockies

197   **Game 34 | December 17, 1981**
Vs. Calgary Flames

204   **Game 35 | December 19, 1981**
Vs. Minnesota North Stars

211   **Game 36 | December 20, 1981**
Vs. Calgary Flames

219   **Game 37 | December 23, 1981**
Vs. Vancouver Canucks

223   **Game 38 | December 27, 1981**
Vs. Los Angeles Kings

229   **Game 39 | December 30, 1981**
Vs. Philadelphia Flyers

248   **His Only Competition is Himself**

273   **Epilogue**

278   **Sources**

282   **Acknowledgements**

283   **Index**

288   **About the Authors**

Introduction

n a sport where wins and losses are determined solely by the team that puts more pucks into the net, the simple act of scoring a goal has always held the highest prominence. The equivalent of a home run in baseball and a touchdown in football, a goal is unquestionably hockey's signature achievement. And for those players who score most often, there is an exalted status, a type of superstardom bestowed on them that dwarves all others. For generations, the most proficient goal scorers also have been hockey's leading men, with fans intently following their every move on the ice. A certain type of excitement clings to those elite goal scorers as fans impatiently anticipate their next goal. As a result, the number of goals scored has always been the sport's most watched statistic, and the top scorers have long been hockey's most celebrated and idolized players.

The adulation surrounding the act of scoring a goal helped make the 50-goal season the most glorified individual triumph in all of hockey. And in much the same way that Babe Ruth transformed hitting a home run into baseball's most popular play, in the 1940s and

1950s Maurice "Rocket" Richard took scoring a goal in hockey to a whole new level of importance and established the standard to which all future goal scorers would aspire.

There had been some outstanding goal scorers before the Rocket. In 1917–18, the NHL's first season, Joe Malone of the Montreal Canadiens posted an incredible 44 goals in just 20 games; and throughout the 1930s, in five different seasons, Toronto Maple Leafs superstar Charlie Conacher led the league in goals. But neither man sparked the excitement the electrifying Richard did. Not a very big man, nor blessed with a wealth of hockey skills, Richard possessed an intense drive and determination, and he channelled it all into one overwhelming obsession: scoring goals.

"That desperation he played with, it was God's gift," remarked teammate Dickie Moore, who skated alongside Richard in the 1950s. The Rocket "was gifted to score goals." That Richard scored in numbers never before seen—and elevated his performance in the games that mattered most—only further endeared him to the fans, who also appreciated his humbleness off the ice, which stood in stark contrast to his fire on it. "He was a hero in that the way he did things was heroic," said Frank Selke Jr., who served as the Canadiens publicity director during Richard's time with the team. "Everything he did had a different touch than what anybody else did."

In his second year in the NHL (and his first full season), skating alongside Toe Blake and Elmer Lach in the famed Punch Line, Richard scored 32 goals and won his first Stanley Cup. The next year, 1944–45, saw him pass Joe Malone's long-standing record of 44 goals in a season. And it was in the last game of the season, with only 2:15 remaining in the third and final period, that Richard, who always had a sense for the dramatic, scored his historic 50th goal.

Like Babe Ruth's single-season record of 60 home runs—set in 1927—Richard's achievement of 50 goals in a single NHL season was viewed at the time, and for a long period afterward, as a transcendent accomplishment. It not only elevated him to a loftier place in the hockey pantheon and established him as the dominant figure in the sport for his era, but it also bestowed on him the status of a living legend. Beyond that, the Rocket's performance firmly set the number 50 as the pinnacle for all goal scorers to come.

Richard himself played another 15 seasons, and his burgeoning legend would only grow larger. He won another seven Stanley Cups and led the league in goals four more times. But never again did he score 50 goals. Although, neither did anyone else in those years. Gordie Howe came closest, with 49 goals in 1952–53.

Ironically, in the year following Richard's retirement, 1960–61, one of his former teammates tied his record: Bernard "Boom Boom" Geoffrion finished the season with 50 goals. A year after that, Bobby Hull of the Chicago Black Hawks became part of the suddenly growing club by scoring 50 goals in the 1961–62 season. Supporters of Richard, however, were quick to point out that both Geoffrion and Hull had scored their 50 goals over the course of 70-game schedules, while the Rocket had scored his in one made up of 50 games.

An ongoing debate over the merits of both Geoffrion's and Hull's 50-goal seasons—when compared with Richard's—mirrored a dispute taking place in Major League Baseball at the same time. In the summer of 1961, the New York Yankees Roger Maris took direct aim at Babe Ruth's long-standing record of 60 home runs in a season. Eventually, the executives who ran baseball decreed that if Maris were to break Ruth's record, he had to do it in 154 games—the length of the schedule during Ruth's record-setting 1927 season. By one home run, Maris fell short of hitting the target imposed from above, but he bettered Ruth's season total by hitting his 61st home run in the 162nd (and last) game of the 1961 season. In the end, Maris's achievement was recognized in record books alongside Ruth's.

Echoes of the Ruth–Maris debate could be heard in the first few months of 1966, when Hull once again took aim at Richard's mark, this time setting a new single-season standard by scoring 54 goals. Not surprisingly, defenders of Richard demanded that the NHL follow baseball's lead and indicate that Hull's record was achieved in a 70-game schedule. And while the NHL refused that request, those who backed Richard argued that Hull had scored his 50th goal in Chicago's 57th game, and so had failed to surpass Richard's feat of 50 goals in 50 games. Hull scored 50 goals on three more occasions in his illustrious career, including when he set a new record with 58 goals in the 1968–69 season, but never again did he come close to matching the increasingly mythical 50 in 50.

Hull's successor as the game's preeminent goal scorer was Phil Esposito of the Boston Bruins. In the 1969–70 season, Esposito began an unprecedented six-year reign as the NHL's top goal scorer. In the second year of that run of dominance, Esposito set a new standard for goals scored in a single season. With 76 goals in 1970–71, he shattered Hull's previous record by 18 goals.

But, like Hull before him, Richard's 50-in-50 milestone repeatedly eluded Esposito. In his record-breaking 1970–71 season, he scored 45 goals in his first 50 games; he got 44 goals in 50 games in 1971–72, 46 in 50 in 1973–74, and finally 46 goals in 50 games in 1974–75.

Esposito wasn't the only one scoring goals at an increased rate throughout the early part of the 1970s, as a combination of rapid expansion, longer schedules, and the birth of the rival World Hockey Association (WHA) all contributed to a mass dilution of talent, with the end result being an evident reduction in the quality of the play and of the players, especially those who guarded the goal.

And just like that, the ranks of those players who had scored 50 goals in a single season, which up until 1970 had consisted of three players—Richard, Geoffrion, and Hull—swelled, as 18 more players reached the mark by the end of the decade. And while in the 1970s the list of 50-goal scorers included such superstar players as Esposito, Guy Lafleur, and Mike Bossy, more than a few players in that decade (including Danny Grant, Jean Pronovost, and Guy Chouinard, each of whom is largely forgotten today) achieved what was considered the greatest offensive achievement. Interestingly enough, this abundance of 50-goal scorers only served to increase the magnitude—in the eyes of the public, at least—of Richard's 50-in-50 achievement in 1944–45, and at the conclusion of the 1979–80 NHL season, 35 years after his record season, appreciation for his feat appeared to be as durable as ever.

And then, in the last month of 1980, unexpectedly, two serious threats simultaneously emerged to challenge Richard's increasingly revered 50 in 50. The challengers' names were Mike Bossy and Charlie Simmer. Both were young. Bossy, 23, was in the midst of his fourth NHL season, and Simmer, three years older, was competing in only his second full season in the league.

Of the two, Bossy was the far more visible and vocal. Chosen by the New York Islanders with the 15th-overall selection of the 1977 NHL Amateur Draft, he immediately caused waves throughout the hockey establishment with his bold prediction that he would score 50 goals in his rookie season. In the end, on his way to winning the

Calder Trophy as the NHL's rookie of the year, he backed up his statement by scoring 53 goals, a rookie record at the time. In his sophomore year, 1978–79, he proved that he wasn't a one-hit wonder, leading all NHL scorers with 69 goals. And while his third season in the NHL saw him "slump" to 51 goals, he was still a vital part of the Islanders' 1980 Stanley Cup championship team.

If Bossy had risen almost instantly into the ranks of elite NHL goal scorers, Simmer's path was more protracted. Drafted by the California Golden Seals with the 39th-overall selection of the 1974 NHL Amateur Draft, Simmer split his first three professional seasons between the Seals, one of the NHL's worst teams, and the Salt Lake Golden Eagles of the Central Professional Hockey League. The financially struggling Seals relocated to Cleveland in 1976, and Simmer remained little more than an afterthought at the NHL level. That began to change in 1977, when he was traded to the Los Angeles Kings. There, after shuffling between the American Hockey League's Springfield Indians and Los Angeles for a season and a half, he finally found a permanent spot on the Kings roster, due in no small part to the chemistry he established with teammates Marcel Dionne, who was widely regarded as one of the top players in the NHL, and Dave Taylor. Soon the three were given the moniker the Triple Crown Line, and they became one of the most potent offensive trios of the era. In 1979–80, Simmer's first full season in the NHL, he scored 56 goals.

This led right into the 1980–81 season, when both Bossy and Simmer would take direct aim at the fabled 50 in 50. While the chase garnered a tremendous amount of media attention, most of it focused solely on Bossy, who, before the season began, publicly proclaimed his desire to reach the 50 in 50. The more reserved Simmer shied away from much of the discussion. "I'd love to do it for sure," he admitted to the press, "but I'm not obsessed by it. It's amazing to me the way Mike puts pressure on himself. I don't enjoy that." As a result, Simmer's quest took a backseat to Bossy's—that is, until the evening of December 27, 1980, when Simmer scored his 38th and 39th goals (in 36 games), overtaking Bossy, who scored his 38th (in 38 games) the same night. Then the media began to cover the "competition" for the coveted 50 in 50.

As fate would have it, the competition reached its climax on Saturday, January 24, 1981. In a quirk of scheduling no doubt welcomed by the media and especially by the television networks, both Simmer and Bossy were scheduled to play their 50th games of the season that day, with Simmer's Kings squaring off against the Boston Bruins in the afternoon, while Bossy's Islanders hosted the Quebec Nordiques that night.

On what had the potential to be the biggest day of his professional career, Bossy began his morning by preparing a hot-cereal breakfast for his then 16-month-old daughter, Josiane. Going back to bed for a little extra sleep, he awoke in time to watch a televised broadcast of the Kings–Bruins game. As could be expected, his attention was entirely focused on Simmer, who entered the game with 46 goals in 49 games, and had the opportunity—however remote—to beat Bossy to the 50-in-50 throne, long occupied by only one other player: Maurice Richard.

As Bossy closely watched, in the game's first 37 minutes Simmer failed to direct a single shot at, much less put a goal past, Bruins goalie Jim Craig. But then—as he had done so many times before—stationed on his own at the edge of the opposing goalie's crease, he notched goal number 47 with a tap-in on a Kings power play. Then, at the start of the third period, in an almost identical situation, he scored goal number 48. Helplessly, nervously, watching from his home in Long Island, Bossy began to squirm in his chair. "I really didn't think he'd get four goals when I tuned in," Bossy later admitted, "but then I began to wonder." Simmer scored a third goal—number 49—into an empty net after the Bruins pulled Craig for an extra attacker, but by then there was only a single second remaining in the game.

And as that second ticked off the clock, Simmer settled for 49 goals in 50 games. "I'm disappointed I came so close and didn't make it," he told reporters in the dressing room following the game, "but getting 50 in 50 games had never been uppermost in my mind. If Mike can do it, more power to him."

Unlike Simmer, the thought of "getting 50 in 50" had always been uppermost in Mike Bossy's mind. Before the season began, he had shared privately with his friends that 50 goals in 50 games was the individual feat that he wanted to accomplish more than any other. As the season wore on, and after he had scored 34 goals in 35 games, 38 in 38, and 40 in 41, the media attention intensified, especially after Bossy went public with his goal, declaring that "Rocket's record is what I'm aiming for."

And thus began the so-called "Bossy Watch" as more than 20 reporters from other NHL cities collectively flew into New York for that night's game, all of them hoping to catch a glimpse of hockey history. The Islanders even offered to cover Richard's expenses if he would join in the festivities. The Rocket gracefully declined, but not before wishing Bossy the best of luck in his quest.

Bossy's objective of reaching 50 in 50 had started to look like a real possibility 11 days earlier, on January 13, when he had scored four goals in an outburst against the Pittsburgh Penguins, and on

January 17 he followed up this performance with a hat trick against the Washington Capitals. By game 47, Bossy had 48 goals. In game 48, and with the hockey world carefully watching his every move, the Islanders soundly defeated the visiting Calgary Flames, 5–0—but in defeat the Flames could claim a moral victory as Bossy failed to score a goal. Such was their success in that respect that some whisperers suggested that the Flames had made winning a secondary ambition—on this particular night, at least—to stopping Bossy.

Game number 49 took place two nights later in Detroit. With the collective attention of the hockey media and fans fixed squarely on him, Bossy was once again held without a goal. Unlike the game against the Flames, though, he could point to a couple of lost opportunities, including a foiled two-on-one rush, and two missed shots at an empty net.

So with Bossy held at 48 goals, and with Simmer's quest for the 50 in 50 over, the eyes of the hockey world, and the gaggle of reporters that formed the Bossy Watch, turned their attention to the Nassau Veterans Memorial Coliseum on Long Island on the night of January 24, 1981, to see whether Mike Bossy could score two goals against the Quebec Nordiques and equal the Rocket's magical 50 in 50. The pressure on Bossy was intense, although a group of appreciative fans tried their best to diffuse the tension by having a bouquet of 51 yellow and red roses delivered to the Islanders dressing room before the game.

Like Simmer earlier that same day, Bossy was a non-factor through the game's first two periods. Despite his teammates' best and repeated efforts to set him up and his coach giving him more ice time than usual, Bossy entered the dressing room 40 minutes into the game without a single shot on goal.

"I wasn't doing anything right," Bossy later admitted. "It was like my hands were taped together. I was thinking I wasn't going to get [the 50 in 50], not even a shot. I had the feeling I was never going to score again. And the thing is, I was the one who had made such a big thing out of this. I was so afraid of coming back in the room after the game without that record. I would've been embarrassed. But then I realized that the biggest thing was not to give anyone the satisfaction of saying I didn't try."

Reinvigorated, throughout the third period Bossy fired shot after shot at Quebec goaltender Ron Grahame, but he was still unable to put one past the netminder. With a little over five minutes remaining in the game, the clock, along with the Nordiques goalie, had become the biggest obstacles to the next 50 in 50.

And then suddenly, with the Islanders on the power play, a loose puck fired at the net somehow found the back end of Bossy's stick as he jostled amongst a cluster of players in front of the Nordiques goal. And just like that, Bossy directed it into the back of the net for goal number 49.

Later on, Bossy freely admitted that he had almost given up any hope of scoring the 50 in 50, but with number 49 out of the way, and time ticking away, he quickly realized that it was now or never. Returning to the ice with less than two minutes left in the game, Bossy veered to the left as the Islanders gained the Nordiques blue line. There, Nordiques defenceman Dave Pichette attempted to clear the puck, but was thwarted when it unintentionally deflected off of Islanders forward John Tonelli and went directly to Bossy's teammate Bryan Trottier near the right boards.

All alone in the left circle, and afraid that Trottier couldn't see him, Bossy hollered for the puck. He needn't have bothered.

"I saw him," said Trottier, whose swift and hard pass came to a rest on the blade of Bossy's stick. And with his patented quick flick of the wrist, Bossy fired the puck right between Grahame's legs for the goal that tied the Rocket's record.

In an instant, Bossy found himself on par with the legendary Rocket. Already on a level with the game's greatest-ever goal scorers, Bossy added another layer of prestige to the 50 in 50 by becoming only the second player to reach the famed mark. Bossy's stunning performance topped many of that night's news broadcasts, received front-page coverage in the next day's newspapers, and was widely celebrated, almost immediately, as not only one of hockey's greatest moments, but as one of the sport's greatest feats, the duplication of a record considered by many impossible to reach.

It had taken over 35 years, but the sacred 50 goals in 50 games had finally been achieved again. Amidst the postgame celebration, a relieved and elated Bossy was handed a telegram from the Rocket himself, which read: "Congratulations from an old recordman to a young recordman. And tons of goals for years to come. I knew one day my record would be surpassed or tied but I had always hoped that it would be done by the player . . . that I have admired from the start."

What no one could have known at the time was that, within less than 12 months, the 50-in-50 standard would be shattered.

———

In late September 1981, Wayne Gretzky took to a secluded Florida condo for five days with a couple of close friends. Barely anyone, including his parents, knew he was there, and he preferred it that way. He was 20 years old and, in the opinion of many, the best hockey player in the world. And yet inside that darkened and isolated condo, he struggled to come to terms with what he would later refer to as "far and away the worst experience I've ever had in hockey."

Despite being barely a year removed from his teens, Gretzky had spent the last decade, roughly half of his life, in the public spotlight. As a 10-year-old, novice-aged player in his hometown of Brantford, Ontario, he had garnered nationwide attention by scoring an astonishing 378 goals in only 85 games. He became the target of autograph hunters and those seeking him out for interviews, which he accepted without complaint. A child prodigy in skates, by the age of 13 he was believed already to have scored over a thousand goals in his fledgling career. Four years later, following a year-long stint in the Ontario Major Junior Hockey League with the Sault Ste. Marie Greyhounds, a 17-year-old Gretzky decided to turn professional, signing a seven-year personal-services contract worth $1.75 million US with the Indianapolis Racers of the WHA.

Gretzky's time in Indianapolis turned out to be far shorter than that. In fact, he played only eight games for the club. Needing a quick financial infusion, Racers owner Nelson Skalbania, through a complicated deal that combined real estate and cash, ended up selling the teenaged prodigy to Peter Pocklington, owner of the WHA's Edmonton Oilers, on November 2, 1978. Re-signed by Pocklington to a 10-year personal-services contract a few months later, Gretzky quickly emerged as the Oilers' leading offensive force, capturing rookie-of-the-year honours in what turned out to be the WHA's final season.

In 1979, the NHL absorbed the Oilers and three other WHA teams. Many within the hockey establishment predicted that the small-in-stature, waifish-looking Gretzky would struggle in what was considered by most to be a league with bigger, stronger, and more talented players. Instead, Gretzky thrived in his first NHL season, tying Marcel Dionne for the league lead in points (137) and becoming the youngest player to ever score 50 goals in a season. At the end of that first year, he was awarded the Hart Trophy as the NHL's most valuable player.

Gretzky repeated his performance as scoring champion in 1980–81 season, and received the Hart Trophy again that year, but his accomplishments didn't end there. His 164 points that season set a new league record (surpassing Phil Esposito's 152, set in 1970–71), as did his 109 assists (breaking Bobby Orr's mark of 102, also set in 1970–71).

No player in hockey history had enjoyed such a start to his professional career. And yet there were critics like Stan Fischler, who dubbed Gretzky "Mr. Waynderful" in the pages of the *Hockey News*, who suggested that the combined offensive and defensive skills of the New York Islanders' Bryan Trottier made him a more valuable player. On his Hamilton-based television show, Dick Beddoes, formerly of the *Globe and Mail* newspaper, repeatedly bashed Gretzky by openly questioning whether he could have achieved any of his scoring feats in the old six-team NHL.

The accolades and criticism served to heighten the drama surrounding the 1981 Canada Cup. This star-studded tournament, a best-on-best affair involving the world's top six hockey nations, represented Gretzky's first experience playing at such a high, international level, and as such the pressure on him, and on Team Canada as a whole, was intense. A state of affairs that Gretzky himself, was well aware of.

"All of us on this team must realize that we're playing the next four years in the next month," said Gretzky on the eve of Team Canada's training camp. "If we win, then everything will be okay because the Canadian fans expect us to win. But if we lose, we're going to hear a great deal about it for the next four years, or at least until the next big tournament like this."

In the beginning, everything went according to script, as Canada pummelled Finland in their first game of the tournament, 9–0, with Gretzky, playing on a line with Guy Lafleur and Gilbert Perreault, scoring two goals and adding an assist. The next game was more of the same as Gretzky had two goals and two assists in Canada's 8–3 win over the United States. Canada's third game of the tournament told a different story, however, as Gretzky was held off the score sheet in the team's 4–4 tie with Czechoslovakia. That lacklustre performance merely set the stage for what came next: a hard-fought, nasty encounter with Sweden that saw Canada emerge with a 4–3 win. But they paid a terrible price in the process, as Perreault suffered a broken ankle, prematurely putting an end to his participation in the tournament, while Gretzky took a hard slash to the elbow that later had him admitting that he'd "never been hurt that badly before in a hockey game."

With Perreault out, Marcel Dionne was elevated to Gretzky's line, and in Canada's next game, their last of the round-robin, against the Soviet Union, the newly formed trio of Gretzky, Lafleur, and Dionne combined for eight points in the 7–3 Canada win. A 4–1 win over the United States in the semifinal round set up the one-game final that everyone had hoped for: Canada and the Soviet Union, to be held within the confines of the historic Montreal Forum.

The first half of this much-anticipated clash lived up to its billing, as Canada enjoyed the better of the play but was repeatedly stymied by Soviet goaltender Vladislav Tretiak, who almost single-handedly kept the score tied at one. And then the roof caved in on Canada, with two Soviet goals late in the second period giving the visitors a 3–1 lead. Five more for the Soviets in the third period resulted in an embarrassing 8–1 loss for Team Canada.

No player took the loss harder than Gretzky, who led all the players in the tournament with 12 points. Despite his prowess on the score sheet, he later confessed, half-jokingly, "I played so badly [in the 1981 Canada Cup that] they should have sent me to Siberia."

Gretzky's frustration only grew in the immediate aftermath of the shocking loss. Just as the players on Team Canada were boarding planes destined for their NHL cities and the start of their upcoming training camps, they were informed that each of them had been invited to a luncheon hosted by Prime Minister Pierre Trudeau in Ottawa. In the end, only three players from the team attended the hastily arranged engagement: Gretzky, Larry Robinson, and Butch Goring. "I don't think I've ever been to a more embarrassing event in my life," Gretzky said later. "Here's the prime minister sitting at a table set for 30 guys, and three of us show up."

From there, Gretzky quietly hopped a flight to Florida and spent the next five days sequestered inside a condo, where he tried to make sense of what had happened during the Canada Cup, along with doing some intense self-analysis.

"Not only had I let down my country, but I'd started people asking all those stupid questions about me again," he wrote in his autobiography a decade later. "Yeah, he can score against the Winnipegs of the world, but what happens to him in the big games? I knew I'd spend the 1981–82 season trying to prove that my Canada Cup series was a fluke . . . instead of the other way around."

Having accomplished more than anyone else ever had in his first two NHL seasons, Gretzky could have been forgiven had he decided not to tinker with his game, but inside that isolated Florida condo he came to the startling conclusion that he had to change his style of play. "I'd been passing 90 per cent of the time," he later declared. "I was too predictable. Every time I'd come down the line, they'd play me to pass, not shoot. The pass was getting too tough and the shot too easy to pass up. Now I decided to shoot more."

Less than a month later, at the onset of the 1981–82 NHL season, Gretzky put his new, overhauled approach to the test.

By the time of his 39th game of that season, played in Edmonton on December 30, 1981, against the Philadelphia Flyers, he had rewritten the record book in a way no one could have imagined.

———

Now more than a decade and a half removed from his final NHL game, 55-year-old Wayne Gretzky can look back at a career unparalleled by any other in North American team sports. He holds an astonishing 60 official NHL records that are absolute in their durability. And yet, when asked what might be the hardest of his records to break, amongst a host of seemingly unbreakable records, Gretzky doesn't hesitate to offer up his opinion.

"People ask me all the time about my records, but to me, [the 50 in 39] is my favourite," Gretzky told the *Edmonton Journal* in 2006. "[Records] are all made to be broken, that's what sports is. That's what's so great about sports, but that's my favourite because I think that will be the hardest to break."

When one considers that, as of the 2015–16 NHL season, no player in the past two decades has reached or surpassed the 50-goal in 50 games barrier, one can see Gretzky's point.

In a career filled with jaw-dropping accomplishments, the 50 in

39 stands out partly because it was the first moment in which Gretzky did something that hadn't yet been dreamed of, that blew apart the much-glorified previous record, and that forced us to reevaluate the parameters of the game and how Gretzky would reshape them.

Many more "Gretzkyian" benchmarks followed: a staggering total of 92 goals by the end of the 1981–82 season; 215 points in a single season a few years later; 1,963 career assists, which is more than any other player has in career points. The list goes on and on. But the 50 in 39 was a particularly spectacular accomplishment. And that Gretzky did it by scoring five goals in the unforgettable 39th game only adds to the aura surrounding his achievement.

The 50 in 39 elevated Gretzky to the very top of the hockey pantheon—past the Rocket, past Gordie Howe, past Bobby Orr. He is the sole player at an elite level no other player has reached. Getting to the 50 in 39, he kept journalists awake at night struggling to find the right superlatives to accurately depict his effect on the sport. "There have been heroes before, summoned from the ice ponds and hockey rinks across the country," reported *Maclean's* magazine in its February 22, 1982, cover feature on Gretzky. "The names of Joliat, Morenz, Richard, Howe, Hull and Orr still conjure 'greatness.' But Wayne Gretzky transcends them all."

"He has overwhelmed the records so completely as to render them irrelevant," proclaimed *Newsweek* magazine in its January 18, 1982, issue. "His point of reference now is himself." Even *Chatelaine* magazine, designed for and primarily sold to a female audience, jumped on the Gretzky bandwagon, publishing an article that claimed, "just as Luciano Pavarotti has touched people with no interest in opera, the name of Wayne Gretzky, barely out of his teens, has suffused the consciousness of the world."

But perhaps it was Bobby Clarke, the proud and tenacious captain of the Philadelphia Flyers, who summed it up best. Entering the Oilers dressing room directly after the historic 39th game, Clarke personally congratulated Gretzky. "I know everything's been written about you," he said. "I think none of it is adequate."

Gretzky later suggested that, in the immediate aftermath of the 50 in 39, he lost whatever remained of his private life. He had long grown used to the attention that had accompanied him since he was a child, but that had always come from "hockey people." Now he saw his picture on the cover of every magazine, and not just those devoted to sports. In every city he visited, he was recognized as he walked down the street. At restaurants, he had to sneak in a few bites between signing autographs. And he had to use alternate entrances and exits to get in and out of NHL arenas. Almost instantly, he was living a life—and enjoying a type of adoration—usually reserved for the most popular of rock stars.

The Oilers estimated that in the last three months of 1981, the duration of the famed 39 games, they sold 5,000 replicas of Gretzky's sweater, and each day they received 500 pieces of mail addressed to him. Not surprisingly, big business had taken note, and it is rumoured that at the time, and following it, endorsements netted Gretzky an additional $650,000 per year. A 7UP soft drink commercial, which featured Gretzky and his younger brother Keith, was the first television ad starring a hockey player ever shown in all the major U.S. markets. His exposure was unprecedented for a hockey player, especially one who played for a Canadian-based team.

By obliterating the magical 50-in-50 mark, Gretzky became the most beloved public figure in Canada and emerged as the country's most prominent ambassador. He accepted the fame, attention, and demands on his time without complaint and with a streak of humility that never wavered, which made everyone in Canada adore him that much more.

And he was only 20 years old.

———

This book tells the story of the fated 39 games: those that forever altered the professional and personal life of Wayne Gretzky, the greatest hockey player who has ever lived; those that forever changed the sport of hockey.

The passage of time has not dulled the awe and wonder that surround Wayne Gretzky's 50 goals in 39 games. It remains an achievement difficult to fathom, with longevity that not even Maurice Richard's famed 50-in-50 record enjoyed. Simply put, the 50 in 39 is as astounding today as it was all those years ago, on that cold night in Edmonton, when Gretzky slid the puck into the Philadelphia Flyers open net and the scoreboard high above the ice began flashing *50 . . . 50 . . . 50 . . .*

Game 1 | October 7, 1981

Vs. Colorado Rockies

Northlands Coliseum, Edmonton, Alberta

At practice, when the Edmonton Oilers held any sort of drill that involved skating, he usually finished, at best, in the middle of the pack. A few years before, during his first season in the NHL, amongst all the other Edmonton players, he tested last in upper-body strength. He was skinny, and when he skated his elbow waved in a way that many observers would have called "awkward." When the team lined up for a shooting drill, his shot was one of the weakest, hardly powerful enough to bulge the twine at the back of the net.

To the untrained hockey eye watching the Oilers practice, the 20-year-old wearing number 99 would not have resembled what he became when the game started: the greatest hockey player in the world. Wayne Gretzky.

———

The start of hockey season is a wonderful time of year, filled with so much promise. There are the contenders, pretenders, and defenders—the defenders being the team that won the Stanley Cup the year before.

No matter which category it slots into, each team shares a common refrain: "All we want to do is make the playoffs, and if we get in, you never know what can happen."

If only it were that simple.

At the outset of the 1981–82 season, the New York Islanders were the defenders, attempting to win the Stanley Cup for a third straight season. They were a dynasty in every sense, and they had it all—size, speed, experience, toughness, not to mention great goaltending. They were the model every other team tried to follow, led by superstars Denis Potvin, Bryan Trottier, and Mike Bossy—who, just the season before, in 1980–81, had scored his 50 goals in 50 games.

In Edmonton, the young Oilers were still very much a work in progress. But in 1980–81 they had finished with a record of 29 wins, 35 losses, and 16 ties, scoring 328 goals while allowing 327. The Oilers took giant strides that season, upsetting the heavily favoured Montreal Canadiens in three straight games in the best-of-five preliminary round of the playoffs before succumbing to the Islanders in six games in the best-of-seven quarter-finals.

Many years after Gretzky retired, he looked back fondly at the start of his third season in the NHL. The Oilers were, overall, a pretty young team to be entertaining the notion of winning the Cup, he admits, but they were having the time of their lives. Occasionally their giddiness got the better of them.

"In some instances, we did show our age," Gretzky said. "You know, I think when we'd go to the Montreal Forum or Maple Leaf Gardens in Toronto and we acted like we were 10 years old, it kind of got the better of us. We were like little kids. We were lucky we were all together, because outside of the locker room and outside of the group, we didn't feel younger; we didn't feel any inexperience. Part of that was to do with Sather and how he treated us, and the other part of it was the older guys that were on the team who led us; guys like Lee Fogolin and Doug Hicks who were consummate professionals. In a lot of ways they were extremely unselfish because they knew the importance of us growing as players and as people. We had the right mix and right group around the young guys who made us feel better about ourselves."

Pumped for the 1981–82 season, Gretzky believed that what the Oilers had accomplished in the previous season—sweeping the Canadiens in Round One of the playoffs and extending the Islanders to six games in Round Two—spoke volumes about where they were as a team.

"I think in our minds, we felt we were ready," Gretzky said in a recent interview. "Even the year we lost to the Islanders in six games, in the locker room we felt we were as good as they were and we should beat them. It's funny how the feeling of the group was, especially after we had gone into Montreal and won two games there. In Game 1 we played really well and caught them flat-footed, and in Game 2 Andy Moog stood on his head and stole the victory. When we came home for Game 3, the whole excitement for the fans really started to percolate and take off. Up to that time most of the fans would come to the game, and they were excited about the team because we were an exciting team to watch, but they didn't really feel that we were ready to compete for the Stanley Cup. Consequently, it was a little quiet in our building throughout the years. But when we played Game 3, our first home game of the playoffs, things were taken to the next level.

"So going into the next season, we really believed we had a chance to compete for the Cup because the Islanders had won and we felt like we were very competitive against them through the entire series, even though we lost in six games."

In his first two NHL seasons Gretzky had already amassed 106 goals and 195 assists for 301 points in 159 games. What could he possibly do for an encore?

Time would tell.

First up for Gretzky and the Oilers as the 1981–82 season kicked off were the ill-fated Colorado Rockies. Previously the Kansas City Scouts, the franchise transferred to Denver in 1976 and would eventually move to New Jersey in 1982. Over six seasons in Colorado, the team only made the playoffs once, in 1977–78, when they lost in the preliminary round to the Philadelphia Flyers in two straight games. Not much of a legacy.

Bill MacMillan, who coached the Rockies in 1980–81, also held the title of general manager that year. The team had one legitimate star: captain Lanny McDonald, formerly of the Toronto Maple Leafs, who, soon after the start of the season, was handed his get-out-of-jail-free card in the form of a trade to the Calgary Flames.

At the insistence of cantankerous Toronto Maple Leafs owner Harold Ballard, Leafs general manager Punch Imlach had banished Lanny McDonald to Colorado in December 1979. Imlach had wanted to trade captain Darryl Sittler, but a no-trade clause in his contract made that impossible—Sittler would have to give his okay to be moved. So, in an effort to diminish his captain's resolve, Imlach traded Sittler's closest friends on the team: McDonald and Dave "Tiger" Williams. Eventually Imlach wore Sittler down and found a way to get rid of him, too, eliminating the nucleus of what some believed could have been the first Maple Leafs team since 1967 with the potential to win the Stanley Cup.

For McDonald, who was 28 and entering the prime of his career, playing with the Rockies was a nightmare. "Our team normally got outshot, and unfortunately giving up 50 shots in a game was not a rare occurrence, either," McDonald recalled.

The Rockies were mostly a bunch of journeymen, sure to be easy pickings for the rapidly developing Oilers. And yes, it was an easy game for Gretzky and company as they blasted the visitors from Colorado, 7–4.

On a night when 21-year-old Walt Poddubny was making his NHL debut with the Oilers, it was not the Great One who led the charge for Edmonton, but 33-year-old veteran Garry Unger, who had joined the team after being traded the previous season by the Los Angeles Kings for a seventh-round pick in the 1981 draft. Earlier in his career, the mop-haired centre had been one of the flashiest scorers in the NHL.

Edmonton defenceman Kevin Lowe, who was just 22 in 1981, recalled seeing a picture of a young Garry Unger wearing jeans and cowboy boots and standing beside a souped-up Corvette Stingray. "He looked so cool," Lowe said. "He was the guy we all wanted to be when we were young."

The oldest player on the Oilers in 1981–82, Unger broke into the NHL with Toronto in 1967–68, but was promptly traded to the Detroit Red Wings in a blockbuster deal that also sent future Hockey Hall of Famer Frank Mahovlich, Peter Stemkowski, and the rights to defenceman Carl Brewer to Detroit in exchange for Norm Ullman, Floyd Smith, Paul Henderson, and Doug Barrie.

In 1969–70, his second full season in the NHL, Unger scored a career-best 42 goals. Unger starred with the St. Louis Blues for more than eight seasons in the 1970s, but in the years leading up to Gretzky's 50-in-39 season, he had bounced around the NHL, landing in Atlanta, Los Angeles, and finally Edmonton, where his role was as more of a journeyman checker than a scorer.

Unger was a close friend of Oilers head coach and GM Glen Sather. The two had played together with the Blues in 1973–74 and had stayed in touch over the years.

"When I joined Edmonton, I felt like I was going home," said the Calgary, Alberta, native. "My career had come full circle and I could play out my NHL career in front of my family and friends."

Unger saw action in 13 games with the Oilers in 1980–81, but was goalless and minus-9. He didn't register a single point in eight playoff games. Not exactly the kind of numbers that inspire confidence in an aging veteran. As of the first game of the 1981–82 season, he had not scored a goal in 43 games, dating back to January 20, 1981. In addition, the Oilers had left him unprotected in the preseason waiver draft, and he was not claimed by another organization.

If Unger had one thing going for him, it was that he'd been around the bend a time or two, whereas most of his Oilers teammates were barely out of their teens. In fact, Unger felt closer to the coaching staff than he did to his teammates. Another thing working in his favour was that, upon his arrival in Edmonton, the Oilers went 7–2–4. Before he was acquired, the Oilers were not assured of a playoff spot. But as a veteran player of 15 years, Unger could ill afford a prolonged scoring drought if his NHL career was going to continue.

Unger's first experience with Gretzky was as an opponent. The first time he lined up against Gretzky in the faceoff circle he thought, "This guy is going to get killed!"

"Wayne wasn't a flashy player; not an end-to-end guy like Bobby Orr," Unger says. "You'd hardly notice Wayne, and then you'd look at the game sheet and he had six or seven points. The thing is, you couldn't hit him. He was so smart, he would find a way to get out of the way. Dave Semenko was there to protect him, but Wayne didn't really need protection."

So two goals in 44 seconds was a decent start to Unger's year. On his first goal of the season, he tipped a shot by teammate Glenn Anderson past Colorado goalie Phil Myre at 7:27 of the second period, and shortly afterward, when Myre wandered from his crease, Unger shot the puck into the empty net. A week earlier, Unger had been in the hospital with kidney stones, and there he was, taking his career off life support. At least temporarily, he got the home fans, who had been booing him, to lighten up.

After the game, Unger was seemingly unimpressed—happy, yes, but not exactly over the moon. "Just because I scored two goals doesn't mean I have arrived," he said. Coincidentally, the game also saw Unger record his 1,000th career penalty minute.

Sather was thrilled that his veteran centre, and former teammate, performed well. "It had been a long time since he scored a goal, but when you do score the people love you for it," Sather said at the time. "Maybe now they'll get off his back. I don't think he has been on for a goal against since we played the Islanders in the playoffs, and he wins more faceoffs than anybody else on the team."

If his early days in Edmonton bothered Unger, he grew to look back at the experience very fondly. "It was a fun time for me," Unger said years later. "I wish I could have been younger. Players hiring personal trainers and all that stuff was on the horizon. If I had that, maybe I could have played a few more years."

Colorado actually took an early lead in the game when Steve Tambellini, who became the Oilers GM more than two and a half decades later, scored for the Rockies on the power play. However, their lead was short-lived.

By the end of the first period, Edmonton had a 2–1 advantage, with goals by Brett Callighen and Jari Kurri, who scored on his fifth shot of the period (he had a total of eight shots on goal in the game). Unger's two goals made it 4–1. McDonald put one in the net for the Rockies, making it 4–2 after the second period, and just 38 seconds into the third period, Tambellini pulled the Rockies to within one. But late in the second period, Glenn "Chico" Resch had replaced Myre in the Colorado goal, and he proceeded to allow three goals— by Pat Hughes, Callighen, and Kurri—on 17 shots in the third period. (Kurri's goal, scored at 2:06 of the third, was the winner, with assists going to Gretzky and Callighen.) So, by the time Joel Quenneville added Colorado's fourth of the game, late in the third period, the game was out of reach for the Rockies. The Oilers emerged victorious by a score of 7–4.

Gretzky had to settle for what *Edmonton Journal* sportswriter Jim Matheson described in his report of the contest as a "measly assist." Not a great start to the Great One's season, but it did keep Gretzky's streak of consecutive games with at least one point alive at 11. He had two shots on goal in the first period, three in the second, and none in the third.

Even though they lost, the Rockies could celebrate the fact that they had limited Gretzky to a single assist. Little did they know that, in a record-breaking season like none before or since, few teams would be able to make such a claim.

"Before every game we would come up with a plan to stop Gretzky, but truth be told, none of them ever worked," McDonald said. "I remember once, we had a guy follow him; later on they would call that shadowing. So Gretzky would enter our zone and our designated guy would follow him, and then Gretzky would skate outside the blue line with our shadow in pursuit and throw us all out of sorts."

The defencemen weren't the only ones to shadow Gretzky. Years after that stellar season, Unger recalled that *Sports Illustrated* had once sent a journalist on an East Coast road trip with the Oilers to report on hockey's new superstar.

"They filmed us practicing, and at the end I was called over to talk with the reporter, and as we were talking he suddenly realized I wasn't Gretzky," Unger says with a laugh. "They had followed me by mistake, so they had to come back the following day and shoot some Gretzky action. The rest of the guys on the Oilers tolerated it because we all loved Wayne. He was just one of the guys; a lot of fun and that is what Glen [Sather] wanted to foster."

There are not too many players who can make the claim that they were mistaken for Wayne Gretzky.

Game 2 | October 9, 1981

Vs. Vancouver Canucks

Pacific Coliseum, Vancouver, British Columbia

f the Colorado Rockies were an easy mark for the Oilers in the opening game of the NHL season, two nights later in Vancouver, the Canucks presented a much greater challenge for the Oilers.

Having joined the league when it expanded to 14 teams in 1970, the Canucks were in their 12th season in the NHL and coming off a disappointing year. The Buffalo Sabres, who had also joined the NHL in 1970, had swept the Canucks in three straight games in the opening round of the 1980–81 playoffs. The Canucks were a team of experienced players with dependable goaltending from veterans Richard Brodeur and Glen Hanlon. At least that's how they opened the season. Hanlon was ultimately traded (on March 9, 1982) to the St. Louis Blues for goaltender Rick Heinz.

On this night it was Brodeur stopping pucks at the Vancouver end of the ice, and at the other end, young Andy Moog tended goal for the Oilers. The Canucks, who opened the season with a 4–2 win over the Rockies and then tied the Calgary Flames, 1–1, would make it three games without a loss at Edmonton's expense, and all because of one player's stellar offence.

The Canucks Thomas Gradin, 24 and in his fourth NHL season, began scoring in the first period with back-to-back goals at 15:47 and, 21 seconds later, at 16:08. And although Mark Messier brought the Oilers to within a goal at 19:31 of the first period, Gradin struck again for his third goal of the game, at 5:14 of the second, putting the Canucks ahead for the rest of the game.

Gradin technically had only one shot on goal. His other two goals deflected in off Edmonton defenders' skates. What made the night even crazier was that Edmonton's Pat Hughes kneed Gradin, and the Swede spent the second half of the game lying on the trainer's table in the medical room, listening to the colour commentary on the radio. Yet when all was said and done, he was named the game's first star.

After Gradin's hat-trick goal, Vancouver scored twice more in the second period: Ivan Boldirev connected at 9:01 and then set up Blair MacDonald to make it 5–1. The Oilers came to life in the final minute of the second period, but barring a miracle, at that point they were out of the game with a period to go.

In his most productive season in the NHL (in which he scored 15 goals and 63 points), Finnish-born Risto Siltanen was a factor in both Edmonton goals, scoring one and adding an assist on the other. Siltanen also led the Oilers that night with six shots on net, while Messier had five. Centre Garry Unger continued his hot start to the year with an assist and Glenn Anderson had a helper, but a goal scored by Vancouver's Ivan Hlinka with less than three minutes remaining in the third period settled the outcome, 6–2 for the Canucks.

Thirty-one-year-old Ivan Hlinka, the great Czechoslovakian, was playing for the Canucks in his first NHL season on the night of October 9, 1981. He would go on to become a valuable member of the team that was destined to go all the way to the Stanley Cup final that spring. His 60 points that season set a franchise record for most points by a rookie, a mark later tied by Pavel Bure.

After his playing career concluded, Hlinka embarked on a successful coaching career in the Czech Republic and ultimately came back to the NHL, where, as only the second European-born head coach in league history, he guided the Pittsburgh Penguins in 2000–01. Inspired by the return of superstar Mario Lemieux from retirement, Hlinka coached the Penguins to a surprise berth in the 2001 Eastern Conference final. However, due to a breach in his relationship with Lemieux, after the Penguins began the 2001–02 schedule with four consecutive losses, he was fired. Less than three years later, on August 16, 2004, Hlinka passed away suddenly in the Czech Republic when the car he was driving collided head-on with a truck. He was 54 years old.

Gretzky's performance in the first game could be described as disappointing—just one assist, albeit on the winning goal. In the Oilers' second game of the season, he took a step backwards. The Canucks held him off the score sheet. He didn't manage a shot on goal in the first two periods, but hit the net three times in the third, and it's no coincidence that his shots came when Thomas Gradin was out of the game. Not only did the slick-skating Gradin lead the way on offence, but he also, very effectively, frustrated Edmonton's most lethal offensive weapon: Gretzky.

"Gradin showed tonight how good a two-way player he is," said Vancouver head coach Harry Neale after the game. "Whenever he had to play Gretzky, he did the job. And he put the puck home when he got chances."

Despite two mediocre games, Gretzky had already established himself as a scoring machine in the NHL, and those around him could see that even better days lay ahead. He was, after all, only a kid. "Wayne was really just figuring things out, like a lot of players on that team," said Unger. "They were young and just going for it. At times it was like playing on a junior hockey team. We had lots of fun. We'd stay out after practice and play 'kids' games'; things like three-on-three. I really saw then how Wayne read the game. He was just so smart and had amazing lateral movement."

Unger chuckled as he recalled his old pal Sather dealing with a talented group of youngsters that he was trying to mould into a championship outfit: "Slats had a different rapport with the players compared to his public image. As a coach, he could be the players' friend one minute, but when things really mattered he could drop the hammer if he needed to. Slats was not an Xs and Os guy. Even his practices were fun. Glen wanted to have fun, but he wanted the fun to be through hard work. He was a father figure who would joke around with the young players, but when the time was right, he'd get serious and they would listen."

Sather wouldn't blow a gasket in order to get the attention of his players, and yet, if he needed to get his message across, he didn't beat around the bush.

"He was really big on the power of positive thinking," says former Oilers defenceman Kevin Lowe. "He would tell us we had to start believing we could win it all. He would say to us that we not only belonged in the league, we had to start thinking about winning championships. The only time he'd be tough on us was when it was called for. It wasn't so much about making a mistake in a certain game; it was more about how you conducted yourself as a teammate and whether you were letting your teammates down by messing around after hours."

When the Oilers lost, 6–2, to the Canucks, Sather felt compelled to make his players accountable.

"A lot of our guys were standing still," Sather said. "For a team that skates as well as we do, they made us look ordinary."

The players got their coach's message.

"He pushed the right buttons," Lowe said. "A couple of times maybe he pushed too hard and it got awkward, but not very often."

Game 3 | October 10, 1981

Vs. Los Angeles Kings

The Forum, Inglewood, California

As a rookie in the NHL in 1979–80, Gretzky didn't score his first goal until his third game. He scored on opening night the following year. By the third game in his third year in the league, he already had 106 goals on his NHL resumé, so nobody was worried that his scoring prowess had suddenly dried up.

Despite his struggles in the first two games of the 1981–82 season, the momentum that he had built in his first two years in the NHL was also beginning to draw attention from the kinds of media outlets that rarely gave *any* attention to *anything* hockey-related.

According to the October 10 edition of the *Globe and Mail* newspaper, published the morning of the Oilers' game in Los Angeles, "editors of at least three U.S. national magazines have dispatched photographers to the wilds of northern Alberta to record the teenybopper good looks of hockey's wunderkind. In the next few weeks, Wayne Gretzky will be cover boy on *Sports Illustrated*, *Inside Sports*, and *Life* magazine. And he has a piece of Page 1 of this week's issue of the *Sporting News*. . . . In an era when the United

States appears to be short of sports heroes, perhaps Gretzky's hockey and public-relations skill will force the U.S. media to take notice."

Of all the magazines featuring Gretzky that flooded North American newsstands, the *Sports Illustrated* cover and the magazine's lengthy profile of the player offered the most revealing glimpse of a 20-year-old at the beginning of his third season in the NHL, one that changed everything.

Written by E.M. Swift and titled "The Best and Getting Better," the article features a timely kicker: "At 20, Wayne Gretzky is without question the NHL's top player. All that's left to ask is. How good will he become?" The profile, based on Swift's observations of Gretzky at the beginning of the recently completed Canada Cup tournament, was not the first time that the magazine had paid attention to Gretzky, but never before had it gone so in-depth, or produced something so lengthy. The piece regurgitated the familiar stories of Gretzky learning to skate on the backyard rink at the age of three and playing with 10-year-old boys by the age of six, and his father's often-quoted advice to "skate to where the puck's going to be, not where it has been." But it also contained a rare look at the 20-year-old away from the rink and was testimony to his profile and popularity that had surged at the start of the 1981–82 season.

In the finished article Swift sets the chaotic scene inside the living room of Gretzky's 14th floor two-bedroom condominium. Normally, the condo is occupied by Gretzky and his roommate/Oilers teammate Kevin Lowe, but on this particular afternoon, mere hours after Gretzky had finished his latest practice with Team Canada, he is joined by his mother, Phyllis, and 18-year-old sister, Kim, who are staying with him for the first week of the Canada Cup.

If Phyllis and Kim, visiting from Brantford, and sitting on opposite ends of the living room couch, represent a link to Gretzky's family and his past, then Gus Badali, a family friend, and Gretzky's agent, and holding court across the room, represents not only his client's rapidly expanding entourage but also Gretzky's immediate future, particularly off the ice. Surrounded by a stack of life-sized cardboard cutouts of his client modeling his preferred brand of jeans, cutouts that will soon take up space in clothing stores throughout Canada, Badali plots strategy with a representative of GWG jeans, the company that has tied up much of their marketing and promotional strategy with Gretzky.

Striving for attention in the crowded, busy room is Vickie Moss, an aspiring singer, and Gretzky's 19-year-old girlfriend. And then there is Gretzky himself, sitting alone at his desk, calmly opening the mail. And while to an outsider, it may seem like he's trying to carve out a quiet space amidst all that's going on around him, the opposite is true. In fact Gretzky feels quite comfortable in the midst of such gatherings. "I'm not big on independency," he admits to Swift who in the article observed that . . .

> "[Gretzky is] outgoing when relaxed. He has been like that ever since he was a kid—always ready with an answer, always striving to be the center of attention."

Within the Edmonton city limits, Gretzky's image was everywhere, on just about everything—jigsaw puzzles, T-shirts, key chains, billboards, magazines—and a person couldn't go more than three steps outside without spotting a Number 99 jersey, either in a shop window or being worn by a passerby. Such was the deluge of all things Gretzky that after spending a few days in the city, *Philadelphia Inquirer* reporter Al Morganti suggested that "they should rename the place Gretmonton."

But Gretzky's increasing popularity was by no means limited to Edmonton.

In the summer of 1981, Gretzky's status and recognition was spreading throughout Canada and starting to gain momentum in the United States. In fact, before he left for the Canada Cup training camp in August, Gretzky had made at least two public appearances in each of Canada's eight largest cities, including a stop at a Montreal shopping centre that drew a crowd of over 7,500 people. That same summer Gretzky also made three separate visits to New York City and one to Las Vegas. On one of these trips, noted artist Leroy Neiman painted his portrait, the original of which was at that time priced at $125,000, with prints being made available for $2,675 in the U.S. and $3,200 in Canada.

Presiding over Gretzky's interests off the ice is Badali, who had represented him since he was 16 years old. As the 1981–82 season beckoned, Badali had secured endorsement deals with seven different products (including GWG jeans) ranging from hockey sticks to chocolate bars, the most noteworthy of which involved a commercial for the soft drink 7UP that featured Gretzky with his 14-year-old brother, Keith.

"One of the first deals we did was with 7UP," said Badali in a recent interview. "It was one of the first times they had ever endorsed a player. The ad even went into the United States in the St. Louis area. Wayne's recognition was gaining momentum all the time. We were bombarded by it, and there was definitely a lot of people wanting his attention."

In his *Sports Illustrated* profile, Swift speculated that Gretzky's off-ice income as of September 1981 almost matched his salary from the Oilers. It's not a conjecture Badali would dispute: "When did Wayne realize he could make a lot of money from endorsements? I got $75,000, which was a lot of money back then, from the Traveler's Insurance Group, and that seemed to provide us with the wow factor at the time. The GWG jeans [company] wanted to have his name on their product, and then other good products and good people kept approaching us. Today $75,000 is like peanuts, but back then it was a lot of money."

But despite all of the appearances and endorsement deals, Gretzky's primary focus always remained on the ice. "As Wayne's popularity soared, it didn't overwhelm him," Badali maintains today. "He just went out on the ice and did his business. Truth be told, I was always more nervous, at any event I was at, for him than he was."

On the night of October 10, and in the Oilers' third game of the season, a brewing rivalry with Los Angeles Kings centre Marcel Dionne lit a fire under Gretzky. Sure, the two had played together in the Canada Cup only a few weeks earlier, but on NHL ice Dionne was Gretzky's main scoring competition. In Gretzky's first two NHL seasons, he and Dionne had waged a two-man battle over the Art Ross Trophy for the league's top scorer. In 1979–80, the 28-year-old Dionne and 18-year-old Gretzky ended up tied with 137 points apiece. But the Art Ross Trophy went to the Kings scoring ace because Dionne got 53 goals to Gretzky's 51. The following season, Dionne again scored more goals than Gretzky, 58–55, but Gretzky had more assists—109 to Dionne's 77—and so the younger man won the scoring title by 29 points.

Years later, Gretzky said that playing against the game's top players motivated him. "That's the way the world works in professional sports. One guy is on top of the mountain. In my case it was Marcel Dionne and Guy Lafleur who were at the top of their games. As a kid I idolized them, and here I was playing against them. It was like, 'Wow!' That is what drives you as a youngster. I would think, 'I've got to be as good as those guys.' Then, as time goes on and the next guy comes along, before you know it you've got this young Mario Lemieux chasing you down. All of a sudden the tide turns and you're the Marcel Dionne and he's the Wayne Gretzky. It's something we all go through in sports, but that is what makes hockey so special. There are players at your level who are trying to be as good as those who have already accomplished great things."

Three days earlier, the Kings had been blown out, 4–1, by the Islanders in their season opener and they presented no match for the supercharged Oilers on this night. Thus, a crowd of under 9,000 people showed up at the Forum for a game in which Gretzky scored his first goal of the season and the Oilers beat the Kings, 7–4.

Andy Moog, just 20, had played goal for the Oilers in the first two games of the season. Perhaps a little worried that Dionne might intimidate the youngster, Edmonton coach Glen Sather chose to put veteran Ron Low, 10 years Moog's senior, in the net to face the Kings.

The previous season wasn't a great one for Low, who broke his thumb twice, watched his goals-against average balloon to 4.43, and ultimately lost the starter's job to Moog. Even so, the other players on the Oilers valued Low's much-needed leadership.

"Glen Sather's big theory on building the team was to have the right veteran players around," Gretzky says. "He felt that would make us a better group. Guys like Lee Fogolin, Doug Hicks, and Ron Low made us better. They showed the younger players how to be professional on and off the ice. He was as concerned about which older players he was going to have on the team as he was about which younger players we had."

Even if he was no longer the Oilers' main man in the crease, the rest of the team looked up to him.

"Ron was very well respected by everyone," Kevin Lowe attested. "He was a great teammate; a classic old western guy. He was a young guy at heart, even though he was 31 years old. He always battled like a madman in practice. He never gave up on a shot in practice. The thing I admired most about him was he never worried about what he looked like. Some guys tried to be too cool. They were afraid to extend themselves and look vulnerable. Ron didn't care as long as he made the save. I learned very early in my career to not be afraid to extend myself and look bad. It was only going to make you a better player. Ronnie taught me that."

For his part, Low let the Kings score four goals. On many nights, and with many teams, that would have led to a loss. Not on this night, though, and not with this offensively gifted team.

The Oilers took a first-period lead on the strength of goals by Jari Kurri and Mark Messier. Gretzky set up the opening goal, at 6:38. The Kings got back into it with a goal by Steve Bozek at 5:43 of the middle frame, but Messier, with his second of the season, restored Edmonton's two-goal lead four minutes later. The seesaw affair continued as the Kings scored two goals in less than two minutes: Doug Smith, just 18 years old and the second-overall pick in the 1981 NHL Entry Draft, made it 3–2, and shortly afterward, with the Oilers playing a man short, Jim Fox tied the game.

Dave Hunter restored Edmonton's lead late in the second period, setting the stage for Gretzky to score the eventual game winner—and his first goal of the season—at 1:12 of the third period when his shot beat Kings goalie Mario Lessard. The power-play goal was originally awarded to Unger, but ultimately, and correctly, was credited to Gretzky. Pat Hughes and Risto Siltanen rounded out the scoring for the Oilers, while Steve Jensen did the same for Los Angeles in the 7–4 defeat.

Gretzky got stronger as the game progressed. He was held shotless in the first period, took one shot in the second, and three more in the third. Bozek led with six shots on goal, while rookie defenceman Larry Murphy of the Kings chipped in five. Murphy would be named the NHL's rookie of the year at the conclusion of the 1981–82 season after establishing NHL records for assists (60) and points (76) by a first-year defenceman. Messier, Gretzky, Anderson, Kurri, and Hughes had four shots each for Oilers, who outshot the Kings, 38–35.

Gretzky's two points this game gave him a total of three in three games—well off his normal production, but he was just getting warmed up. In typical fashion, he put a team spin on the start of his individual season. "We're 2–1, and that is what is important," Gretzky said at the time. "If we win two of every three and I only score once in a while, so what?"

The lure of the Los Angeles nightlife caused more than a few NHL players to stray from their usual way of life after games there, and the young Oilers were no exception. At the team practice Sunday morning, the day after defeating the Kings, Messier, Lowe, Curt Brackenbury, and Dave Semenko were late.

Defenceman Doug Hicks jokingly suggested, "I think we should string them up."

The guilty players were fined.

Boys will be boys.

Game 4 | October 14, 1981

Vs. Winnipeg Jets

Northlands Coliseum, Edmonton, Alberta

ooking back on the Oilers' amazing roster in 1981–82, it's hard to believe they ever lost a game—and yet, the core of the hockey team was extremely young.

By season's end, Edmonton's top four scorers—Gretzky, Glenn Anderson, Paul Coffey, and Mark Messier—were just 20 years old. The elder statesman in fifth place was 21-year-old Jari Kurri.

While other expansion teams favoured leaning on veterans, often those playing the back nine of their careers, the Oilers opted to depend mostly on kids. In 1981–82, Risto Siltanen, Kevin Lowe, and Charlie Huddy were 22; Dave Hunter was 23; Dave Semenko was 24; Randy Gregg and Matti Hagman were 25; and Pat Hughes was 26.

"We really didn't have a sense of how young we were," Lowe said. "By then, we were third-year pros. I always describe the start of my career like this: the first year it is just a blur . . . you are just surviving. I was lucky to be part of an expansion team; otherwise, on any other team, I probably would have been in the minors. By year three, it's kind of like when you were in junior, you are an established player. Then, of course, Gretz was doing what he was doing. He led the league twice in scoring and we were beating just about everybody. We had our challenges against the Islanders, the Flyers, and the Bruins, but we were beating everybody else."

Looking back on his third NHL season, Messier said on some level the players understood how young they were, but on the other hand, they felt as though they belonged in the NHL.

"Well, Wayne and I were in the WHA as 17-year-olds, so we were a good three years into our pro careers," Messier says. "If you look at history, many players' most productive years are between the ages of 20 and 25. I don't know if we felt super-young at that particular time, but on some level we knew we were entering the peak years of our careers."

Were the Oilers too naive to fully comprehend how hard it was going to be to unseat an older, more experienced team such as the New York Islanders as NHL champs?

"It's the same old story," Messier insisted. "You don't know what you don't know. It was our goal. I mean, we got a taste of what playoff hockey was like our first season in the NHL, having been eliminated by the Philadelphia Flyers. Then winning the playoff series against Montreal and taking another step with a tough series loss to the Islanders had us thinking we could win. If you had asked us back then, I am sure we would have insisted we were ready, but in hindsight we weren't anywhere near being ready to win the Cup.

"There were still a lot of lessons to be learned. We were winning a lot of games on talent and trying to figure out a way to play a more team-oriented game. We didn't have anybody on our team that had won the Stanley Cup, so we were basically learning on the fly.

"Our real role models, the guys we were learning from, were our fierce opponents on the Islanders. They were a test sample. They were the guys that were winning Cups, and when we were up against them and they were beating us, we were trying to figure out how and why."

Coffey, who would soon emerge as one of the most offensively gifted defencemen in NHL history, was as wide-eyed and naive as any of his tender-aged teammates. "Truthfully, we had no real sense of how young we were," Coffey said, "but we knew we were having a lot of fun. You have to remember, back then there wasn't the massive coverage of the sport there is today. You never had what these guys have today, with everybody either telling you you're great or that you stink. And you certainly didn't have million-dollar guaranteed contracts like you see today. That all came later. All we knew at the time was, if we wanted to get paid, we had to produce. It's just the way it was. That's why we placed such an emphasis on scoring goals. Slats brought that in from Sam Pollock. It was basically 'Give us four or five good years and you'll get your money.'"

According to Coffey, players at that time relied heavily on trying to earn the bonuses that were in their contracts. "If you got 20 goals, you might get $3,500 or $5,000. We loved it because that would pay for your trip after the season ended. That was our motivation. That's why I think that brand of hockey was so exciting; if you didn't produce, you didn't get paid. It was plain and simple. Besides, when your best player derives as much excitement out of scoring as Wayne did, it becomes pretty contagious."

Even when they didn't win, the Oilers entertained.

"We were starting to feel like we belonged and we deserved success," Lowe said. "Glen had turned the team over to the younger players by 1981–82. In the first few years, he had gone with more veterans, including some holdovers from the WHA. Slowly, those guys had gone away and we became a very young team."

It was even more shocking that a team with so many young skaters would put two kids between the pipes: Andy Moog and 19-year-old Grant Fuhr. In 1981–82, the Oilers also used 31-year-old Ron Low, who had bounced around the minors for a number of years before becoming an NHL journeyman, making stops in Toronto, Washington, Detroit, Edmonton, Quebec, and finally Edmonton again before finishing his career in New Jersey. In keeping with his intention to go young or go home, Sather made a wise decision to retain Low, but put him in a rare three-goalie system with Moog and Fuhr, who had played the previous two seasons in junior with the Victoria Cougars of the Western Hockey League until being chosen eighth overall by the Oilers in the 1981 NHL Entry Draft. Fuhr had been so impressive in the preseason that he replaced veteran stopper Eddie Mio, whom the Oilers sent back to the minors.

Some were surprised by Sather's decision to keep Fuhr, given Moog's impressive performance in the previous season's playoffs, but not everyone marvelled.

"Andy, although he played great in that year's playoffs, he really didn't have Grant's pedigree," Lowe said. "Besides, Slats was always big in justifying his drafts, too."

In a season when the young Oilers took a gigantic step towards respectability, Fuhr eventually did make his individual mark, but not in his NHL debut.

The Winnipeg Jets had not adapted well to the NHL after joining the league in 1979 along with the other teams from the defunct World Hockey Association: Edmonton, Quebec, and Hartford. The Jets had been a powerhouse in the WHA, with the likes of Bobby Hull, Anders Hedberg, and Ulf Nilsson, and had won three Avco Cup championships in the league's seven-year existence. In their first, frustrating NHL season, however, the Jets were 20–49–11, and they bottomed out in their second year, suffering through a miserable 9–57–14 campaign, good enough for consecutive last-place finishes in the 21-team league.

The Jets' 1981–82 season opened with a loss to the Toronto Maple Leafs, but they got themselves back to .500 with a victory over the New York Rangers. Now they were up against their old WHA foes, the Oilers. Moog had played poorly in the team's first two games of the season, and Low had played Game 3. Sather, noting the Jets' weak and developing roster, figured this game was the perfect opportunity to give Fuhr his first taste of big-league action.

Fuhr, an Edmonton native, gave a good account of himself that night, making 32 saves. He stopped two breakaways in the game and also had a little luck on his side as the Jets hit the post three times, but the Oilers were beaten 4–2 at the Northlands Coliseum in what would be the team's only non-sellout home game of the season.

Perhaps his teammates forgot about their responsibility to try for a victory during Fuhr's first NHL showing. Early in the game, they stood around, not registering a single shot on goal until nearly seven minutes had ticked off the clock. The pattern repeated in the second period, when it took them nearly eight minutes to get a shot on goal.

Speedy right winger Paul MacLean gave the visitors a 1–0 lead with a power-play goal at 8:29 of the first period, but Gretzky tied the contest with his second of the season two minutes and 26 seconds later, deking a befuddled Ed Staniowski in the Jets goal. After Ron Wilson restored the Jets' one-goal lead at 16:26 of the first period, Morris Lukowich scored the eventual game winner at 16:12 of the second, beating Fuhr on a breakaway.

Mark Messier struck midway through the third period when his shot banked off a few skates and past Staniowski for point number 100 of his young NHL career, but the Jets put the game away when Lucien DeBlois scored while Fuhr was on the bench in favour of an extra skater.

Gretzky and Hagman led the Oilers with four shots apiece, while Norm Dupont and Willy Lindström had five shots each for the Jets, who outshot their hosts, 36–28. Despite the result, Sather felt justified in going with Fuhr in goal. "I think you will see some great things from that youngster," Sather said. "It's a shame the rest of our players didn't put in the same effort he did." He later amended his evaluation to include Hagman and Pat Hughes, along with Fuhr, as those who showed up for the game. He cited a lack of concentration and complained that his defencemen, specifically Coffey and Siltanen, overhandled the puck. Sitting with a 2–2–0 record, and with a game against the Calgary Flames coming up in two nights, clearly had the coach-GM frustrated.

Gretzky had scored two goals and four points in his first four games, which wasn't an exemplary showing from the player who would go on to become the Great One. His early-season record was proving to indicate very little about what magic might lie ahead.

Game 5 | October 16, 1981

Vs. Calgary Flames

Northlands Coliseum, Edmonton, Alberta

T he Battle of Alberta, one of hockey's all-time great rivalries, had not yet reached the heights it would soon attain, but in the early stages of the 1981–82 season it was off to a good start. Any time the two Alberta-based NHL teams faced off, bragging rights were on the line.

The team having transferred to Calgary from Atlanta the season before, the Flames had an excellent 1980–81 season wherein they reached the semifinals before losing in six games to the Minnesota North Stars, who ultimately lost in five games to the Islanders in the Stanley Cup final.

The Flames were led by the Magic Man, Kent Nilsson, who in 1980–81 placed third in NHL scoring with 49 goals and 131 points in 80 games. Only Gretzky, with 164 points, and Dionne, with 135, produced more than the gifted Swede who had cut his teeth in North America playing two seasons with the Winnipeg Jets in the WHA, before Atlanta claimed him when the NHL and WHA merged.

A young, but experienced, supporting cast that included Guy

Chouinard, Willi Plett, Eric Vail, Bob MacMillan, Don Lever, and Ken Houston ably assisted Nilsson. The Flames were solid in net with the trio of Pat Riggin, Reggie Lemelin, and Dan Bouchard. Standout defenceman Paul Reinhart was only 20, but already had two NHL seasons under his belt and promised to have a long, prosperous career.

With defenceman Al MacInnis chosen in the first round of the 1981 draft and goaltender Mike Vernon in the third, the team that in time became Stanley Cup champions, and the Oilers' fiercest rivals, was starting to come together. General manager Cliff Fletcher added to the Flames' arsenal later in the 1981–82 season by acquiring veteran right winger Lanny McDonald in a trade with the Colorado Rockies. For now, though, the Flames remained a work in progress.

The Flames had opened the 1981–82 season with a tie and a win, but had stalled and were on a three-game losing streak when they travelled to Edmonton for their October 16 meeting with the Oilers. On this night, their fortunes did not improve.

With Ron Low back in goal for the Oilers, Paul Coffey and Mark Messier staked the veteran stopper to a 2–0 first-period lead.

Gretzky failed to register a shot on goal in the opening 20 minutes of this night's game, but after Nilsson scored four minutes into the second period, Gretzky restored Edmonton's two-goal lead at the 6:21 mark. It continued to be a back-and-forth game through the remainder of the middle frame: Lever scored for Calgary at 8:31 to again draw the visitors to within a goal of the Oilers. Unhappy with the way things were going, at the start of the third Sather pulled Low from the Edmonton net and replaced him with Andy Moog. It was Sather's job to worry about his team's goaltending. As for the Oilers skaters, well, they had their minds on other things.

"It was interesting because as a group we really didn't worry too much about goaltending," Gretzky said. "We knew that our goalies were going to be good, but if we had to, we'd win 7–6. Unfortunately, you weren't going to win a Stanley Cup thinking that way. We had a great deal of confidence in both of them. We never looked at them in terms of their age or who was number one and number two, or in the case of 1981–82, who was number three. We always looked at our goalies as being in a healthy competition. In 1981–82 we just knew we had three good goalies who were making each other better."

Swapping Low for Moog did not have the desired results; at the start of the third period, Nilsson tied the game after just one minute had gone by. Glenn Anderson (with assists from Gretzky and Kevin Lowe) and Messier then scored 17 seconds apart to give the Oilers a little breathing room, but the Flames refused to go away and defenceman Phil Russell scored to make it 5–4 with just over 10 minutes left to go in the game. Gretzky responded a minute later by setting up left winger Brett Callighen at the 10:27 mark, and goals by Matti Hagman and Stan Weir concluded what developed into a third-period offensive assault on the Flames.

This is how things were in the '80s: despite being thumped and allowing Gretzky to score once and set up two other goals, the Flames declared after the game that they had done a great job of keeping the Great One in check.

"We were pretty rotten," Nilsson admitted more recently. "We didn't let Gretzky hurt us too much, but we didn't stop their other guys."

Perhaps he was referring to Messier, who scored twice, or Jari Kurri who had four assists.

Jari Kurri was just one of the Oilers scratching the surface of what would eventually become a Hall of Fame career. "Jari was very quiet early in his career," recalled Kevin Lowe. "It wasn't until around 1988 that he actually started to become more vocal in the dressing room. He didn't have great command of the English language when he first came to North America, and he hardly ever spoke. He let his play on the ice do his speaking for him."

Messier and Kurri's big nights were still more examples of exactly how tight the Oilers were. Stopping Gretzky didn't guarantee a win. But Gretzky's three-point night was a relief for the team, and its fans. "When your offence stalls like we did against Winnipeg it's a good sign to bust out with eight goals in the next game," said Gretzky, who now had three goals and eight points in five games.

Game 6 | October 18, 1981

Vs. Chicago Black Hawks

Chicago Stadium, Chicago, Illinois

Just like Billy Joel, Wayne Gretzky and the Edmonton Oilers didn't start the fire. But they did fan the flames.

Not only were they young and fast—not to mention rapidly becoming famous—but they loved nothing more than to score goals. Defence be damned!

In Gretzky's first year in the NHL, 1979–80, the average NHL team scored 3.50 goals per game. The rate climbed marginally to 3.51 the following season, before increasing sharply to 4.01 in 1981–82.

This was well before the awful "dead puck era," when stifling defence threatened to suck the life out of the sport. That mind-numbing era—when holding, interference, and clutching and grabbing all combined to reduce goal scoring—began in 1993–94 and lasted until a lockout cancelled the 2004–05 season. It was a time when third- and fourth-liners had as much impact on the outcome of games as the sport's superstars. It has often been said that you cannot teach a player how to score goals, but you can teach him to prevent them. Coaches certainly took that axiom to heart during this period.

In 1992–93, teams combined for an average of 7.26 goals per game. The following year that dipped to 6.48, and, for the most part, there was a steady decline in scoring that resulted in just 5.12 goals being scored in the average game by the time of the 2003–04 campaign.

It wasn't until the 2004–05 lockout that those charged with running and playing in the world's best hockey league decided to crack down on obstruction in an effort to generate more scoring chances. The NHL also introduced the rule that allowed shootouts to decide games that were still tied after overtime.

In the early '80s, however, the dead puck was not an issue, especially for the young, freewheeling Oilers who really didn't give a hoot about trying to keep pucks out of their net. Their attitude was simple, if somewhat naive: Score four against us? That's fine. We'll score five. Score six against us? Huh! We'll score seven.

It was not a winning formula by any stretch of the imagination, but it was fun to watch. Coming off their 8–4 victory over the Flames at home, the Oilers travelled to Chicago to face the Black Hawks, who had been swept by Calgary in three straight games in the preliminary round of the previous season's playoffs and were off to a slow 1–3–1 start in 1981–82.

Like the Oilers, the Black Hawks were led by a 20-year-old, Denis Savard, who the season before had placed second in team scoring with 28 goals and 75 points in 76 games. The Black Hawks were an interesting collection of players that included four future NHL general managers: Tony Esposito, Doug Wilson, Darryl Sutter, and Bob Murray.

During the off-season, the NHL had realigned its divisions and the Black Hawks were on the move, shifting from the Smythe Division to the Norris Division, which included the Detroit Red Wings, Minnesota North Stars, St. Louis Blues, Toronto Maple Leafs, and Winnipeg Jets. With three losses in their last four games the Black Hawks were getting a little itchy for a victory, so things did not look good when Gretzky scored 1:36 into the first period to give the visiting Oilers the early lead.

Fortunately for the Black Hawks, Gretzky's goal was not a harbinger of things to come, although it set the wheels in motion for the Great One's most productive games of the early season and led to the young scoring genius being chosen as one of a game's three stars for the first time in 1981–82.

The night, however, belonged to the Black Hawk's Darryl Sutter. After a 40-goal campaign the season before, Sutter hadn't scored yet in 1981–82, but in this game he potted two first-period goals, including one of two shorthanded efforts he tallied for the Black Hawks that evening. He tied the game at 3:21 and then, when Kevin Lowe restored Edmonton's lead by making it 2–1, Sutter struck again at 16:33, with the Oilers on the power play.

Chicago took over the game in the middle period, outscoring Edmonton, 3–2, as the Oilers' goaltending woes became a point of concern. Not that it was all the fault of Andy Moog, who was in net that night. He, like Low and Fuhr, was a victim of his teammates' costly, wide-open play that gave odd-man rushes and repeated scoring opportunities to the opposition. Doug Wilson, Tim Higgins, and Al Secord scored for Chicago while Gretzky drew assists on goals by Paul Coffey and Brett Callighen.

In the third period, at 11:13, Gretzky set up Matti Hagman for his fourth point of the night, which tied the score at 5–5, but Chicago's Rich Preston scored the game winner before Sutter added insult to injury by completing a hat trick with his second short-handed marker of the night—an empty-net goal, as the Oilers had pulled Moog for an extra skater to gain a two-man advantage.

Not surprisingly, Sutter led all skaters with eight shots on goal. It was a big night indeed for a player who had been goalless in the season up until then. All told, the Black Hawks outshot the Oilers 45–35, with Hawks goalie Esposito making 30 saves.

Coffey had a big offensive night with a goal and two assists, but it was his giveaway in the game's dying moments that allowed Sutter to score in an empty net. "We always make it harder on ourselves than we should," said Coffey about his team letting in two goals while skating on the power play.

Sather, meanwhile, did his best to maintain a positive attitude. Despite being 3–3–0 out of the gate, the Oilers shared the Smythe Division lead with the Vancouver Canucks, who had played one more game than Edmonton. "We're so close to being a hell of a team; a winning team," Sather insisted after the game, "but we still lose our composure and let mistakes kill us. We could use a defence-man like Larry Robinson [of the Montreal Canadiens] to slow the game down. Either that or have all the players skip a few years and suddenly be 24 instead of 20."

Former Black Hawks superstar and Hockey Hall of Fame member Stan Mikita watched the game and, despite the Chicago victory, was enthralled by Gretzky, telling reporters afterward that he was surprised to see the youngster dominating the sport at such a tender age and going on to compare him to the likes of Bobby Orr, Gordie Howe, Bobby Hull, Maurice Richard, and Guy Lafleur.

"His biggest asset is that he controls the play," Mikita said at the time. "He can speed it way up or he can slow it down; whatever he needs to do to accomplish his objective. I won't say he's unstoppable, but he's awfully close to it right now."

Against Chicago, Sather played Gretzky with just about every other forward on the team. "Tonight might be the most I shifted him around," Sather said. "Sometimes his quickness and stick skills intimidate defenders and sometimes they hypnotize them."

According to Paul Coffey, every player on the team had to be ready to be pulled into the game by Gretzky. It didn't matter where you were on the ice or in the pecking order. "The thing that always impressed me about Wayne was he never passed to a face, he always passed to a jersey," Coffey said in a recent interview. "In other words, if it was me going down the ice and Lee Fogolin is beside me in a better scoring position, Fogolin is getting the puck. It doesn't matter that I am an offensive defenceman and Fogolin is a defensive defence-man. Wayne made the right play. That's what made him so special."

Future Black Hawks captain Troy Murray, who would get into one game with Chicago later that season, was, like everyone else in the hockey world, keenly watching Gretzky to see how high he'd raise the goal-scoring standard. A few years later, Murray would be charged with trying to keep the Great One in check.

"If I held him to three points a game I was happy," said Murray, jokingly patting himself on the back. "The thing about the Oilers back then is they didn't run up the score on teams purposely; they were just that good. Think about it: they had the five best players in the world, all on one team. No wonder they were so difficult to beat."

Game 7 | October 20, 1981

Vs. Calgary Flames

Stampede Corral, Calgary, Alberta

T he Edmonton Oilers, Saskatoon's team?

In a poll conducted by the *Saskatoon Star-Phoenix* and published on October 20, 1981, newspaper readers were asked which Canadian team they cheered for in the National Hockey League. In a city without a team of it own, sports editor John Cherneski said he expected that the Oilers would top the list, and they did. But what really surprised him when he pored over the results was that the Oilers had received more votes than all of the other Canadian teams combined. Here's how the teams ranked:

Edmonton Oilers:	176
Montreal Canadiens:	62
Calgary Flames:	34
Toronto Maple Leafs:	28
Vancouver Canucks:	8
Winnipeg Jets:	6
Quebec Nordiques:	0

So despite being separated from Edmonton by a five-hour drive along the Yellowhead Highway, the city of Saskatoon could officially be considered "Oiler Country." Gretzky might have had a thing or two to do with that.

Six games into the 1981–82 NHL season, Wayne Gretzky had very quietly positioned himself for another solid campaign. Thanks to two goals and seven points in his last two games, he now had a total of four goals and 11 points on the season and was on pace for a 53-goal, 147-point season.

For most players, that would have been a glittering prospect. For Gretzky, though, it represented a slight dip from the 55 goals and 164 points he had amassed the season before. There was absolutely no indication of anything special unfolding, which was what ultimately made Gretzky's dream season so extraordinary. Even so, after having just one assist in his first two games of the season, Gretzky had been on a roll and had now scored in four straight games, while setting up six other goals for his teammates in that span.

Furthermore, his Oilers were only marginally above the .500 mark and were continually being victimized by countless defensive lapses. Ah, the joys of having a very young roster in the NHL. Despite all that, Glen Sather was not about to point the finger at his trio of goaltenders, even though the Oilers had allowed 29 goals in six games.

Sather remarked that the only breather Moog could have been given in the 7–5 loss to the Black Hawks two nights before—a game in which he faced 45 shots—would have come if the Zamboni had "gouged a big hole in the ice."

Reporter Jim Matheson, who covered the Oilers for the *Edmonton Journal*, summed it up best: "Their defence has played more like Bobby Orr than Bobby Baun," he wrote, "and the forwards think a check is something that arrives twice a month."

For this particular game against the Flames in Calgary, Sather put the veteran, Ron Low, in goal once again. It would turn out to be another long, albeit successful, night for the guy charged with keeping pucks out of the net. Low had taken three shots in the groin region the last time he started against the Flames, so, needless to say, Sather's decision to give him the start this night, too, raised a few eyebrows.

Gretzky didn't waste any time extending his points streak to five games when, 4:55 into the first period, he set up Paul Coffey for a goal. Thirty-four seconds later, Matti Hagman followed with a goal, his third of the season, when he tipped a Mark Messier shot past Calgary goaltender Pat Riggin. Flames defenceman Paul Reinhart scored at 6:05, pulling the Flames to within a goal of their rivals. Later in the game, however, Reinhart, who was developing into one of the best young two-way defenders in the NHL, suffered a knee injury and was expected to be out of action for at least three weeks.

Don Lever tied the game for the Flames early in the second period, but the Oilers stormed back and took command with the next two goals: Gretzky scored at 11:28 and checking forward Dave Hunter tallied his second of the year at 17:12, when his long shot deflected off Calgary defenceman Pekka Rautakallio and fooled Riggin. Low kept his team in the game, even while the Flames outshot the visitors from Edmonton, 16–10, in the second period.

Calgary continued to push the pace in the third period, outshooting Edmonton, 11–8, and outscoring the Oilers, 2–1, but the Oilers hung on for the victory. For the Flames, Swedish-born left winger Dan Labraaten scored, as did Guy Chouinard, with Glenn

Anderson replying for the Oilers with the game-winning goal, at 6:21 of the period with an assist from Messier.

Looking back many years later, Calgary general manager Cliff Fletcher said he wasn't the least bit surprised his team was able to score four goals—which should have been enough for a victory— but that the Flames lost because the Oilers scored eight.

"That's what it was like playing the Oilers," Fletcher said. "They beat us one night in Calgary where it was 6–6 and we got a power play with just under two minutes to go in the third period—and we had a good power play. They scored a shorthanded goal and all four of their players were below the hash marks in front of our net. I mean, they had nobody back. One bad bounce for Edmonton and we would have had a four-on-none. The [neutral zone] trap was a foreign word back then." And the people who benefited most, especially in Alberta, were the fans. "It was the most exciting hockey I've ever seen in my life," Fletcher said.

The Oilers were now 4–3–0, starting the year with a victory and winning every second game since. Gretzky, for one, was a little concerned with his team's inability to string consecutive wins together.

In 1980–81, rookie Glenn Anderson, a fourth-round pick by the Oilers (and the 69th choice overall), scored 30 goals and 53 points in 58 games. He was clearly poised to take his game to the next level as a sophomore. With blazing speed and infinite determination, Anderson registered a point in each of the first seven games of the 1981–82 season. It would not be long before the future Hockey Hall of Famer had established himself as one of the best left wingers in the NHL.

"It is very important for us to get off to a good start," Gretzky said at the time. "The first 10 games [of the season] are vitally important and we have to climb a steady pace over 80 games, peaking for the playoffs. Hopefully we'll get the home-ice advantage in the playoffs so we don't have to travel too much." Throughout his 21-year professional career, Gretzky was very uneasy with air travel, so it's no surprise to hear that the youngster enjoyed playing home games.

It's funny how a mere two points can change the context of a season. Following the win over Calgary, Gretzky was suddenly on pace for 57 goals and 160 points. Still, he had given no indication of the greatness that would ultimately unfold, but he was certainly trending in the right direction.

Game 8 | October 21, 1981

Vs. Hartford Whalers

Northlands Coliseum, Edmonton, Alberta

What do Paul Coffey, Dave Keon, Gordie Howe, Mark Howe, Bobby Hull, Ron Francis, and Brendan Shanahan have in common?

You guessed it: they've all been elected to the Hockey Hall of Fame. Plus, at one time each played for the Hartford Whalers. Although, to be fair, many of those legendary names played the bulk of their Hall of Fame careers elsewhere, and that fact, along with a host of others, contributed to the Hartford Whalers never really amounting to much as an NHL franchise.

Established in 1972–73, the then New England Whalers won the first Avco Cup in the World Hockey Association's inaugural season. They played their first two seasons in Boston before settling in Hartford. After joining the NHL in 1979, when the WHA folded into that league, the Whalers played 18 seasons in Hartford before becoming the Carolina Hurricanes in 1997. In those 18 years, they won exactly one playoff series: in 1985–86, the Whalers swept the Quebec Nordiques in three games in the best-of-five preliminary round before being beaten in seven games by the Montreal Canadiens in the Adams Division final.

While Glen Sather had a strategy for building his team out of the ashes of the defunct WHA, developing his young players' skills regardless of the growing pains, Larry Pleau, who took over as the Whalers coach/GM partway through the 1980–81 season, was pretty much playing the hand he had been dealt. And it wasn't pretty.

The Whalers were led by Blaine Stoughton, who had been a scoring ace with the junior Flin Flon Bombers of the Western Hockey League and with the WHA's Cincinnati Stingers. Stoughton was a pro hockey journeyman, but he scored a respectable 258 goals and 449 points in 526 NHL games.

The Whalers lineup, like that of the Oilers, featured a few kids who would later emerge as NHL stars: 18-year-old Ron Francis started the season in junior with Gretzky's former team, the Sault Ste. Marie Greyhounds, but after scoring 18 goals and 48 points in 25 games, the Whalers decided he was NHL-ready. They were right. Francis wound up with 28 goals and 68 points in 59 games. Mark Howe, 26, made a successful transition from forward to defence and was becoming a solid NHLer who would ultimately be elected to the Hockey Hall of Fame. Doug Sulliman, 22 and a solid NHL worker bee, enjoyed his best NHL season in 1981–82, with 29 goals and 69 points in 77 games. Another young defenceman for the Whalers, Mickey Volcan, was just 19, but his career never really got off the ground after the team brought him up the season before.

As for Hartford's veterans, Dave Keon was at one time one of the best and most complete players ever to skate in the NHL, but he was now 41 years old and in his final season—there wasn't a whole lot left in the tank. Rick MacLeish had tasted glory with the Philadelphia

Flyers' Stanley Cup teams of the mid-1970s, but was mostly ineffective at this stage of his career with Hartford. Defenceman Paul Shmyr, at 35, was an experienced tough guy, also in his final year of pro hockey.

The Whalers' goaltending duo of John Garrett and Greg Millen were both graduates of the Ontario Hockey League's Peterborough Petes. Coincidentally, both would transition to the role of television hockey analyst.

Basically, the Whalers had enough skill and experience to be in games, but were nowhere near a threat to win the Stanley Cup—or even to make the playoffs. Early in the 1981–82 season, they appeared to be competitive, managing two ties and a one-goal defeat before the wheels started to come off. By time of their sixth game of the season, in Edmonton, they were riding a two-game losing streak. Montreal had beaten them, 7–2, and Detroit, 8–1.

Though the Oilers were at 4–3–0, they had yet to win back-to-back games. But on this night the Oilers did get their second consecutive victory, though Gretzky had no hand in it. He played in the game, but didn't register a point or even a single shot on goal. It was the fifth time in his young NHL career that this happened. Credit Hartford checking centre Rick Meagher with keeping the Great One silent for the evening. Meagher, on the other hand, had an assist and four shots on goal.

"We did a good job on Gretzky," said Hartford coach Larry Pleau afterward, "but this game proved they are not a one-man team. They've got a lot of guys that can hurt you."

Indeed, the Oilers did have a lot of weapons, and two of their hottest in the early going were Mark Messier and Matti Hagman. The first period opened with Messier scoring his seventh goal of the season at 6:11. Hagman connected at 19:01 with his fourth goal in four games. Hagman, who was 26 years old and in his fourth and final NHL season, broke in past startled Whalers defencemen Paul Shmyr and Jack McIlhargey and beat Garrett with a shot from five feet out.

The Whalers outscored the Oilers, 2–1, in the second period, with Stoughton and Sulliman scoring for Hartford and Garry Unger sending one across the crease for the Oilers. For Unger it was his second goal of the season and first since opening night. It wasn't a happy night for him, however. Later in the game, he tried to block a shot by Hartford defenceman Chris Kotsopoulos, and although the puck missed him, the defender's skate hit him in the face and Unger left the game with a suspected broken cheek. Doug Hicks and Paul Coffey scored for the Oilers in the third period.

If Gretzky had a rare night to forget, it was Hagman who stole the spotlight. He added to his goal with two assists, for a three-point night, and afterward Edmonton assistant coach Billy Harris described him as being effective at critical times. Glen Sather went a step farther, stating Hagman "controlled the game."

Messier, who played left wing for the first few years of his NHL career before becoming one of the most dominant centres in NHL-league history, felt lucky to be playing with Hagman, underrated though he was. "I was playing left wing on a line with Glenn Anderson and Matti Hagman and we had some really good chemistry," Messier recently recalled. "Matti was a great distributor of the puck and he would find Andy or me in full stride in open ice. A good winger always needs a good centre, so he provided that ability to distribute the puck."

Also celebrating was defenceman Risto Siltonen, who, with three assists, not only matched Hagman in points but registered his one-hundredth NHL point.

It was also a significant night for Grant Fuhr, who had his first NHL victory. While each team managed 28 shots on goal, Fuhr stopped all but two, for a 5–2 win. He was particularly strong in the third period, when the Whalers pumped 17 shots his way and he turned them all aside.

Coffey recalled being thrilled for Fuhr, but conceded that the first time he saw the young goalie play, he wasn't impressed. "I remember going to a Memorial Cup game in Windsor to see my old junior team, the Kitchener Rangers, play," Coffey said. "I was sitting high in the corner of the rink with the Oilers chief scout Barry Fraser, and he says to me, 'What do you think of the kid in net?' I say, 'Which end?' He says, 'Victoria.' They were losing, 8–3, so I say, 'Uh, I don't know.' Barry says, 'We're going to pick him.' I turn to Barry and say, 'I don't know about that. I don't block a whole lot of shots and I ain't about to start now.' Barry laughs and says, 'You can't go on just one game,' and that is what made him such a great scout."

Game 9 | October 23, 1981

Vs. Pittsburgh Penguins

Northlands Coliseum, Edmonton, Alberta

O ne of the great advantages of playing on a team with Wayne Gretzky was that the opposition was so consumed with trying to stop him that they often forgot about the other players.

After a three-point effort two nights earlier against the Hartford Whalers—in which Gretzky didn't produce a point or even a shot on goal—Matti Hagman continued to hold a hot hand when Pittsburgh came to town on October 23, scoring two goals and drawing two assists. The six-foot-one, 185-pound native of Helsinki, Finland, came to North America to play for the Boston Bruins in the 1976–77 season, during which he scored 11 goals and 28 points in 75 games. Decent numbers for a third- and fourth-liner. The next year he started the season with the Bruins and had four goals and five points in 15 games before Boston sold his contract to the Quebec Nordiques, then of the World Hockey Association.

Although Hagman played well in the WHA, scoring 25 goals and 56 points in 53 games, he decided to return to Finland to play with the Sports Club Comrades (HIFK Helsinki) for the next two seasons before taking a second stab at an NHL career. Playing in the top Finnish league was nothing new to Hagman. He first played for HIFK Helsinki when he was 17 years old—a boy against men.

Glen Sather had an ulterior motive for bringing Hagman back to the NHL. The Oilers had an emerging young winger from Finland, Jari Kurri, who didn't speak a lick of English when he arrived in Edmonton in 1980. Sather felt it was important to surround Kurri with fellow countrymen, so, to help make the transition to living and playing in North America a little easier for the future Hockey Hall of Famer, he acquired Hagman and defenceman Risto Siltanen.

"I thought I'd need more experience back home, but Matti was a big reason I decided to come to the NHL that first year," Kurri said.

In fact, Hagman made the pass that set up Kurri for his first of 601 NHL goals.

While Gretzky and Mark Messier eventually formed one of the greatest one-two punches at centre for the Oilers, for the time being Hagman was the team's number-two centre, while Messier played on his left side. In his first season with the Oilers, Hagman scored 20 goals and 53 points in 70 games. He looked much more comfortable playing at the NHL level as a 24-year-old than he had four years earlier.

After having suffered a broken foot and being held pointless in the Oilers first three games of the 1981–82 season, Hagman finally scored his first goal, and then there was no stopping him. He briefly put up numbers at a Gretzky-like pace, and his two goals against the Penguins on this night gave him six in five games.

The Penguins were 3–4–2 heading into the game against Edmonton, but had little chance of winning after the Oilers scored on three of their first five shots against Pittsburgh goalie Paul

Harrison. Glenn Anderson, Hagman, and Gretzky each landed one in the first 8:25 of the game. The score, however, didn't accurately reflect the game, as the Penguins outshot the Oilers, 15–10, in the first period.

For the second game in a row, Fuhr started and, as would be the case for years to come, supplied his team with saves while the skaters in front of him generally ignored defensive play. Even the Penguins were suitably impressed with the young stopper's performance: "He was unconscious in the first period," Pittsburgh left winger Paul Mulvey said. "It should have been 3–2 or 3–3. When we came back to score twice in the second, he could have let down, but he got even stronger." Throughout his career, Fuhr would often bend, but rarely break.

The Penguins did put a bit of a scare into Edmonton by outscoring them, 3–2, in the second period with goals from Randy Carlyle and Mark Johnson. But the Oilers responded with goals from Dave Hunter and Pat Hughes. Hughes's goal was noteworthy because Fuhr drew an assist—his first in the NHL. Pat Boutette completed the Penguins' scoring at 18:11 of the second.

The Oilers gained the momentum in the third period, and the result was three unanswered goals in their eventual 8–3 win. Hagman struck again, as did Messier for his eighth goal of the season, and with four minutes left to play, Gretzky set up Coffey for Edmonton's eighth goal of the game.

Today, Fuhr is in the record books as the third-highest-scoring goalie of all time, with 46 assists, trailing only Tom Barrasso (48 points) and Martin Brodeur (47 points, including two goals).

With two points added to his score sheet that night, Gretzky enjoyed his fifth multi-point game of the season and, one game after being denied a shot on goal, directed five shots at the Penguins net.

A two-point night by the greatest goal scorer in NHL history, even after a game in which he was held without one, didn't dominate the headlines. Even a big four-point night by Hagman, considered a secondary scorer on a team full of young guns, was overshadowed by back-to-back wins from a 19-year-old goaltender. The Penguins outshot the Oilers, 38–27, but Fuhr was spectacular.

The following day, the headline in the *Edmonton Journal* shouted, THE FUHR GOALS THE BETTER!

"He made some game-saving saves and that's the difference between an ordinary goalie and a good one," Sather said at the time.

Added defenceman Paul Coffey: "To me he's playing like he's been in the league for 10 years instead of three weeks."

Years later, Coffey still chuckled when he thought of the rookie goalie who now holds a place in the Hall of Fame. There would be ups and downs to come—off the ice more than on it—for Fuhr, who battled substance-abuse issues, but no one could deny his ability to win hockey games.

"Grant has not changed a bit," Coffey said in a recent interview. "He was the perfect goalie for that team and that group. We had fun when he first broke in . . . just treated him like any other rookie, even though he was a first-round pick. Fuhrsie would just shrug his shoulders and roll with it. His first few seasons, he battled his weight a little bit, and one time [in his sophomore season] Glen Sather sent him down to the Moncton Alpines of the American Hockey League as a wake-up call. Grant just said, 'No worries; I'll be back.'

"He was incredible because he instilled so much confidence in us as players. Nothing fazed him. We'd be down 4–2 at home with the fans getting on our case, and between periods Grant would say, 'Don't worry boys, they ain't getting any more.' Our eyes would light up and we'd win, 8–4."

Game 10 | October 24, 1981

Vs. Colorado Rockies

McNichols Sports Arena, Denver, Colorado

I t was just a matter of time until youthful Mark Messier's hands caught up with the rest of his rapidly developing man's body. And when they did, there was no turning back. As a teenager, Messier was an emerging power forward who made a rare jump from Tier II junior, with the Alberta Junior Hockey League's St. Albert Saints, directly to professional hockey with the World Hockey Association's Indianapolis Racers. When he signed his contract, he was 17 years old, the same age as Wayne Gretzky had been during his brief stint with the Racers a year before.

The two shared an instant mutual admiration and a bond that grew quickly.

"Mess said that one year in the WHA, although he didn't accomplish much, was so important for his development," said former Oilers defenceman Kevin Lowe. "It made his first few years in the NHL easier. Wayne really accepted Mess, and that was the great thing about the two of them. Mark respected Wayne so much. The Messiers, Mark and his dad, Doug, knew how great Wayne was.

There was never any envy. Conversely, Wayne really accepted Mark as his peer. I really think that helped with Mark's development. That helped expedite Mark to becoming a great player."

The son of career minor leaguer Doug Messier, Mark Messier was a beast of a teenager, a strong and mean competitor whose physical prowess attracted the attention of former NHL defenceman Pat Stapleton, head coach of the Racers. Stapleton had played with Doug Messier, and he signed his son to a pro contract for $30,000. The WHA, in a desperate effort to attract talent, targeted the players deemed too young and therefore ineligible by the NHL. Messier, at 17 years old, clearly had "professional" written all over him, and if the NHL wouldn't let him play, then the WHA would.

Messier didn't get a point in his five games with Indianapolis and was released just before the franchise folded. Not long afterward, the WHA's Cincinnati Stingers signed him, and with them he played 47 games, scoring a goal and adding 10 assists for a very modest 11 points with 58 penalty minutes. It wasn't his scoring output but his physical play and determination that were the greatest indicators of better days ahead.

Unlike Gretzky, whose magical scoring ability was evident right from the get-go, Messier's bread and butter was his ferocity. At six foot one and more than 200 pounds, he was a horse of a player. Or, as he became known, a Moose.

"Bobby Clarke [of the Philadelphia Flyers] said after our first playoff series in 1980 something along the lines of, 'Yes, that team is going to be really good, and obviously Gretzky is amazing, but watch out for Messier,'" Kevin Lowe recalled. "Mess started to exert himself physically even though he was only 18 years old. The nastiness comes naturally from his dad and how he believes the game should be played. He had the body to do it. He was a man-child at a young age."

In his first two NHL seasons, Messier continued to assert himself physically while the offensive side of his game improved at a steady pace. He scored 12 goals and 33 points with 120 penalty minutes in 1979–80 and nearly doubled his offensive numbers—23 goals and 63 points—as a sophomore in 1980–81. Like his other young Oilers teammates, Messier was ready to bust out in 1981–82.

Messier was always going to be a superstar. It was in the cards and it didn't matter where or with whom he played. That said, it didn't hurt to have Gretzky playing ahead of him. Teams that drew up a game plan to defeat the Oilers always placed a high priority on trying to stop Number 99. They played their best checking forwards and top defensive pairs against him. Messier and those not fortunate enough to play on Gretzky's line had more freedom to manoeuvre on the ice.

By 1981–82, Messier was ready to take his game to the next level. He scored six goals in Games 2 through 5 of the season. He didn't score in Game 6 or 7, though he drew his first two assists of the season in Edmonton's 5–4 win over the Calgary Flames, but in Games 8 and 9, Messier was back at it again—after nine games, the hulking left winger had eight goals and 10 points. Suddenly, the Oilers' opponents had more than Gretzky to worry about.

On opening night, the Colorado Rockies limited Messier to just two shots on goal, but in the rematch, a mere two weeks and two days later, this time in Denver, he owned the ice.

Having come in to relieve starter Phil Myre in the season opener, Rockies goalie Chico Resch was given the start this time against the Oilers, who were riding a three-game winning streak.

On some level it was a good decision, as Resch made 50 saves. The problem for Colorado was that he allowed three goals—two by Messier—and the Rockies only found the back of the net once. The loss dropped Colorado's woeful early season record to one win, six losses, and two ties.

It was a frustrating night for Gretzky, who pumped shot after shot Resch's way, only to have the veteran stopper boot each one back. Gretzky got a goal—his second game winner of the season, mind you—to go with an assist, marking the second straight game he finished with one and one.

"I had eight shots against Resch and I probably could have scored on six of them if he hadn't been so hot," Gretzky proclaimed after the game. "We won and that makes any game enjoyable, but watching Resch play like that was a treat, even though it was frustrating."

After a scoreless first period, during which Resch made 16 saves to Oilers starter Ron Low's nine, Messier opened the scoring at 8:52 of the second: Resch had stopped Gretzky on a breakaway and then thwarted defenceman Lee Fogolin, but Messier charged the net and swatted home the rebound.

Colorado's Tapio Levo tied the score at one, with a power-play goal a minute and 10 seconds later, but Gretzky struck at 14:34 with the only goal the Oilers needed to claim their fourth straight victory.

"[Gretzky] messes you up something awful," said Resch, who was chosen first star of the game. "Instead of coming right at you with his shot, he comes laterally catching a goalie in between as he moves across the goal line."

Still, it was Messier who, at 5:54 of the third period, capped the scoring with his second goal of the game and 10th of the season—in the team's first 10 games. The previous season, when he scored a total of 23 goals, he did not register his 10th of the season until January.

Incidentally, Messier was three goals ahead of Gretzky at this point.

"I don't know what the secret is," Messier admitted. "It's just that I seem to be shooting the puck better and more often."

Quietly celebrating his first multi-point game of the season, captain Lee Fogolin, with two assists, registered his 100th career assist in the win over the Rockies.

At the end of the night, though, everyone was talking about the losing goalie, who put on a magical display against some of the best sharpshooters in the NHL.

"This is the kind of game when you might expect to fatten up your statistics," defenceman Paul Coffey claimed. "But when a goalie plays like that you just feel lucky to get out with a win."

Throughout his career, Resch was a scrapper—a survivor—who constructed a respectable 231–224–82 record with a 3.27 goals-against average (high by today's standards, but a reflection of the era he played in) and .867 save percentage.

Those who had the pleasure of playing on the same team as Resch had a great appreciation of his ability and contributions.

"Chico Resch was a competitor," said Lanny McDonald. "He kind of reminded me of Johnny Bower in that he hated to give up goals. Coming from the Islanders, he had to change his whole approach to the game. Playing for the Rockies was definitely a pressure situation in that you were going to see a lot of pucks. But Chico enjoyed that; he relished that particular challenge, and when it came to playing a team like the Oilers, he couldn't wait to play them."

Ten games into the 1981–82 NHL season, and Wayne Gretzky and the Oilers had a win-loss record of 7–3 and were in first place in the

Smythe Division by six points. Offensively, they had scored the most goals of any team in the NHL, and five Oilers were in the league's top 20 in the individual scoring race, with Gretzky in the lead.

However, next on the calendar was a date with the two-time defending Stanley Cup champion New York Islanders, the team that, the previous spring, had ended the Oilers' season.

Game 11 | October 27, 1981

Vs. New York Islanders

Nassau Veterans Memorial Coliseum, Uniondale, New York

O n November 8, 1971, the NHL awarded two new expansion franchises—one to the city of Atlanta, the other to be based on Long Island in New York—bringing the number of teams in the league to 16. Both teams began playing in the NHL at the start of the 1972–73 season. The Atlanta team was nicknamed the Flames, while the team in Long Island was christened the New York Islanders.

Now in their 10th season in the NHL, the Islanders were unquestionably the league's model franchise, as well as the two-time defending Stanley Cup champions and the team that had ended the Edmonton Oilers' season the previous spring.

The Islanders' success story began when they hired Bill Torrey, who was brought in as the team's general manager on February 14, 1972, almost eight months before the franchise's first-ever game. From the very beginning, Torrey was committed to building the Islanders through the draft, though he knew how many agonizing seasons there would be before the team would taste success. The Islanders finished dead last in each of their first two seasons, 1972–73 and 1973–74, but in the third year they reached the playoffs, and quickly, almost absurdly so, emerged as one of the NHL's top teams.

True to his word, Torrey built a championship team, mostly by choosing in the draft the likes of Denis Potvin, Bryan Trottier, Mike Bossy, and Clark Gillies (each of whom would one day be enshrined in the Hockey Hall of Fame), along with a strong supporting cast of Bob Nystrom, John Tonelli, Garry Howatt, Ken Morrow, Dave Langevin, and Bob Lorimer. In 1980, Torrey also made a deal that shuffled centre Billy Harris and defenceman Dave Lewis to the Los Angeles Kings and brought the excellent two-way centre Robert "Butch" Goring to New York. It has been suggested that Goring was the final piece of Torrey's championship puzzle, and the trade has been held up over the years as one of the best deadline deals ever.

Torrey had also wisely hired Al Arbour as his head coach in 1973–74. Arbour had been a bespectacled defenceman who played 626 NHL games before becoming the head coach of the St. Louis Blues. He had a calm demeanour behind the bench and the young Islanders seemed to feed off him. Working in tandem, Torrey and Arbour built a dynasty.

While the young Edmonton Oilers played the game with reckless abandon and little regard for defence, the Islanders were a big, strong, fast, physical, and disciplined team. Trottier, 23 years old when the Islanders won their first Cup in the spring of 1980, was rapidly becoming the best two-way centre in the NHL. Bossy, all of 22 years old when he first sipped champagne from the Cup that same spring, scored like a machine and had 241 goals in his first four NHL seasons.

If the Oilers were going to supplant the Islanders as Stanley Cup champions, they would have to mature and play a more refined game. Their day would eventually come in the spring of 1984, but not before the Islanders won two more Stanley Cups, in 1982 and 1983, respectively, to make it four championships in a row. In fact, when the Islanders won the Stanley Cup in 1983, it was against the emerging Oilers, in four straight games. As the story goes, when the defeated Oilers made their way out of the rink, they passed the Islanders dressing room and saw a beaten and battered championship team sitting in their stalls, trying to summon the energy to shower and change. Right then and there, the Oilers realized what type of commitment it takes to win a championship in the greatest hockey league in the world.

Denis Potvin, who boasted one of the NHL's all-time great combinations of skill and toughness, looked back on those days and concluded, "Our game was more complete. It was pretty well known we could play a speed game, a physical game, a high-intensity game, a defensive game. We could play it any way you want it.

"We went from beating the Flyers and Bruins, who were tough teams, to beating the Oilers, who were a speed team, to beating a young Minnesota team that had great players like Dino Ciccarelli and Bobby Smith. We could play any style. That was really the cornerstone of why we could stay on top of the game for so long."

The Islanders fired on all cylinders. Bossy, who two years before had dipped to 51 goals from the 69 he scored in 1978–79, was coming off his miraculous 50-goals-in-50-games season, during which he tallied a total of 68 goals.

Having had a front-row seat for all of Bossy's heroics, Potvin recalled, in a recent interview, the utter lack of complication in his teammate's game. "In my view he always shot at the same spot—he always went five-hole," Potvin said. "You didn't have the butterfly goaltenders back then. I'll never forget, we were at the Hockey Hall of Fame one time and we were taking some questions. Somebody said to Mike, 'Geez, with the new style of goaltending they'd take the five-hole away from you; do you think you would have scored as many goals as you did?' Boss, looked at him, smiled and said, 'I would have found another hole.' And he would have.

"He had such an amazing release, but really, the bottom line is, you are talking about a guy who lived to score goals. That was what he wanted to do the most, and he expected to score. He would never let up, not even in practice. He would score in practice and he would score in games. He wanted to score every time he took a shot. His intensity was all about scoring goals. He had the hands for it, he had the confidence, and he had the quick release. It never stopped until the back injury and he couldn't do it anymore."

Bossy would ultimately finish the 1981–82 season with 64 goals, adding 17 more in 19 playoff games to claim the Conn Smythe Trophy as most valuable player in the playoffs while the Islanders skated off with their third consecutive Stanley Cup.

When the Oilers and Islanders met for the first time in the 1981–82 season on the evening of October 27, Edmonton was riding a four-game winning streak, while New York was 6–1–1. This game was the Oilers' biggest challenge of the young season.

And Wayne Gretzky did not have a banner night. For the second time in four games, he was held without a shot on goal. Not only that, but Gretzky learned firsthand about the hazard of hanging around the Islanders' goal crease when Billy Smith was between the pipes.

Better known as "Battling Billy" because of his penchant for using his goalie stick to chop at opponents who dared invade his space, Smith whacked Gretzky across the knee at 7:17 of the second period. There was no penalty on the play, much to Gretzky and the Oilers' chagrin.

Gretzky crumpled to the ice in pain and couldn't bring himself to finish the game. He tried, playing two more shifts, but eventually headed to the Oilers dressing room. Still, he did not leave pointless. Paul Coffey gave Edmonton a 1–0 lead at 4:46 of the opening period, and Gretzky set up the goal. The Islanders' John Tonelli tied it on the power play at 9:22 of the second period, but Edmonton stormed back, scoring twice more: Mark Messier got his 11th, and Risto Siltanen subsequently made it a two-goal lead. Siltanen would end up leading all the night's players with nine shots on goal.

Bossy made it 3–2 in the final minute of the middle frame, and from that point forward, all the scoring belonged to the Islanders. Moog, who hadn't played since October 18, raced out of his net after a loose puck and actually beat Bossy to it. Rather than freezing the puck, Moog shot it, and, unluckily, it hit Bossy, who deposited it into the Oilers' empty net. Wayne Merrick scored twice in the third to secure an Islanders' victory. The first was the result of a bad clear by Moog and the second—the game winner—was a tip-in. With Gretzky out of the third, the Islanders outshot the visitors, 16–5, for a 34–28 advantage in the game.

Afterward, Glen Sather was incensed that Smith had chopped down his team's best player. "That was bull," Sather snarled. "Smith could have ended Wayne's career like that. I don't care who it is, Wayne Gretzky or a rookie up in his first NHL game, you don't do that. It's not the way this game is played. It was a typical Smith cheap shot that he has been getting away with for 10 years."

Sather promised to send a tape of the play to the NHL head office in an effort to have Smith fined or suspended. (He did exactly that, and the NHL office did not feel supplemental discipline was necessary. As Sather surmised, Smith got away with another one.)

For his part, the Islander goalie was far from repentant. Then in his 11th NHL season, Billy Smith had chopped more than a few opponents with his goal stick, and he didn't issue apologies. "He's a crybaby," Smith said of Gretzky. "He goes looking for the refs every time he gets touched. He might be a great player, but you don't treat him any different than anybody else. Gretzky is known for scoring goals from behind the net. Am I supposed to just let him score?" Smith didn't stop there. "Gretzky's a little shit," he said, "and he put on an act. Look, he's trying to beat me and I'm trying to beat him. If what I did was as terrible as he claimed, I would have gotten a penalty. Look at the films and you'll see what I mean."

Gretzky limped out of Nassau Coliseum, and some feared he might not recover to face the Rangers at Madison Square Garden the following evening. But despite Smith's insinuations, Gretzky was quickly garnering a reputation for defending his own honour. When told what Smith said about him after the game, Gretzky smiled and said, "I guess you have to consider the source. Billy should be talking about crybabies. All he did was complain and moan every day at Team Canada camp [for the 1981 Canada Cup]. He was trying to break up the team." Then he cut Smith a little slack. "Billy swung at me on purpose," Gretzky says, "but I told people I don't think he meant to hurt me; just scare me off."

Game 12 | October 28, 1981

Vs. New York Rangers

Madison Square Garden, New York, New York

I n contrast to their neighbours, the two-time defending champion Islanders, the New York Rangers hadn't won the Stanley Cup since 1940. They had, however, enjoyed a highly successful season in 1980–81, having reached the Stanley Cup semifinals, only to be eliminated in four straight games by, you guessed it, the Islanders.

That success from the spring of 1981 hadn't, at least so far, continued, as the Rangers opened the 1981–82 season with three consecutive losses and were in the midst of a two-game losing streak when the visiting Oilers arrived in the city.

But, good news for the Rangers, Edmonton's best player—Gretzky—was still suffering from his bang-up on Long Island the night before, when Islanders goaltender Billy Smith slashed him across the leg. Following that game, it didn't look very likely that Gretzky would suit up for the game against the Rangers.

Gretzky, however, had other plans. While many other players might have begged off for the night to rest a sore leg, Gretzky did not surrender to the pain. "My dad always told me pros are paid to play," Gretzky told the media after facing the Rangers. "I'm making good money, and even though the leg was sore, I had to try to play."

In an effort to make sure he was healthy enough to face the Rangers, Gretzky had spent the previous night with his swollen leg bent and tied with a string to keep it in position, all the while attempting to get a bit of sleep. In addition to nursing an injured knee, the Great One also had to face his dissatisfaction with his numbers from the last four games.

One of the things that separate the truly great players from the rest of the pack is their ability to perform at a high level under less than perfect circumstances. During his career, time and again Gretzky was considered down and out, only to rise to the occasion when the chips were down. The 12th game of the 1981–82 season, against the Rangers, at Madison Square Garden, was one such occasion. And he had an additional incentive to go out and have a grand night: earlier in the day, he had agreed to a contract extension with the Oilers that made him the highest-paid player in the NHL.

Gretzky's salary was $150,000 in 1980–81, and he was set to get $280,000 for the 1981–82 season, which was a pittance compared to the $450,000 that the Los Angeles Kings were paying Marcel Dionne. Negotiations for his new deal had taken place during the summer, but had lagged. Oilers owner Peter Pocklington was under no obligation to tear up Gretzky's old deal and significantly increase his pay, but in light of Gretzky's unparalleled accomplishments in his first two NHL seasons, as well as the widespread acknowledgement that he was the best player in the sport, Pocklington realized that sweetening the deal for Gretzky was the strategic thing to do.

Gretzky would publicly admit his surprise at how long it took to get the finished deal done. But apparently the terms pleased him in the end. "It's a very nice contract," Gretzky cracked with his typical grin.

No details about the contract were shared with the public, but speculation was that Gretzky would be paid $550,000. The two sides had come to an agreement on October 27, with the details leaking out on the day of the game versus the Rangers, the 28th, with Pocklington telling the media, "In the next 10 years he'll make over $10 million subject to today's rate of inflation, and team and personal bonuses."

Money aside, Gretzky had a job to do on the night of October 28, and despite his sore leg, he was ready for the Rangers. In fact, the game against the Rangers heralded the real start of his march toward being the only player in history to score 50 goals in 39 games.

And it all started with his wearing a girdle to protect a swollen knee. In the opening 20 minutes of the game, Gretzky was visibly slowed by the injury and didn't register a shot on goal in the period.

With teenage goaltender Grant Fuhr back in net for the fourth start of his young professional career, the evening did not begin well for the goalie . . . or the rest of the Oilers, for that matter. New York defenceman Tom Laidlaw opened the scoring at 1:29 when his shot hit a skate and found a hole between Fuhr's pads—and then winger Pat Hickey gave the Rangers a two-goal lead at 12:03.

With veteran centre Garry Unger nursing a facial injury, the Oilers summoned Tom Roulston from the Wichita Wind of the Central Hockey League. A third-round draft pick in 1977—in both the NHL (St. Louis Blues) and WHA (Quebec Nordiques)—Roulston was emerging as a minor-league scoring sensation, having notched 63 goals in 69 regular-season games and 15 more in 18 playoff games. In an 11-game trial with the Oilers in 1980–81, Roulston managed a goal and two points. His second-ever NHL goal, a little over three minutes after Hickey's, narrowed the Ranger lead to 2–1. Even though the Rangers' Mike Rogers responded with another first-period goal, Gretzky and company were just getting warmed up, and their goalie Fuhr was settling into his game, too.

In the second period, Gretzky was clearly feeling better and began making up for lost time. With the strength in his leg improving with each shift, Gretzky set up Paul Coffey for the defenceman's seventh goal of the season, and then proceeded to score two goals in 42 seconds, both inside the final minute of the period, beating Rangers goalie Steve Baker. Both goals also happened with the Oilers on the power play, the first coming while they had a five-on-three advantage. "In a situation where we're two men up, we try to make sure Wayne is handling the puck," Coffey said after the game. "There's no one better with it anyway and when you give us that much edge, Wayne's going to get us a goal."

Gretzky added a fourth point in the last minute of the game when he assisted Dave Hunter on his fourth goal of the season to give Edmonton a 5–3 victory. And typical of Gretzky, instead of celebrating a four-point night after the game, he lamented what could have been a fifth point earlier in the third, when he had a chance for a hat trick but failed to connect on a breakaway. "I don't know what my record is on [breakaways], maybe two-for-eight," Gretzky said. "It's not good; I know that."

Rangers defenceman and captain Barry Beck acknowledged Gretzky's outstanding performance, but said he and his teammates needed to look in the mirror. "Gretzky could have scored five goals tonight with all the chances we gave him," Beck claimed. "We played stupid, and you just don't do that against Wayne Gretzky or a team which scores like the Oilers. They will jump all over your mistakes."

Glen Sather, who had grown accustomed to watching the bud-ding superstar pull rabbits out of hats, acknowledged Gretzky's great-ness and ability to rise to the occasion.

"He's really chipped out of something special," Sather said. "I'm not sure he's mortal." Of course he was mortal, but he was also driven. His teammates saw his ambition on a daily basis. "We had no sense of what was unfolding right in front of us," Kevin Lowe recently recalled. "It was just expected. He won the scoring his first year, really, even though he ended up tied with Marcel Dionne. Although there were naysayers when he first joined the NHL, he basically shut them down his first year in the league. He kept raising the bar. If you saw him in games, there was no selfishness in his game. For Wayne, the game was never over until it was over. If he had five goals, he was gunning for eight. Why stop? That was obviously engrained in him at a young age."

With his two goals and four points, Gretzky had raised his season totals to nine goals and 23 points in 12 games. Scoring at this rate, he'd finish with 60 goals and 153 points in the season, and yet he was not content with his play.

"It's about time I started to do something," Gretzky told the reporters in the Edmonton dressing room after the game. "I haven't really been jumping; maybe just in Colorado last week. I don't know what it is, but I haven't played as well as I should."

Game 13 | October 31, 1981

Vs. Quebec Nordiques

Northlands Coliseum, Edmonton, Alberta

With five wins in their past six games, the Oilers were feeling good about themselves. Gretzky, in particular, was hitting his stride, even though he suggested he hadn't been particularly thrilled with his overall performance through the season's first 11 games.

But a two-goal, four-point performance on an injured leg three nights earlier, when the Oilers played the Rangers, had him smiling on the return home to host the Quebec Nordiques on Halloween night. The Nordiques represented an intriguing test as an opponent that skated easily with the speedy young Oilers and had enough firepower to match them goal for goal.

Led by the three Šťastný brothers—Marián, Peter, and Anton—as well as Michel Goulet, the Nordiques' biggest concern, much like the Oilers', was keeping the puck out of their net. The Nordiques also had a few young guns of their own, including 19-year-old defenceman Randy Moller and 22-year-old sophomore centre Dale Hunter. Réal Cloutier and Wilf Paiement, both 26, were established and dependable forwards, while veterans André Dupont, 33, and Jean Hamel, 30, anchored the blue line. Left winger Marc Tardif, who had been a scoring ace in the WHA with impressive seasons of 71 and 65 goals, in 1975–76 and 1977–78, respectively, still had plenty of gas left in the tank at the age of 33.

Dan Bouchard, 31, was the team's number-one goaltender—a good netminder by NHL standards, but not great. By the time he concluded his NHL career, with the Winnipeg Jets following the 1985–86 season, the native of Val-d'Or, Quebec, had a 286–232–113 record in the regular season with a 3.26 goals-against average. In the playoffs, he was 13–30 with a 3.46 average.

After losing to the Philadelphia Flyers in the preliminary round of the playoffs the spring before, the Nordiques, who had begun the 1981–82 season with a 7–5–0 record in their first 12 games, were seen as a team on the rise, albeit one with some weaknesses, as exhibited in an 8–7 loss to the Los Angeles Kings three nights earlier. That game showed just how badly things could go for the Nordiques when they went into full-offence mode and didn't get good goaltending.

After using his younger goaltenders, Andy Moog against the Islanders and Grant Fuhr against the Rangers, Glen Sather gave Ron Low his first start in a week against the potentially dangerous Nordiques.

Edmonton completely overwhelmed Quebec in the opening period, outshooting the Nordiques, 15–5, and taking a 2–0 lead. Matti Hagman got the Oilers rolling at 2:50 of the opening period while Brett Callighen doubled the score at the 12-minute mark. Gretzky was held without a shot on goal in the first period, but he wouldn't remain quiet for long.

At 4:09 of the second period, Gretzky scored to give the Oilers a 3–0 lead. With each team playing a man short a minute and a half later, Quebec's Marián Šťastný got one in the net for the visitors, but the Oilers stormed back with goals by Matti Hagman and Glenn Anderson to give the Oilers a 5–1 lead after two periods of play. The score doesn't reflect the action on the ice, though. The Nordiques had turned the tables on the Oilers in the middle frame, outshooting Edmonton, 16–8, but Low played superbly.

In the 1981–82 season, teams scored an average of four goals per game, so it wasn't unusual for two teams to be lighting it up on the same night. The Oilers and Nordiques had already combined for six, and the game still had 20 minutes left to play. Gretzky scored his second of the game 1:54 into the third period, which prompted Quebec coach Michel Bergeron to pull Bouchard from the Quebec net and replace him with veteran Michel Plasse. Following Bergeron's move, Dale Hunter and Jacques Richard both scored goals to cut the Oilers lead to 6–3. But the Nordiques' comeback was short-lived.

Glenn Anderson scored his second of the game at 8:12 to give the Oilers a four-goal lead, and Jari Kurri added a pair of goals just 26 seconds apart, at 13:50 and 14:16, with the second featuring an assist from Gretzky. For Kurri, it was a big night, and one filled with relief, as he snapped a frustrating nine-game goalless drought.

With the Oilers leading 9–3, and Gretzky in possession of two goals and an assist, it would have been easy for him to coast to the finish. Instead, he notched his third goal of the night and 12th of the season at the 16:06 mark, and then his 13th goal—in 13 games—at 17:29. Anton Šťastný completed the scoring for the Nordiques on what was, for the visiting team, a night to forget.

Low was at his comical best in the wake of the 11–4 Edmonton win. Most goalies who had allowed four goals would be sullen, but not this Oiler. "It's really tough playing goal on this team when you know you can let in 10 goals and still win," he joked afterward. Low was one of just five Oilers who didn't get a point in the game. (Tom Roulston, Pat Hughes, Dave Hunter, and Curt Brackenbury were the other four.) "That's what really burns me," Low said. "Eleven goals and I don't get a point."

Bergeron wasn't feeling quite as bubbly. He was completely miffed with his team's abundant turnovers of the puck. "Seventeen times in our own end in the first period alone," the Nordiques coach lamented after the game. Bergeron revealed that the game plan had been to run with the bulls. The Nordiques were young and fast and could score goals, so it made sense to engage the Oilers in a good, old-fashioned shootout. "What can you do?" Bergeron said at the time. "We play our style because that is our best chance to win. Edmonton plays that style better than we do and they get 11 goals."

The Oilers' scoring outburst allowed them to maintain their first-place standing in the Smythe Division and set four team records:

Most goals in a game: 11

Most goals scored by both teams in a period: 9

Fastest four goals: scored in 3 minutes, 39 seconds

Fastest five goals: scored in 9 minutes, 17 seconds

With regards to Gretzky, he now had six goals and nine points in the last two games, and season totals of 13 goals and 28 points, all of which put him in first place in the NHL. Since that fateful night in Hartford 10 nights earlier, when he was held without a point or even a shot on goal, Gretzky had amassed eight goals and 14 points in five games.

Also noteworthy, with two goals against the Nordiques, Matti Hagman achieved 100 career NHL points. Unger, who returned from his facial injury, had an assist on Gretzky's hat-trick goal. The veteran paid tribute to Gretzky's determination to shoot the puck more often and gave a tip of the cap to the younger man's passing ability: "He sees everything and makes those soft little passes that look like they would be easy for a defenceman to pick off. But he puts them right by the defenceman and a second later a teammate is there to pick it up. Most guys who handle the puck aren't good goal-scorers, too. But Wayne is shooting more and he has a terrific touch when he shoots."

Gretzky's strategy to make shooting a priority was paying off. Years later, he looked back at the 1981–82 season and was thankful that those close to him encouraged him to alter the way he played the game. "The people around me—mostly Glen Sather, my dad, and my agent, Gus Badali—when they complained about my play at that time, they'd say I needed to shoot more," Gretzky said. "They felt I was passing way too much and I was passing up scoring opportunities. I didn't sit there and say, 'I need to get 50 goals in 50 games and try to tie Mike Bossy and Rocket Richard.' But the fact was these three guys who I respect are telling me I need to shoot more. so that was going to be a goal of mine: to make sure I shot the puck a heck of a lot more than I did the previous season.

"If you ask somebody if they could name one thing about Wayne Gretzky as a player, what would it be? Probably the first response would be, 'He's a playmaker.' That's probably a fair assessment, so there was a little bit of an adjustment for me. There were times when, if it was 50-50 in terms of me shooting or passing, I would lean toward making the pass. At the start of that season, I started consciously thinking to myself, if I have just as good a chance to shoot as I do to make a pass, I'm going to shoot."

Gretzky had just recorded his seventh hat trick and his second four-goal game of his NHL career. The young Oilers celebrated their victory, while the Nordiques tried to figure out what had gone wrong. That is the beauty of an NHL season: just when you think you have things figured out, along comes a curve ball. Things aren't always as they seem.

Game 14 | November 4, 1981

Vs. Toronto Maple Leafs

Northlands Coliseum, Edmonton, Alberta

L ove the Toronto Maple Leafs or hate them, there is no denying that a game against the team from Hogtown has special meaning. It doesn't matter whether they're a good team or out of playoff contention early in the season, the Leafs always draw a huge audience—even when they play on the road. In Canada, they have fans from coast to coast. Over the years, teams have been infuriated, playing home games and seeing half the fans in the seats wearing Toronto jerseys—and the Leafs haven't even won the Stanley Cup since 1967.

The 1981–82 version of the Maple Leafs was a lousy hockey team. Just four years earlier, led by Darryl Sittler, Börje Salming, Ian Turnbull, Tiger Williams, Ron Ellis, and Lanny McDonald, they made it all the way to the Stanley Cup semifinals. Roger Neilson was a respected defensive coach, about whom it was said that he would rather lose a game 1–0 than win one 7–6, and goalie Mike Palmateer had given the team a fighting chance on most nights. But by 1981–82, the Maple Leafs were once again on the latest of what would become a never-ending cycle of youth kicks, turning over the leadership of the club to the likes of 22-year-old Rick Vaive and 23-year-old Bill Derlago. At 30, Salming was still an impactful player, but he was in the last act of what amounted to a Hall of Fame career, and Sittler, also 30, was in the process of playing his final games with the team. He was dealt to the Philadelphia Flyers in January 1982. Others, like Turnbull, Wilf Paiement, Pat Hickey, and Laurie Boschman, shared the same fate.

Their replacements, mostly youngsters such as Rocky Saganiuk, Jim Benning, Norm Aubin, Fred Boimistruck, Bob McGill, and Miroslav Fryčer, all 21 or under, were ill prepared to face the no less youthful, but fast and terrifically talented Oilers, including Gretzky—the hottest player in the NHL.

In goal, the Leafs tandem of Michel "Bunny" Larocque and Vincent Tremblay was one of the weakest in the NHL. Larocque, who had won four Stanley Cups as the backup goalie for the Montreal Canadiens between 1976 and 1979, was now in over his head as the starter with Toronto.

Just 46 seconds after everyone sang the national anthem, Glenn Anderson scored his sixth goal of the season. Then, after six minutes of play, Gretzky tipped a pass from Kurri into the net to give Edmonton a quick 2–0 lead. Falling behind early in games was a problem for the Maple Leafs, who had been drubbed, 9–4, by the Chicago Black Hawks three nights earlier. "It's kind of discouraging," said Toronto coach Mike Nykoluk. "We've been down two goals in the first five minutes of our last four games."

Toronto defenceman Bob McGill put his team on the board at 9:45, cutting the Oilers' lead in half, and in the process notching the first goal of his NHL career. A teenager chosen for his toughness and fighting ability, McGill would never score more than four goals a season in a career that spanned 705 games, so to get his first in a game against and Gretzky and Fuhr, with whom he'd played the season before with the Victoria Cougars, was significant.

"Halfway through the first period we were down 2–0, and I took a penalty and I didn't think it was a very good call by the official, so I chirped at him a little bit and ended up with a double minor [for unsportsmanlike conduct]," McGill recently recalled. "Needless to say, I am sitting in the penalty box, sweating big time, thinking I'm going to be in big trouble if they score a goal just because I was stupid. At the end of the power play, they tried to make a pass across and Wilf Paiement dove and chipped the puck away.

"I stepped out of the penalty box and the puck was right on my tape. I had such a clear-cut breakaway that I don't think I took a stride from the blue line in. Here I am, skating in alone on Grant Fuhr. I was going to go five-hole, but he kind of moved his leg so I slid it along the ice on his stick side and scored my first NHL goal. I only scored 17 goals in my whole career, so to score my first on a breakaway was really quite something special for me."

When Tom Roulston scored to give Edmonton a 3–1 lead at the 11:07 mark of the first period, it looked like the game would be a cakewalk for the Oilers. But the Maple Leafs had other ideas, and while Fuhr made a few big saves, he clearly wasn't as sharp as he had been in his previous four starts. In the middle period, Toronto took full advantage, outscoring Edmonton, 3–1, to put the teams on even terms at 4–4 after 40 minutes: Börje Salming, Bill Derlago, and Rick Vaive scored for the visitors and Pat Hughes responded for the hosts. The Maple Leafs argued that an offside pass had preceded Hughes's goal, but to no avail. "We got up 3–1 and assumed the game was over; like we had it in the bag," said Garry Unger.

The second period had belonged to the Maple Leafs, but the third clearly belonged to the Oilers. A Larocque miscue led to the Oilers' winning goal 3:21 into the frame. The beleaguered goalie attempted to clear the puck, but inadvertently shot it at Glenn Anderson. The puck bounced to a waiting Brett Callighen at the side of the net, and he simply tapped it home. Gretzky would conclude the scoring and ice the 6–4 Edmonton win with an empty-netter at 19:56.

Wilf Paiement drew an assist for the Maple Leafs in Game 14. The rugged Toronto right winger was one of only six players in the history of the NHL to wear 99, the number that Gretzky made famous. Paiement would discard the number when he was traded to the Quebec Nordiques on March 9, 1982. Others who at one time wore the famed number were Léo Bourgault, Joe Lamb, Desse Roche (each of these three wore it for the Montreal Canadiens during the 1934–35 NHL season), and Rick Dudley, who sported the number for 30 games with the Winnipeg Jets at the end of the 1980–81 season. When Gretzky retired in 1999, his number did, too.

While the Oilers secured two points in the third, they were not thrilled with their performance overall. "It was definitely a struggle," Glen Sather said after the game, adding that it was the team's second-worst outing of the season. Only Edmonton's 6–2 loss to the Canucks in Game 2 of the season was worse, he claimed.

And yet, the Oilers now had as many points in the standings as they had on December 20 of the previous season (putting them a full 46 days ahead of their 1980–81 pace) and had the most points of any team in the NHL.

The Maple Leafs, on the other hand, were pleased to get out of Edmonton without being totally humiliated. "The Oilers were scary," McGill said in a recent interview. "If you weren't on the top of your game, they'd hit double digits in goals. And they only got better as they went on. Over the years when they had those teams and we had some bad teams in Toronto, before games against them we literally would be saying, 'We have to be sure we keep these guys in single digits.' Going on the road to Calgary and Edmonton, where they both had good teams, was like going through Death Valley. The Oilers had arguably the best six players in the world playing on their hockey club."

Gretzky's second goal of the game, and eighth in his past three games, meant he had 15 goals in 14 games. For the remainder of the 1981–82 season, he would not slip below a goal-per-game pace.

Looking back at that season, McGill—not the least bit surprised at Gretzky's performance—said, "He was unbelievable. We used to play the Oilers in preseason and then again in the regular season, and one year in a preseason game he scored a goal where he came across the blue line and deked a guy, then he went through the four other guys, plus the guy he had deked in the first place, and scored a goal. The guys on the bench were going, 'Ooo . . . ah . . . uh . . . ooo . . . ' as we watched the play unfold. When he scored, you wanted to jump up and cheer, but you had to give it the old 'Ah, crap.' It was such an amazing goal. It was like he had four sets of eyes."

Game 15 | November 7, 1981

Vs. Colorado Rockies

Northlands Coliseum, Edmonton, Alberta

An impressive and increasing goals-per-game average gets tongues wagging. With 15 goals in his first 14 games of the 1981–82 season, Wayne Gretzky suddenly made people wonder: Could this young prodigy become the third player in the history of the National Hockey League to score 50 goals in 50 games?

On a tear with eight goals in his last three games, Gretzky was an amazing playmaker who had averaged 3.3 shots per game in the 1980–81 season and had vowed to shoot more in 1981–82. But the reality was that he was averaging only 3.6 shots per game in Edmonton's first 14 outings. Such a slight improvement was not exactly what he was aiming for. Still, if he kept scoring at his current rate, he would have a record-breaking 86-goal campaign.

Jim Matheson, who covered the Oilers for the *Edmonton Journal* and won the Elmer Ferguson Memorial Award in 2000 for his body of work, was the first to ask Gretzky about the possibility of scoring 50 in 50.

"It's a little too early to say I'm shooting for it," the modest young man responded. "I'm scoring more than I normally do. My breakdown is usually 40-60 in terms of goals and assists." Gretzky scored 106 goals in his first two NHL seasons—55 in 1980–81 and 51 in 1979–80—but was still regarded more as a pass-first centre than a shooter, perhaps because he had assisted on 109 goals in '80–81, breaking Bobby Orr's record of 102, set in 1970–71.

Gretzky reasoned that if he shot more, he'd score more, and even though his shots-per-game ratio was only up slightly, his recent goals-per-game was sizzling.

"I'm consciously trying to shoot more," Gretzky said at the time. "Other teams figure I'm going to pass 90 percent of the time so I've started shooting. The goal I scored against [Toronto's] Bunny [Larocque] the other night was a perfect example. Two guys went with Jari Kurri so I just walked in. There didn't seem to be any sense in passing."

If Gretzky was having a blast courtesy of his newfound scoring prowess, others outside of Edmonton already wished the season would come to a close. The month of November proved to be a miserable one for the woeful Colorado Rockies—with one exception. The Rockies, who were 2–7–2 in October, actually got worse in November, when they went 1–10–3.

Their one victory? It was against the Oilers in Edmonton.

The man of the hour was Colorado goaltender Chico Resch. After Phil Myre lost to the Oilers, 7–4, on October 7, the season's opening night, Resch played superbly, making 50 saves in a 3–1 loss to Edmonton on October 24. Resch got the start again in Edmonton on November 7, and for the second straight game against the Oilers,

Resch was the first star. The guy at the other end of the ice, Andy Moog, had a night he'd never want to relive.

With 17,490 avid Oilers fans in the stands, Paul Coffey opened the scoring, swooping in off the rush at 18:04 of the first period, but Colorado defenceman Rob Ramage tied the score only 44 seconds later. In the second period, at the 13:19 mark, Pat Hughes scored from a scramble in front of the Colorado goal, and Glenn Anderson made it 3–1 from in tight with only 24 seconds left in the middle stanza. When tough guy Dave Semenko got one past Resch, sending the puck between the pads with a 40-foot shot at 7:16 of the third period, the Oilers held a 4–1 lead and should have been able to put it on cruise control. On this night, though, their youth and inexperience got the better of them.

Finnish defenceman Tapio Levo kicked it into high gear for the Rockies when his long shot found the back of the net after whizzing past Moog's outstretched trapper. Twenty-one seconds later, Oilers defenceman Lee Fogolin's clearing attempt hit Rockies sophomore Paul Gagné's skate and the puck slid past a surprised Moog.

Colorado now full of momentum, Merlin Malinowski scored on a breakaway at 13:42 to tie the game at four. With fans in shock—and the Oilers apparently stunned, too—Lanny McDonald completed the comeback a minute and 40 seconds later when he banked a shot in off Edmonton defenceman Doug Hicks's skate. It was a rough night all around for Hicks, who broke his finger in the last few minutes of the game.

The victory went to Resch, and equally important, he kept Gretzky off the score sheet. For the second time this season, Gretzky led the Oilers with eight shots on goal, but none found their way past the Rockies goaltender.

"Winning this game the way we did was the best thing that's happened to us all year," Resch proclaimed. As for blanking the Great One, Resch bubbled with enthusiasm about it after the game. "I like to play Edmonton," Resch said. "In fact when Number 99 is on the other side he fires everybody up. It's a challenge to keep him off the scoreboard."

For his part, Gretzky was suitably impressed with his foes. "Colorado played well, especially down the stretch, and we didn't," he concluded. "I don't know why we've had tough times with them except that Resch has been so tough. Resch made some fabulous saves. That kept them close and then we just let up. It shouldn't happen to a professional team, but it does."

His goal-scoring streak snapped, Gretzky pointed the finger at himself for the loss. "Any time you lose you get frustrated," Gretzky said. "Professional athletes are paid to win and losing is no fun. I have a lot of pride as a professional athlete and I would be lying if I said I didn't care about my contributions. If I score it helps the team."

Gretzky was disappointed at the end of Game 15, but Moog was devastated. Following the game, the Oilers sent him to the minors. In a what-have-you-done-for-us-lately league, Moog had gone from being the Oilers' playoff hero in 1980–81 to the low man on the totem pole in a three-goalie rotation in 1981–82. Many had assumed Moog would be the Oilers' number-one goalie after his playoff heroics the previous spring, but through the team's 15 games he had suffered four losses and recorded only two victories. Three goalies on an NHL team was one too many, and Glen Sather decided the 21-year-old could benefit from some time in the Central Hockey League with the Wichita Thunder.

"It was a little awkward in the dressing room, that's for sure," recalled Kevin Lowe. "But truthfully, in those days there really wasn't a lot of attention paid to those sort of things. Based on how Grant played out of the gate, it was pretty hard to argue with Sather's decision to go with him as our number-one goalie."

It was of little comfort for Moog when, after the loss to Colorado, Sather declared, "Everyone was to blame. It was a total collapse." But only Moog was on his way to Wichita.

Game 16 | November 11, 1981

Vs. Hartford Whalers

Hartford Civic Center, Hartford, Connecticut

The Oilers' youthful 1981–82 team was loaded with natural talent and ability, not to mention enthusiasm, but there were definitely a few bumps on their road to respectability. Then again, there were nights when Glen Sather could just stand back and proudly watch his inexperienced kids make miracles. After all, he had the genius Gretzky and a handful of future Hall of Famers at his disposal. Pleasantly memorable games abounded. Unfortunately, after the 5–4 home loss to the vastly inferior Colorado Rockies, the Oilers bombed again. This time in Hartford.

On November 11, the Whalers proved themselves to be a difficult team to play. They may not have been able to seriously compete for the Stanley Cup, but they had enough veterans and satisfactory experience to be challenging to a young team. The Whalers had managed just two victories in their first 14 games of the season, but things weren't as dreary as one might expect. Against six losses, they also had six ties, including one with the Buffalo Sabres, 2–2, in their previous game.

In his preparation for this road game, Glen Sather specifically pointed out to the Oilers that when the Whalers fell behind, they leaned heavily on Blaine Stoughton. The 28-year-old right winger with a big shot had produced three game-tying goals for the Whalers already. So Sather was less than impressed when, despite his pregame warnings, the Whalers winger foiled his team on this night—not once, but twice. For Gretzky, game number 16 on the schedule wasn't so bad. Coming off his third game of the season without a point, he responded against the Whalers with a three-point night, producing two goals and adding an assist.

The game between Hartford and Edmonton opened with Matti Hagman giving the Oilers an early lead at 1:45 of the opening period, but veteran right winger Rick MacLeish tied the score for the Whalers with a power-play goal at 12:40.

The score remained deadlocked until 2:09 into the second period, when Gretzky potted his 16th goal of the year, with the assists going to Jari Kurri and Brett Callighen. That 2–1 lead for Edmonton would hold for most of the second period, but not all of it. With the clock showing only 17 seconds remaining in the period, Sather watched helplessly from behind the Edmonton bench, and with utter disdain, as Stoughton—on a breakaway—tied the score at two.

In the third period, Edmonton regained the lead at the 7:19 mark on a goal by Dave Hunter, which was assisted by Gretzky, but Hartford's Rick Meagher responded a little over two minutes later, scoring at 9:38 and once again tying the game.

With time winding down and the score knotted at three, the table was set for what looked to be the game-winner by Gretzky: his second goal of the game (and 17th of the season) transpired with a little help from the wonky boards at the Hartford Civic Center. Almost as if scripted, an Oilers wide shot hit the end boards and scooted directly to Gretzky in front of the net. Hartford goalie Greg Millen had abandoned his crease in an effort to corral the puck and was caught flat-footed when it unexpectedly careened in front of the net, where a waiting Gretzky casually deposited the puck into the vacated Hartford goal. "It didn't surprise me when the puck bounced out front," Gretzky said. "Slats had us shooting pucks into the four corners in the morning practice because of the way the boards are here."

In fact, Millen had been victimized by bad bounces a few times already this season, and he had even approached arena management, asking them to do something to fix the boards so that they wouldn't cause unpredictable rebounds, but to no avail.

With Edmonton seemingly en route to a 4–3 win, Stoughton exasperated Glen Sather yet again. Only 62 seconds remained in the third period when Stoughton got a second breakaway with the puck, putting it past Fuhr for his second goal of the game and closing out the scoring in what would end as a 4–4 tie. Afterward, Risto Siltanen was left shaking his head. Adding insult to injury, the goal was scored with the Oilers on the power play. "I can't believe he could do this to us not once, but twice in the same game," a dejected Siltanen said.

Defenceman Paul Coffey had entered the game with eight goals and 20 points. One of the best skaters ever to play in the NHL, offence was this defenceman's priority, but Sather wanted him to be defensively responsible when the game was on the line. And yet there was Stoughton, alone on a breakaway, and Coffey and his defence partner, Siltanen, were caught napping. For his part, Coffey felt badly about his defensive miscue. "I didn't even see him," said Coffey, who could think of about 50 more pleasant ways to celebrate his 100th NHL career game. "Where was he?"

The game-tying goal was already Stoughton's 11th of the season. "I wasn't out there to do anything but save the game," he said after the game. "My first concern was to get away from Coffey and Siltanen and the next was to score. I only had time for one look."

"I told every guy when I called the timeout exactly what Stoughton would try to do," Sather huffed to the assembled media after the game. "It's hard to imagine what goes through a guy's mind when you're telling him the way it's going to be."

After a few inconsistent efforts in the Edmonton goal, Fuhr had a solid outing in Hartford with 39 saves, but there would have been a much happier ending had he been able to stop Stoughton. The Hartford star ultimately led skaters from both teams with nine shots on goal that night. Gretzky followed with eight, including four in the all-important third period.

The Oilers, in their third NHL season, were off to their best start ever with a 10–5–1 record, but on this night Sather didn't take any pleasure in the big picture. He couldn't shake out of his head the vision of Stoughton's game-tying goal, saying, "The way this game ended, it might drive me to drink."

Game 17 | November 12, 1981

Vs. Boston Bruins

Boston Garden, Boston, Massachusetts

Since they had joined the NHL at the start of the 1979–80 season, the Oilers had found trips to the Boston Garden to meet the Bruins downright tormenting. In four meetings—two in each of their first two NHL seasons—the Oilers returned home empty-handed: Four games, four losses, zero points. Not only that, but the Bruins had embarrassed the usually high-scoring kids from Edmonton in those four games, outscoring the Oilers by a total of 24–8. Things weren't much better when Edmonton played the Bruins at home, where Boston had won three out of four and outscored its hosts, 16–11.

Those were the numbers rolling around in the minds of the Oilers as they departed Hartford for a game the very next night against the Bruins, who had been off for three days since losing, 4–1, to the Minnesota North Stars and were looking to get back on the winning track.

In 1981–82 the Bruins, who had captured two Stanley Cups the decade before and appeared in the finals on three other occasions, were still a talented group, and the Garden, with its "cozy"

191-by-83-foot ice surface (the standard NHL ice surface by contrast was, and still is, 200 by 85 feet), remained a very difficult arena for the road team to play in. The Bruins had opened the season playing seven of their first nine games on the road, including a gruelling six-game trip during which they went 4–1–1, but had settled in nicely and were 5–2–1 at home when the Oilers came to town.

Like the Oilers, the Bruins were in a transitional period that included adding youth to their lineup. Ray Bourque and Barry Pederson, both 20; 19-year-olds Tom Fergus and Steve Kasper; and 18-year-old Normand Léveillé were pushing the veterans, who included Wayne Cashman, goalie Rogatien Vachon, Don Marcotte, Brad Park, and Terry O'Reilly, all in their 30s, and 29-year-old Mike Milbury.

With Andy Moog temporarily recalled from Wichita to serve as the backup to Ron Low, who got the start, the Oilers fell behind Boston, 3–0, after 40 minutes of play, but they refused to fade away. Cashman gave the Bruins the early lead at 4:39 of the first period with a power-play goal. Stan Jonathan deflected a shot past Low at the 6:35 mark of the second period, and Pederson scored on a rebound 35 seconds later, at 7:10—half a minute the Oilers wished they could take back.

Despite appearing to be headed for a fifth straight loss, the Oilers began to exert themselves physically. If they weren't going to win, they were going to go down kicking and scratching. Hulking Dave Semenko, who was quickly earning a much-deserved reputation as Gretzky's caretaker, scored huge points with his teammates when he emerged victorious from a one-sided fight against Boston tough guy Terry O'Reilly, one in which O'Reilly's teammate Barry Pederson came to the Bruin enforcer's aide and was banished from the game for being the third man in on an altercation.

"In previous games it wasn't so much that we were afraid," said Edmonton defenceman Kevin Lowe at the time, "we just sat back and let the Bruins run the show. We were almost in awe of their reputation here."

Added Oilers captain Lee Fogolin: "I saw a lot of their guys on the bench with eyes the size of quarters when Semenko went off the ice with a misconduct."

With his penalty minutes against the Bruins, Semenko cracked the 300 barrier for his career, on his way toward a total that eventually reached 1,175. Two nights later, his teammate Pat Hughes joined Semenko in the 300-minute club, and three nights after that, captain Lee Fogolin hit 700. Toughness was not an issue with the upstart Oilers.

Glenn Anderson finally got the Oilers on the board at the 3:32 mark of the third period with a power-play marker—Edmonton's 20th goal of the season with the man advantage—beating Boston goaltender Marco Baron, but Tom Fergus restored Boston's three-goal lead a minute and 17 seconds later with a low shot through the five-hole that the Edmonton goaltender felt he should have turned aside. "I thought he was going to walk out front, but he didn't," said Low after suffering his first defeat of the season. "I should have stayed along the post."

Matti Hagman then scored for Edmonton, but Boston's Peter McNab scored into the empty net with 36 seconds remaining on the clock to secure a 5–2 win for the Bruins. Having stood up physically to the Bruins and limited their hosts to just 10 shots on goal through the game's final 40 minutes, the Oilers actually felt pretty good about their overall effort. Even the Bruins were impressed. "The Oilers' young players have really matured and have become a strong club,"

McNab said after the game. "They skate well and their big plus is they have Gretzky. Wayne is unbelievable. He's marvelous to watch."

As for Gretzky, he assisted on both of Edmonton goals, raising his league-leading points total to 34, but was frustrated most of the night by teenaged checking sensation Steve Kasper. During that time, it was not uncommon for teams to have a player spend the game shadowing the opposition's best player. Bryan "Bugsy" Watson used to drive Bobby Hull to distraction with his close and pesky checking, and Kasper did the same thing to Gretzky. A scoring star with the Verdun/ Sorel Blackhawks of the Quebec Major Junior Hockey League, Kasper was asked to play a two-way game with the Bruins. His speed and intelligence made him an excellent multipurpose player, even at the tender age of 19 and in just his second NHL season.

The season before, as a rookie, Kasper had held Gretzky to a goal and four points in four meetings. Such was Kasper's proficiency at both ends of the ice that Bruins head coach Gerry Cheevers went public with his belief that Kasper should have been the recipient of the Frank J. Selke Trophy as the NHL's best defensive forward in 1980–81, an award that instead went to Bob Gainey of the Montreal Canadiens.

"The kid is a dream," Cheevers said of Kasper. "We've put him head-to-head against some of the toughest people in the league and he's done a number on them. Not just Gretzky, but Marcel Dionne, Bobby Smith, and Peter Šťastný. He's handled them all."

Kasper was the type of player who relied on his smarts and was not the type to cheap-shot an opponent. Instead, he tried to get them off their game using other methods. "I didn't clutch and grab," Kasper said recently. "I was similar to a defensive back in football, where I'd try to get one bump and knock him off stride."

Even though he had two assists, Gretzky got just one shot on goal, and he was concerned with the way the game shook down. "It's easier to check when you're always up two– or three–nothing," Gretzky said. "Just once I'd like to see us ahead here." He added, "[Kasper] plays hard and clean and if a guy stops me or anybody else playing that way, there are no complaints. I don't know why he does well against me and against us. If I did, he wouldn't do so well anymore, would he?"

Long after his playing career was over, Kasper recalled his many one-on-one battles with Gretzky. "Wayne used to circle to the wing, and I'd have to keep my head up because somebody was always running a pick on me; often a hard one. Wayne just went about his business. He never tried to punch me or anything."

Game 18 | November 14, 1981

Vs. New York Islanders

Nassau Veterans Memorial Coliseum, Uniondale, New York

After 17 games, Wayne Gretzky had a stranglehold on the NHL's scoring race. Still, the Bruins' Steve Kasper had done a masterful job of checking him two nights before in Boston, and now he was about to face the two-time defending Stanley Cup champion New York Islanders, with their arsenal of tight-checking and determined two-way threats.

An easy game against the Islanders—who were in the midst of the most successful run in franchise history, and in hockey history, for that matter—was unheard of. They had two Cups down, two more yet to come.

Having lost 4–3 to the Islanders already this season, the Oilers were looking to make amends and gauge where their overall game was.

The 10–2–3 Islanders were riding a two-game winning streak when Gretzky and the Oilers rolled into town to play their third game in four nights. Memories of the last time the two teams hooked up, with Islanders goaltender Billy Smith cutting Gretzky's evening short when he cracked the rising superstar across the leg with his stick, were still vivid. There had been no penalty called on the play, and it triggered a war of words between the two teams.

On this particular night, the Islanders made the decision to go with backup goalie Roland Melanson. And even though he had the night off, Smith didn't miss the opportunity to relive his last run-in with Gretzky for anyone who asked. "I didn't even know who it was until he came around in front and laid there like a dead whale," Smith railed, the scorn in his voice hard to miss. "How was I to know he had a boo boo and I hit it? I went through a lot of crap about it. Because of the press I was persecuted about it. But I swung while I was looking straight out in front of the net. I hit something, but I couldn't have been swinging any higher than the kneecap. If I had hit him anywhere up here [pointing to the groin area], okay, then crucify me. But the kneecap? The films show what I mean."

The NHL must have believed Smith's version of the incident, since they hadn't disciplined the stopper. With Smith sitting at the end of the bench for this game, the visiting Oilers turned their attention to Melanson, who was emerging as a solid goaltender in his own right. Melanson, still considered a rookie despite having appeared in 11 games (with a record of 8–1–1) with the Islanders the year before, had first made Glenn "Chico" Resch expendable and now was giving Smith a run for his money in terms of playing time. Of course, when you have a lineup as powerful as the Islanders did, it isn't overly difficult to look good.

Grant Fuhr, on the other hand, was only starting to emerge as a bona fide NHL starter, and he came under heavy fire early in the game as the Islanders came out gunning.

Islanders captain Denis Potvin, who had been sidelined with hip and groin issues up until this point in the season, wasted no time making his presence felt in his season debut. With 5:42 having gone by in the first period, he spotted New York an early 1–0 lead, bouncing a shot off Edmonton centre Garry Unger and beating Fuhr. Bryan Trottier increased New York's lead with a 35-foot shot that eluded Fuhr four minutes later, but the Oilers came back at the 14:12 mark, when Pat Hughes scored with help from Gretzky and Dave Hunter. The Islanders outshot the Oilers, 19–9, in the first period.

The second period was slightly better for the visitors. While they cut down the Islanders' shots to 13 and raised their own total to 12, the home team built a 4–1 lead with goals by Mike Bossy (his 14th of the season), just 90 seconds into the period on a 10-foot backhand shot, and Trottier on another long shot that handcuffed Fuhr at the 8:03 mark of the middle frame. Hughes, a solid secondary scorer who didn't shy away from the rough going, kept the Oilers' hopes alive with his second goal, which featured an assist from Gretzky, one minute and 25 seconds after Trottier had made it 4–1. Unfortunately Hughes's night ended poorly when he was forced to leave the game after suffering sprained knee ligaments in a collision with New York's Dave Langevin. Just 65 seconds after Hughes's goal, Garry Unger scored off a faceoff to make it 4–3, and the Oilers, trailing by only one goal, headed to the dressing room with renewed hopes after the second period.

Evidence that the Oilers were maturing as a group came in the third. Despite falling behind, 5–3, after John Tonelli scored from a scramble at 9:36, the Oilers continued on the attack. Mark Messier scored on a 20-foot slap shot at the 12:03 mark to bring Edmonton back within one goal, and with an assist, Gretzky collected his third point of the night. And then, with time running out and Fuhr on the bench in favour of an extra skater, Unger kept a clearing attempt by the home team in the Islanders zone, and the puck eventually ended up on Gretzky's stick. Not surprisingly, Gretzky took full advantage of the opportunity, beating Melanson with a deke and completing a four-point effort with his 18th goal in 18 games. The game ended in a 5–5 tie. As Kevin Lowe said, "When it comes down to the clutch he just doesn't miss."

But Al Arbour, the Islanders coach, was grumbling. "It went to the wrong guy at the wrong time," he said to the media after the game.

Arbour's biggest concern following the tie was the way his team reacted to the flashy Oilers. In the past, they had used their speed and physicality to throw Edmonton off its game, but on this night, the Oilers turned the tables on them. "We allowed them to dictate the pace," Arbour said. "It was stupid for us to do that, but we got caught up in a real shootout and that's what the Oilers like best."

Gretzky concurred. "Once it started to get wide open I knew we had a chance. The Islanders like to keep it tight, but we proved tonight we can set the pace even against the best teams."

For the paying fan, it was a night to remember. Gretzky's four-point game brought him to a league-leading 39 points, but Bossy matched him point for point with a goal and three assists. Trottier chipped in two goals and an assist, raising his NHL career points total to 650 in his seventh season.

Years later, Potvin, one of the most physical players in the NHL and one of the greatest players of his generation, recalled how difficult Gretzky was to play against, particularly if your intention was to hit him. "The thing that never changed about Gretzky was he was always so frustrating to play against because it was like he wasn't real," Potvin recently said. "You could never get a piece of him. You knew he was somewhere out there on the ice, and when you found him, he'd just pass the puck. You were always in between with him, which was what made it so very, very difficult. When we beat them in the 1983 Stanley Cup final, it really came down to trying to take away his targets. He wasn't going to beat me, or most defencemen, one on one. He would come at a defenceman with great speed, and that's how he would be able to get around the defenceman and get that incredible shot away. He had a better shot than I think anybody gave him credit for. He had a lot of speed and weight to his shot."

Never did Potvin play a game against Gretzky wherein he didn't try to nail him, but thinking about hitting the Great One and actually doing it were two different things.

"I tried a lot, and he'll tell you that," Potvin said with a laugh. "In the 1983 Stanley Cup final my job was basically to try to meet him at centre ice and not let him get behind us. He got behind us a few times, as Wayne Gretzky would. The frustrating thing about playing against the Oilers in 1983 and 1984 was that they got to be pretty good in the defensive zone, too, and if you tried to put pressure on them, that's when Gretzky would sneak out past the blue line and all of a sudden they had a breakaway.

"He was not easy to hit. It was like he was invisible on the ice. You couldn't find him because he was skating behind you. He would go to the areas where he felt the puck was going to be, and when I would turn and find him and I'd take a run at him, he'd move the puck right away. I'd be two steps too late. I once said playing hockey against Gretzky was like playing hockey on the foggy moors of Scotland. It was like a fog everywhere and you are reaching out, trying to grab something, but he's never really there."

Gretzky wasn't the only Oilers star in Edmonton's 5–5 tie against the Islanders. It is also worth noting that, despite allowing five goals, Fuhr stopped five Islanders on breakaways and boosted his record on the season to 5-1-2. It is the type of wide-open, fast-paced action that the young goaltender would master in years to come.

Long after retiring, Gretzky looks back with fondness at the games the Oilers played against the Islanders. He credits the Islanders for showing the young Oilers the way. "I say this all the time: if it wasn't for the New York Islanders, I'm not sure we would have won the Stanley Cup," the Great One said recently. "There was—not a hatred—but a dislike between the Islanders and the Oilers because they were so good and we were coming at them and they had what we wanted. I look at their teams and the players they had—from Billy Smith to Potvin to Trottier and Bossy. We knew we had to be as good as they were if we were going to take that Cup away from them. I think as much as we wanted to beat them, we respected them tremendously and we dissected everything they did and how they did it and why they became successful. The biggest thing we learned from them was that they were unselfish and they had the desire to play better in big games. They had a willingness to do whatever it took to win. We didn't know how to do that until we were taught that lesson by that team. That is the big reason why we got over the hump."

Game 19 | November 15, 1981

Vs. New York Rangers

Madison Square Garden, New York, New York

Brought into the limelight by Gretzky's exploits and the team's explosive offence, the Edmonton Oilers had become like gold for hockey journalists in the early 1980s. Names like Messier, Coffey, Fuhr, Anderson, and Kurri would all eventually become household names and members of the Hockey Hall of Fame.

But Dave Lumley was not a name usually associated with his high-profile teammates. And yet, when the Oilers travelled to Madison Square Garden to play the Rangers on the evening of November 15, he had long occupied a special place in the estimation of Glen Sather: the doghouse.

In his third season with the Oilers, having been chosen in the 12th round of the 1974 NHL Amateur Draft by the Montreal Canadiens, the 27-year-old Lumley had played in the first two games of the 1981–82 season and registered five shots on goal. He sat out the following two games, and then played in the team's fifth game—Edmonton's 8–4 win over Calgary—without a shot on goal.

Since then, he had found a regular place in the press box as a healthy scratch. Pretty humiliating stuff for a guy who, just two years earlier, had scored 20 goals and 58 points while registering 138 penalty minutes with the Oilers. With numbers like those, he should have been established as a regular on the team's roster, but unfortunately Lumley's production in 1980–81 slipped to just seven goals and 16 points, his minus-15 comparing unfavourably to his plus-15 of the season before. With Lumley trending in the wrong direction, Sather kept a tight rein on him. Lumley was in competition for playing time on a high-scoring team that was only improving. But the knee injury Pat Hughes had sustained the night before against the Islanders had opened the door for Lumley's return against the Rangers. Given a chance to dress, Lumley knew he had to make the most of his opportunity: Sather helped him further by placing him on Gretzky's line.

That a player who had fallen into disfavour with the team's head coach was suddenly playing on a line with him was not strange to Gretzky: "You know what, it's funny that as a group we didn't concern ourselves about who was playing with whom," Gretzky said recently. "It never even crossed our minds. You'd get to practice and you'd check in the dressing room to see what colour jersey you were wearing that day. Glen would usually have four different colour lines. One day you might be this colour with that guy, and the next day it could change. We never even thought about it. It wasn't even anything we discussed as players in the room. It was just sort of, 'Okay, I'm playing with him . . . let's go.' I think everyone on the team had that feeling that we just wanted to play and it didn't matter who we played with. Obviously, I'd change my game a little bit if I was playing with Dave Hunter instead of Jari Kurri, but we didn't worry about it. I think it was a pretty special and unselfish group if that's the way all the guys thought. Nobody ever went into the coach's room and said, 'I've got to play with so-and-so' or 'Why am I playing with this guy?' There wasn't one guy who ever thought that way."

Lumley wasted no time making an impact as he, along with Number 99, set up Mark Messier to give the Oilers a 1–0 lead at 3:36 of the first period. The lead lasted exactly 70 seconds, as hulking Rangers defenceman Barry Beck beat Grant Fuhr with a 30-foot blast at the 4:46 mark.

Gretzky restored Edmonton's slim lead a little less than 10 minutes later, at 14:42—his 19th goal in 19 games. Mike Rogers of the Rangers and Stan Weir of the Oilers then swapped goals in the middle period, followed by a score from New York defenceman Reijo Ruotsalainen, who tied the game at 2:07 of the third period by beating Fuhr on a breakaway.

One of the great benefits of playing on a line with Gretzky was that if you were open, he'd find you. For as much as he concentrated on raising his shot and goal totals, passing was still his most polished skill. Twenty-five seconds after Ruotsalainen had tied the contest, Gretzky used his amazing vision to weave a pass to Lumley through a maze of bodies. In the clear, Lumley drilled home a hard shot—his first goal of the season, and the eventual game winner. Lumley told reporters after the game that it was the best shot he'd had in three years.

A relieved Lumley then set up Dave Hunter for the insurance goal with Rangers goalie Steve Weeks on the bench for an additional skater with nine seconds left in the game.

It was nothing less than a dream night for a Lumley. Not only did he score a goal and add two assists, but he was on the ice for all five of the Oilers' goals and was not on for any Ranger goals, which made him a plus-5 for the game. "The thrill of a lifetime," Lumley proclaimed afterward. "I said earlier that if I got to play a game and scored and was on the ice for five goals for and none against, it would be my ultimate and it happened." And he was quick to credit his centre. "It's easy [playing] with Gretzky."

Once again, Sather looked like a genius. Placing Lumley on a line with Gretzky paid obvious dividends.

"Lumley played tremendously well and made a lot of good plays," Sather said. "The thing that surprised me most was that he looked relaxed. Actually, he . . . [had] no trouble keeping up with the play and it was a hell of a fast game."

Many years later, Lumley fondly recalled his golden opportunity to play with Gretzky and get himself back in his coach's good books. "It was amazing," Lumley says today with a laugh. "I'm playing on Wayne's line. I score a goal and add an assist and I'm plus-5 on the night. Going into the game I had goose eggs across the board—no goals, assists, or points—and I was minus-5 on the year. I wipe out all the negatives in one game and suddenly I am back to even."

Lumley was all the rage inside the Edmonton dressing room after the game, but the Rangers couldn't stop talking about Gretzky, who was now 11 points ahead of his record-setting 164-point pace from the 1980–81 season. "On that fourth goal I got him in the corner," said New York defenceman Dave Maloney. "I took him off the puck and out of the play. The next thing I know he's got [the puck] again and throws it through five guys to Lumley and they score."

Following his first-ever start against Gretzky, goaltender Steve Weeks tipped his cap to the Great One. "He's unbelievably tricky," Weeks said. "You have to be aware of where he is. You hope the rest of the guys are keeping track of him all the time because you can't be watching one guy. But if you try that, he'd be the one you had to watch. It's scary because you get the feeling he knows what you're thinking and what you're trying to do."

With comparisons between Gretzky and Mike Bossy beginning to multiply, Gretzky demurred. "Well, 50 in 50 is a long way to go," he said after the game. "Mike Bossy is a heck of a goal-scorer. I don't think there's anybody comparable to him. I'm sure I'm the same as he is; if I get the opportunity I'd like to break it and I'm sure he would, too. Nineteen in 19, well I need a couple of hat tricks here and there to get me going; to give me a cushion."

Game 20 | November 17, 1981

Vs. St. Louis Blues

Checkerdome, St. Louis, Missouri

When the Soviet Union humiliated Team Canada, 8–1, in the concluding game of the 1981 Canada Cup, the two players shamed the most were Wayne Gretzky and St. Louis Blues goaltender Mike Liut.

Just a few months earlier, the two had been the strongest candidates in the race for the Hart Trophy for the NHL's most valuable player, with Gretzky winning his second of eight Harts in a row. For Gretzky, the loss to the Soviets was a kick to the gut, but a game he bounced back from. Better days, including four Stanley Cup championships, lay ahead for the explosive point producer. Liut was a different story; he went on to play 11 more seasons in the NHL, but never again ranked amongst the best goalies in hockey. He still was a very good goaltender, but with one crushing defeat, his career went down a different path than it had been on. He was no longer the golden boy of the goal crease. Liut never again played on a team that made it as far as the third round of the Stanley Cup playoffs, and on a more personal note, Liut was never again named to an

NHL All-Star team and never the recipient of an individual award. Who knows what might have happened in his career had Canada won that hockey game?

In 1980–81, the St. Louis Blues had captured the Smythe Division title and finished second overall in the NHL with a 45–18–17 record, but lost in the second round of the playoffs, four games to two, to the New York Rangers. They had high hopes to bounce back with a more successful campaign in 1981–82, but things were not off to a good start. The Blues had won just two of their first nine games of the year, opening 2–5–2. Their biggest issue? What had been a strength the season before was turning out to be a weakness. Simply put, the Blues couldn't keep the puck out of their net. In their first 18 games, coach Red Berenson's Blues had allowed six goals five times, five goals three times, and four goals three times.

That said, with their 4–2 win over the Colorado Rockies three nights earlier, the Blues had won three of their last four games and were starting to feel a little better about themselves. Playing against the Oilers was going to be a real litmus test to prove whether the Blues' recent success was "for real." With Liut starting in goal for St. Louis and Gretzky riding high, the game within the game was also worth keeping tabs on. Liut's one advantage was the Oilers' track record: since joining the NHL, Edmonton hadn't yet won in St. Louis, posting a record of 0–3–1 at the Checkerdome.

In a hard-fought opening period, the Oilers went about trying to rectify that, outshooting the Blues, 15–13, and outscoring them, 2–1. Matti Hagman gave the Oilers a quick 1–0 lead just 33 seconds after the puck was dropped and Dave Hunter made it 2–0 less than five minutes later, with a little help from Gretzky and a still-resurgent Lumley. Hunter was also on a roll, with seven points in his last seven games. Then Brian Sutter's goal at the 14:31 mark of the first period against Edmonton goaltender Ron Low cut the Oilers' lead to one goal.

Edmonton right winger Jari Kurri got a monkey off his back when he scored the lone goal of the second period, connecting for his first past the crease in seven games. The 20-foot shot also gave Kurri his first point in his last three games. Despite owning the ice in the second period and outshooting the Blues, 13–4, the Oilers held only a 3–1 lead heading into the third period.

But the Oilers continued their dominance of the Blues in the third. And even though Gretzky hadn't recorded a shot on goal through the first 40 minutes of play, he made up for it in the third, taking two shots and scoring on both against the beleaguered Liut. The first goal, at the 12:50 mark, came directly off a faceoff, and the second, at 15:49, came from the side of the net. "The third goal [by Kurri] really hurt," Berenson said, "but Gretzky's off the faceoff killed us."

With the 5–1 win, the Oilers now led the entire NHL with 26 points, had scored the most goals thus far in the season, with 102, and were tied for the league lead with six road victories, the latest of which was the organization's first-ever win in St. Louis.

Despite scoring two goals and adding an assist for a three-point night, Gretzky took the opportunity after the game to talk to the media about his defensive game, all in an effort to let the hockey world know that he was concentrating on being more of a 200-foot player. "There are some people, not the fans, but general managers around the league, who say I can't play both ways," Gretzky said, with some indignation. "I have worked hard for three years on my defence and nobody can tell me I can't play effectively offensively and defensively." He did, nevertheless, oblige some discussion of his scoring. "Last year I had about 10 goals by this time, now I have 21 in 20 games," Gretzky acknowledged. "I can't believe it. I'm going to have to pinch myself to see if I'm for real.

"I'm consciously shooting more from a bad position on the ice or from a bad angle. Where I might have tried to make a fine pass in the same situation last year, I'm now shooting more and fortunately the puck has been going in. The better the team does, the better I do."

Berenson, the Blues head coach, whose claim to fame as a player with St. Louis was scoring six goals in a November 7, 1968, game against the Philadelphia Flyers, could not believe what he saw that night from Gretzky, who was practically a kid in the coach's eyes. "I'm convinced he's the greatest player in the game and, at his age, that's phenomenal," said Berenson, who had a long and successful career coaching Michigan State after he left the Blues. "He's not the greatest goal-scorer and he isn't the greatest skater, although he is deceptive. His greatness lies in the fact he'll do things nobody else will. He has that second and third level of deception of what is taking place within the framework of the game.

"Most in the NHL are aware of the initial play as it is happening. Others—the outstanding players—see the level beyond the initial play. But Gretzky constantly goes beyond that second level. Anything he does, any numbers he puts up there, wouldn't surprise me. He's that far ahead of everyone else."

Game 21 | November 19, 1981

Vs. Minnesota North Stars

Metropolitan Sports Center, Bloomington, Minnesota

n 1981–82, if there was one team that was seen as being in competition with the Edmonton Oilers for the mythical crown as the best young team in hockey, it was the Minnesota North Stars. In fact, the North Stars already seemed to be the more likely contender as both teams headed into their encounter in Minnesota on the evening of November 19. In the spring of 1980, the North Stars had ended the Montreal Canadiens' last dynasty, knocking off the four-time defending Stanley Cup champions with a shocking victory in the seventh game of their quarter-final playoff series at the Montreal Forum. And just last season, the North Stars had advanced all the way to the Stanley Cup final, only to bow out to the New York Islanders in five games.

At the onset of the 1981–82 season, many observers thought that Minnesota was ready to win the Cup, and the well-balanced North Stars, led by 23-year-old Bobby Smith, seemed to be proving the wisdom of that prediction by getting off to a blazing 11–3–3 start. Like the Oilers, the North Stars were also a team trying to build on their youth. Smith, who had a brilliant junior career with the Ottawa

67's, transitioned smoothly to the pro ranks and now, in his fourth NHL season, was taking his game to a higher level. Though 26-year-old Tim Young was officially the North Stars captain, nobody doubted that they were Bobby Smith's team. Smith was joined up front by his former Ottawa teammate, Steve Payne, also 23, who had scored 17 goals in the North Stars' 19 playoff games the spring before. The duo of Dino Ciccarelli and Neal Broten, both 21, ended the 1981–82 season with 106 and 98 points, respectively, while Craig Hartsburg and Curt Giles, each 22, along with 23-year-old Gordie Roberts, were developing into trustworthy defencemen.

The encounter with Minnesota was Edmonton's sixth straight road game—in eight days, no less. Heading into the game against the North Stars, Gretzky had been on a roll, with points in his last five games, for a total of six goals and nine assists over that span, and he had already begun to garner more than the usual media attention for his on-ice performance. After the game in Minnesota, he would embark on a glorious streak of play that propelled his hockey status to legendary. But on this night, the North Stars successfully kept Gretzky off the scoreboard and limited him to a single shot on goal.

With Gretzky enduring a rare quiet night, it was left to others, in particular the Oilers teenaged goaltender, Grant Fuhr, to pick up the slack. At the other end of the ice, guarding the Minnesota net, was Don Beaupre, himself all of 20 years old and in the second year of what would be a solid professional career. One year earlier, Beaupre had been the starting goaltender in the NHL All-Star Game. On this evening, with some of the most potent scorers on the planet sharing the ice, he and Fuhr both did their utmost to keep the puck out of the net.

Adding to the pressure for the young Beaupre was the fact that this game against Edmonton marked his very first start of the season. In the preseason, he had pulled cartilage in his ribs while sneezing, so veteran goaltender Gilles Meloche had been forced to carry the load in the early stages of the season for Minnesota.

As soon as the puck was dropped, the Oilers and North Stars played each other at a breakneck pace, with plenty of hard hitting. Afterward, Edmonton captain Lee Fogolin suggested the game felt more like a playoff game than a regular-season outing. Even if Gretzky didn't produce, the two kids in goal gave the 15,784 fans in attendance their money's worth with terrific performances.

The Oilers came out with their guns blazing, putting Beaupre on the hot spot to try to take advantage of his recent inactivity. The Kitchener, Ontario, native stopped a stellar 14 of the 15 shots the Oilers fired his way, but Mark Messier got one past him at the 18:23 mark. Fuhr, making his third start in the Oilers past four games, responded with 11 saves of his own.

Steve Christoff's power-play goal for the North Stars at 9:56 of the second period tied the game, but Jari Kurri restored Edmonton's lead with his sixth goal of the season at the 17:18 mark. Stan Weir drew an assist on the goal, earning the 300th point of his NHL career. Minnesota's Kent-Erik Andersson connected on a backhand shot at the 5:43 mark of the third period to tie the score at two, and Fuhr and Beaupre both shut the doors the rest of the way.

With 18 seconds remaining, the Oilers had the best opportunity to win the game when Gretzky set up Dave Hunter, who in the season's first 20 games already had two game winners to his credit—only to have Beaupre stop him cold.

Following the game, a frustrated Hunter said he was convinced he had the winner in his hip pocket. "Gretz laid it out nice, right on my stick," Hunter said, "and I had a couple of feet of open net, or at least I thought I did. Somehow he made the save."

Even Beaupre admitted to surprise at stopping Hunter's blast. "It went right off my toe," the Minnesota goaltender told the media after the game. "I saw the puck on his stick, saw him wind up, then I just reacted."

While hardly a grizzled veteran himself, Beaupre had kind words to say about Fuhr. "What I like about him is he's quick; he has really good concentration; he challenges the shooter and he has a really good [glove]," Beaupre observed.

Overall, Glen Sather was pleased with the trip. "We've learned what it takes to win [in the NHL] and we've had a taste of life at the top," Sather said. "I just wish it were April 2." The tie with Minnesota left the Oilers with a 2–1–3 record to show for their six-game road trip.

They were on their way back to Edmonton to begin a four-game home stand. Gaining seven of a possible 12 points allowed them to maintained their hold on first place in the NHL's overall standings with 27 points. Unfortunately, in the third period Messier collided with Minnesota's Brad Maxwell and injured his ankle. It was doubtful that he would play in the Oilers' next game, against the Vancouver Canucks two nights later.

Game 22 | November 21, 1981

Vs. Vancouver Canucks

Northlands Coliseum, Edmonton, Alberta

Though the 1981–82 edition of the Edmonton Oilers was viewed by most as a young, talented, and offensively gifted squad with its best days ahead of it, not all of the players on the team fit so comfortably into that widespread perception. Take Dave Lumley, for example. On a team propped up primarily by kids, Lumley was 27, in his third season with the team, and still had not really established himself as someone who would have a long and fruitful NHL career. Glen Sather liked Lumley's talent, grit, and enthusiasm, but he wasn't convinced of his commitment or that Lumley was right for the team.

"My rookie year, I score 20 goals and 38 assists and I'm thinking to myself, 'This league is a piece of cake,'" Lumley recalled some 26 years after he retired. "I had gone to the University of New Hampshire, so after we got knocked out of the playoffs by Philadelphia I went down to UNH to visit my buddies. A guy invites me down to Cape Cod for the Memorial Day weekend and says, 'We'll go down on Thursday to miss the Friday traffic, and we'll come back on Tuesday to miss the Monday traffic.' I didn't know anybody down there, so I decide to drive my own car and follow my buddy just in case I'm not having a good time and want to go back to New Hampshire. You know when I got out of there? The middle of August!

"I was there for two and a half months, and the only reason I left was because training camp was in two weeks. Oh my God, it was unbelievable. I came back 10 pounds overweight. Probably closer to 15 pounds. Somebody tries to tell me the extra 15 pounds will help me in the corners and in front of the net, but you've got to get there first. I had the best tan in the league."

After this summer of fun, Lumley slipped to seven goals and 16 points in 53 games during the 1980–81 season. He went from plus-15 as a rookie to minus-15 as a sophomore.

"I was in the doghouse that whole second year," Lumley said. "I worked out really hard the next summer to prepare for the 1981–82 season, and in the first five or six games it was Murphy's Law for me. You've heard the old saying when a team gets scored on—'I had my man.' Well, I did have my man, and somebody else didn't have theirs and suddenly I've got no goals, no assists, and no points, and I'm minus-5. Then I did an ill-advised drop pass at the other team's blue line, and the other team goes down the ice and scores. Now I'm in the press box for 11 straight games."

When athletes say they don't want to profit from the misery of a teammate, they lie. The only way for Lumley to get back into the lineup was for a teammate to start playing lousily or to get hurt.

Pat Hughes's injury, sustained in the game against the New York Islanders on November 14, allowed Lumley back into the Oilers lineup the very next night. Not only that, but he was placed at right wing on a line with Wayne Gretzky. Lumley immediately took advantage of the unexpected opportunity, scoring a goal and adding two assists in Edmonton's 5–3 win over the Rangers in New York on November 15.

Little did Lumley know that his season would take a sudden, positive turn. How could it not? He was, after all, now skating on a line with the NHL's leading point producer. At the same time, Lumley knew his time with Gretzky would probably be short-lived, so he'd better make hay.

"I'm enjoying it while it lasts," Lumley said at the time. "All I have to do is go to open spaces and somehow he'll get me the puck. It boggles the mind how he does it all the time."

Happy to be within the friendly confines of the Northlands Coliseum again, though with only one day off since they had played the high-tempo game in Minnesota, the Oilers struck first against the visiting Canucks—and with only 87 seconds having ticked off the clock—when Lumley flipped the puck over Vancouver goaltender Richard Brodeur. This kicked off a string of goals, as Edmonton took a 4–0 first-period lead after only 10:59 of play, with Glenn Anderson, Brett Callighen, and Matti Hagman also beating a besieged Brodeur.

After being blanked by the Minnesota North Stars two nights before, Gretzky bounced back with a big game against the Canucks. He got his evening rolling by assisting on Callighen's first-period goal, and continued his assault when he scored his 22nd goal of the season nearly six minutes into the second period, with Lumley garnering an assist on the play. Neither Gretzky nor Lumley was done for the night. Vancouver's Darcy Rota and Curt Fraser notched goals against Grant Fuhr, but the Oilers responded with a goal from Matti Hagman, whose second of the night was his 13th of the season.

The Oilers entered the third period leading, 6–2. Lumley scored his second of the game and third of the season at the 1:29 mark, and Gretzky followed with his second goal of the game at 15:27. Lumley and Dave Semenko drew assists. Ivan Hlinka capped the scoring for the Canucks in the third, and the visitors left with their tail between their legs, courtesy of an 8–3 defeat.

Though he suffered an injury in the game against the North Stars two nights ago, Messier did end up playing the first two periods against the Canucks, though he didn't have a shot on goal. His sore ankle flared up in the third period, so he sat out the last 20 minutes.

After just one shot on goal in the 2–2 draw against Minnesota, Gretzky was back, pumping rubber at the opposition. He had nine shots on the Canucks goal, scoring on his second and eighth shots in the game. Both Gretzky and Lumley enjoyed four-point nights, with each of them scoring two goals and adding two assists.

Lumley's terrific play is a testament to how Gretzky elevated the level of the whole team. In the four games since he came out of the press box and was paired with Gretzky, Lumley had scored three goals and eight points, reflecting a level of offensive output from the winger that he hadn't attained in some time.

For Lumley, who managed four shots on goal against the Canucks, it was the best of times. For this season, anyway, the bad times were behind him. His two goals against the Canucks heralded the most productive goal-scoring run of his career.

Somewhat lost in the shadow of Gretzky and Lumley's dual four-point night was a three-point effort by Oilers defenceman Kevin Lowe. For Lowe, it was business as usual. Gretzky, Messier, Anderson, Fuhr, Kurri, and Lowe were all part of the Oilers' youth movement, but Lowe received the least amount of notice from the public and the media. In fact, he probably received more attention for his status as Gretzky's roommate than he did for his skills as a defensive defenceman on the NHL's most "offensive" team.

Lowe, who had been the Oilers' first-ever NHL draft pick (the 21st choice in the 1979 Entry Draft) and had scored the franchise's first-ever NHL goal (assisted by Gretzky), was now in his third year and was quickly establishing himself as the team's defensive conscience, with his plus/minus going from a minus-10 in 1980–81 to what would be a plus-46 by the end of the 1981–82 season.

"Every time we played Edmonton, I thought Kevin was the guy who really held the Oiler defence together," said former Islander Mike Bossy recently. "You always knew he would take somebody out of the play, he'd take a hit, he'd block a shot. He never played on the fringes."

On a team full of budding superstars, Lowe's contribution sometimes went unrecognized by those on the outside, but not by those within the club. "Kevin was never about getting the headlines or setting the records for scoring goals," Glen Sather reflected years later. "He was the consummate team guy who helped keep everything together when things got a little bit scratchy."

"He was always the best guy on the team to give a speech and make us all look smart," Gretzky said of his former teammate. "Kevin was a guy who came up bigger and bigger as the games got more and more important."

Game 23 | November 23, 1981

Vs. Detroit Red Wings

Northlands Coliseum, Edmonton, Alberta

Glen Sather had heard the question many times over. After every game, every practice, any time a microphone or a tape recorder was thrust toward him, a reporter would invariably ask it, and he would gladly answer. After all, what NHL head coach wouldn't want what Sather had on his team: Wayne Gretzky? And after having fielded the question many times, he had fine-tuned his answer, repeated it so often that, when what seemed like thousandth reporter asked him, "What makes Wayne Gretzky great?" Sather was more than ready to answer.

"There is no one area that makes him superior, it's a unique combination of all areas. Technically, he is the best player I have ever seen. Watch him move the puck from side to side on his stick; watch him pass to the left, to the right. His hand–eye coordination is extraordinary, his reflexes are uncanny. He doesn't look like the fastest skater, but when he plays between Jari Kurri and Glenn Anderson, who are exceptionally fast, and they're never ahead of him . . . where he's unmatched is in the reflexes, the split–second acrobatics, in doing instantly what his brain says has got to be done."

Throughout the hockey world, Sather had a reputation for being cocky and brash, for being a tad arrogant. And his team would soon be tarred with the same brush by many. But in his answers about what made Gretzky "great," Sather took pains not to mention himself and retained a humbleness that many thought he didn't possess. He was also selling himself short.

For it was Sather who controlled Gretzky's ice time, who manoeuvred him between lines and played him with a multitude of wingers, and not only put him on every power play, which any coach would have done, but also sent him out when the team was shorthanded, something most coaches would have avoided.

Unlike the vast majority of teams in the NHL, the Oilers were so fast and skilled that even when they were a player short, they pressed the offensive attack. Traditionally, the strategy behind penalty killing had been to maintain possession of the puck long enough for the penalty time to run out. With the Oilers, Sather discarded this pearl of conventional hockey wisdom. He taught them to take advantage of the extra skating room a shorthanded situation afforded, to disrupt the other team's momentum, and above all, to look for scoring chances. Gretzky would embrace this strategy and score six short-handed goals in 1981–82, tops in the NHL. Clearly, Sather's singular focus on scoring goals would have a profound effect on Gretzky and NHL history, but Number 99 was far from the only one on the Oilers to benefit.

Take Glenn Anderson, for example.

More than once over the course of his 16-year, Hockey Hall of Fame career with the Edmonton Oilers, Toronto Maple Leafs, New York Rangers, and St. Louis Blues, the renegade Anderson was described as being "out there." When the Oilers drafted him with the

69th-overall pick in the 1979 NHL Entry Draft, after he had led the University of Denver in scoring with 26 goals and 58 points in 41 games, he took the road less travelled. Instead of playing for the Oilers that year, he opted to join the Canadian national team and play in the 1980 Olympic Games—the "Miracle on Ice" Games in Lake Placid.

Anderson could have turned pro in 1980, but he loved the thrill of representing his country, and his amazing skating ability made him a great fit for the larger ice surface used in international hockey. The combination of his blazing speed and fearless drive for the net was the calling card for which he became known.

Many years later, Oilers defenceman Kevin Lowe spoke glowingly of Anderson and his impact on the team. "Andy played the game the way I admired—take no prisoners and go hard to the net," Lowe said. "He was a nice complement to what we had. Let's face it: Jari and Gretzky were not take-it-hard-to-the-net guys. They were shoot-it-at-the-net guys. Andy became a great complement to Mark Messier. He was a fun, happy-go-lucky guy."

If a player had a reputation for being a wild card, others might not count on him. Lowe said that was not the case with Anderson. He wanted to win as badly as anybody; he just didn't consider winning a matter of life or death. "It's not that he didn't take the game as seriously as everybody else, but he and Randy Gregg, who both came through the Olympic program, there was a sense that there was more to life than hockey," Lowe said. "It was like life is bigger than the NHL for those guys. It was a refreshing way to look at things. When he was on the ice, he was all business."

After Anderson finally joined the Oilers in time for the 1980–81 season, he scored 30 goals and 53 points (tied for fifth best on the team) in 58 games. More important, he popped five goals and 12 points in nine playoff games, giving an early indication that he per-formed his very best at the most important time of the season.

In his sophomore season, Anderson got off to a slow start, failing to score in the first five games and managing just three goals in Edmonton's first 12 games. He seemed to have been jump-started with his two-goal effort on Halloween night against Quebec, and after that the goals started coming with more regularity.

With the Oilers sitting atop the NHL standings, boasting a 13–6–3 record, nobody surrounding the team was particularly worried about the statistics of one player. There was the feeling that a player with Anderson's offensive gifts would eventually find his way. This was affirmed when Anderson erupted with a hat trick—the third of his young career—in an 8–4 victory over the Detroit Red Wings on November 23.

Recent history hadn't been good to the Red Wings—or, as they were often referred to in this era, the Dead Things. Detroit missed the playoffs in 12 of 13 years, from 1970–71 to 1983–84, including a run of seven consecutive seasons. And yet, when they arrived in Edmonton for a meeting with the Oilers, their play was not half bad. The Red Wings' 7–9–5 record suggested that the young Oilers would be negligent if they treated their visitors too casually.

Still, the 1981–82 Red Wings were a hodgepodge of veterans and youngsters who basically threw whatever they had against a wall and hoped it would stick. They counted on junior scoring ace Dale McCourt to lead them, but he never developed into a top-flight pro. In fact, later in the season, the Red Wings traded 24-year-old McCourt, along with another young up-and-comer, 22-year-old Mike Foligno, and utility forward Brent Peterson to Buffalo for veter-ans Jim Schoenfeld, Danny Gare, and Derek Smith. Gare became the

Red Wings' captain, but his best years were left behind in Buffalo. McCourt flamed out as an NHLer, but Foligno developed into a quality player—the type the Red Wings could have used moving forward. The ill-fated deal was one of a handful that Detroit's general manager, Jimmy Skinner, made in an effort to get his team into the playoffs, but neither head coach Wayne Maxner nor his midseason replacement, Billy Dea, had a legitimate chance at success with this group.

The Oilers wasted little time in taking control of the game. Dave Lumley and Anderson scored goals a little over two minutes apart, at 11:42 and 13:58 of the first period. Lumley, whose goal featured a Gretzky assist, was still reaping the benefits of having Number 99 by his side.

Typical of most Oilers games, this one quickly turned into a wide-open, run-and-gun affair. Foligno got the Red Wings on the board at the 14:11 mark with a goal against Edmonton's Ron Low, followed by Edmonton's Matti Hagman and Detroit's Greg Smith at 18:16 and 18:50, respectively. The Red Wings made things interesting when John Ogrodnick connected only 34 seconds into the second period to tie the game at three, but Gretzky countered with his 24th goal of the year at 6:05, followed by a goal from Stan Weir at the 7:50 mark, which gave Edmonton a 5–3 lead after two periods of play.

The Oilers pulled away from Detroit in the third period, when Paul Coffey scored at the 4:38 mark and Anderson got his second of the night a little over four minutes later. Greg Smith scored his second of the game for Detroit a little over halfway through the period, and Anderson concluded the scoring with his hat-trick goal with 40 seconds remaining. It was the third hat trick of Anderson's two-year NHL career. All told that night, Anderson beat Detroit goaltender Gilles Gilbert with two splendid dekes and a shot from about

10 feet out for the third goal. He ended the game with six shots on goal; Coffey had eight and Gretzky had seven.

"At least I found the net," said Anderson. "I guess you could say I was capitalizing." With an assist on Matti Hagman's first-period goal, Anderson's four points on the night shot him into ninth place in league scoring, with 12 goals and 31 points.

Gretzky was delighted to see his pal Anderson light it up against the Red Wings. "Is there anyone who enjoys playing the game more than Glenn Anderson?" Gretzky wondered aloud after the game. "He's a pleasure to play with and a pleasure to watch. He hustles every minute and he has a good time at it."

Four goals in a road game is a decent output, but any time a team surrenders eight goals, it's going to be hard to win. The loss in Edmonton marked the struggling Red Wings' 13th consecutive road game without a victory.

"We've had five games on the road where we've given up at least eight goals," Wayne Maxner said after the game. In those five games—against Hartford, Quebec, Los Angeles, Vancouver, and Edmonton—Detroit had been outscored, 40–12.

But Maxner was suitably impressed with Edmonton's ferocious attack. "If you're going to contain them you can't let them play in your zone. If you let them play in your zone you're going to get beat because they jump in the holes, the react to situations and they have got some very heady hockey players."

Gretzky's two points against the Red Wings gave him an even 50 on the season, 10 more than the second-highest point scorer in the NHL, Los Angeles Kings winger Dave Taylor. At the end of the night, though, Gretzky was more concerned about his team's sloppy play than his league-leading point total. He agreed with Oilers assistant coach Ted Green, who suggested they gave away the puck too often.

"Both teams were sloppy in their own end," Gretzky declared. "It certainly wasn't a classic defensive-minded game."

In the 1944–45 season, Maurice (The Rocket) Richard set a standard that many thought would never be equaled – 50 goals in 50 games.

Richard's long-standing mark was finally matched in the 1980–81 season by Mike Bossy of the New York Islanders.

Jerry Wachter/Getty Images

In Edmonton, Gretzky found himself surrounded by hockey's finest collection of young talent, including Mark Messier (on Gretzky's right) and Jari Kurri (on his left).

Bruce Bennett/Getty Images

On the road to 50 in 39 . . .

Gretzky entered the December 30th game against the Philadelphia
Flyers with 45 goals in 38 games.

Sixty minutes later, after scoring five goals, he had reached the 50 goal mark in just his 39th game.

The morning after the game saw a group of enterprising *Toronto Star* photographers rush to Gretzky's childhood home in Brantford, Ontario, where they posed members of his family (from left to right): mum, Phyllis; sister, Kim; father, Walter; and brother, Keith, with a copy of that morning's paper.

Wayne Gretzky's 77th goal of the 1981–82 season, which broke Phil Esposito's single season scoring record, was scored at the Buffalo Memorial Auditorium on the evening of February 24th, against the Buffalo Sabres.

With all of his success, Gretzky's popularity knew no bounds, even in opposition rinks when fans tried to catch a glimpse of The Great One.

Game 24 | November 25, 1981

Vs. Los Angeles Kings

Northlands Coliseum, Edmonton, Alberta

With 24 goals in the Oilers' first 23 games of the season, Wayne Gretzky was showing everyone he had a genuine chance at achieving the hallowed mark of 50 goals in 50 games. And after Game 24, an 11–4 home-ice thrashing of Los Angeles, the Great One's odds of breaking the record increased greatly. Against the Kings, Gretzky got four goals—his seventh multiple-goal game of the season and second four-goal outburst. He also added an assist to give him his second five-point game of the season. Gretzky's linemates on that particular night included Dave Lumley and Dave Hunter—grinders of a decent level, but hardly candidates to challenge for the Art Ross Trophy. Nonetheless, Lumley continued to hold a hot hand, scoring a goal and adding three assists in the game, while Hunter, who never had a 50-point season in his 10-year NHL career, had three assists, giving him 10 points in the last seven games.

For the Oilers, it was the second time in their last 12 games that the team had scored 11 goals. Remember that on October 31, they had popped that number when they played at home against the

Quebec Nordiques. And if that impresses you, consider that the Oilers had barely started their motor. The team went on to score an NHL-record 417 goals in the 1981–82 season, a record they broke the following year when they scored 424 times, before besting that yet again in 1983–84, with an output of 446 goals, a record that still stands today. Taken together over a five-year period, from 1981–82 through 1985–86, the Edmonton Oilers scored an astonishing 2,114 goals.

At the conclusion of this game against the Kings, Gretzky had 28 goals of his own and was suddenly on track for a mind-boggling 97-goal season. If he maintained that torrid pace, he would blow Phil Esposito's 1970–71 single-season record of 76 goals out of the water. He was also now on pace to score 183 points, which would annihilate Esposito's record of 152, also set in 1970–71. But Gretzky was aiming even higher. "I think 200 is realistic. I don't think it's impossible. The fans like to see goals, the teams and players are more offensive-minded and the coaches are opening things up more. . . . If anyone is ever going to get 200 [points in a season] it would be last season, this, or next," Gretzky said after the Oilers' rout of the Kings. "The league is going through a transition right now with so many young players. They'll be better and tougher in the next couple of years."

Gretzky pointed to the Oilers' youth and speed, saying they simply wore down the opposition's defence. So far on the season, in 14 of their 15 victories, the Oilers had scored five or more goals. And that constant pressure certainly wore down the Kings blue line on this particular night—wore down the whole team, for that matter.

The evening of November 25 was a wild and crazy night indeed for everyone on the ice except for goaltender Jim Rutherford. At 32, Rutherford found himself in his 12th year in the league and was at the tail end of a pretty good NHL playing career. For the majority of the 1981–82 season, Rutherford tended goal in the American Hockey League with the New Haven Nighthawks. He probably wished he had remained there by the end of this game, one of his seven NHL appearances in 1981–82. Rutherford was scorched, caught in the net for all of Edmonton's 11 goals.

The Oilers kicked things off with three first-period goals, two courtesy of Gretzky (on his only two shots of the period) at 5:06 and 11:08, with another scored in between by Brett Callighen at the 7:46 mark. Gretzky's first goal came as he flipped a rebound past Rutherford, and his second was a 10-foot blast while his team was on the power play.

Kings superstar Marcel Dionne, who always seemed to come up with solid performances when he was up against Number 99, got the Kings on the board at 1:18 of the second period, but exactly four minutes later Gretzky responded with his hat-trick goal, connecting on a rebound.

Sophomore Kings defenceman Larry Murphy, who a year earlier had set NHL records for points (76) and assists (60) by a rookie defender, scored to make it 4–2, but the Oilers responded with three more before the end of the second period. Coffey netted two and Risto Siltanen got the third. Eighteen-year-old centre Marc Habscheid, who spent most of the season with the Saskatoon Blades of the Western Hockey League, scoring 64 goals and 151 points in 55 games, played in his first NHL game on this night and drew an assist on the Siltanen goal. No shock, really. Habscheid had produced points in 18 straight games with the Blades before joining the Oilers.

In the third period, Gretzky notched his fourth of the game, just 90 seconds in, when he stickhandled past Murphy and then pulled Rutherford out of the net with a shifty move. The Kings responded with a pair by defenceman Trevor Johansen and left winger Steve Bozek, which only served to set off a final outburst of three more goals by the Oilers: two by Mark Messier and the last by Lumley, coming at the 18:26 mark of the final period.

On a night where, for the Kings, positives were hard to find, Dionne had finished the game with a goal and two assists, while his Triple Crown linemate, right winger Dave Taylor, chipped in three assists and now sat in second place in NHL scoring with 43 points, 12 behind Gretzky.

In contrast, almost every player on the Oilers registered points on this night. Only goaltender Grant Fuhr, defenceman Kevin Lowe, and forwards Mike Forbes and junior call-up Todd Strueby were the exceptions.

Fuhr may not have drawn a point in the game, but his night was a success nonetheless. The Kings were no slouches when it came to offence, so he had to be on his toes, and he was, making 34 saves. Not only that, but the game was a benchmark because it was Fuhr's 11th of the season, and as a result he could no longer be sent back to junior hockey. On November 25, 1981, Grant Fuhr became a bona fide NHL goaltender.

While the Oilers were all smiles after the game, Kings head coach Parker MacDonald saw no humour in watching his team allow so many goals. He did come to the defence of Rutherford, though. "I don't think you can blame our goalie tonight," MacDonald said. "I don't know how many times their players were standing all alone in front of the net or how many times we were beaten one-on-one." And then MacDonald stated the obvious: "Too much Gretzky! How many points did that guy get, anyway? I don't think you can play much better than he did. He was deking and darting and diving around. That fourth goal he got was a tough one to swallow, but a great thing to watch."

All told, Gretzky scored the eighth NHL hat trick of his career and recorded his third-ever four-goal game. Having been on an unstoppable tear, and with 28 goals in 24 games Gretzky had started fielding questions about scoring 50 in 50 with an increased frequency, but he insisted that his main priority was on the team's success, not on his personal statistics. "I don't go looking for records," Gretzky said in the dressing room afterward. "The main thing is winning games. Records don't mean a thing if you are losing. There's still a long way to go, but I have a cushion. I'm not going to lose any sleep over it, though."

After the game, Gretzky also suggested professional hockey was becoming more like junior hockey for its wide-open, high-scoring potential. "I don't mind offensive hockey," he said with a smile.

At 30, Dionne had been an elite NHL scorer going on 11 years. He had played with and against the best players in the world and was not easily impressed. He was blown away by the skinny kid from Brantford, Ontario, though. "He's amazing," Dionne told reporters after the game. "You have to think he'll be setting all kinds of records every year, the way he's going. I don't know who's going to win the scoring title again, other than him, for a long time."

Even at 20 years old, Gretzky had a good perspective about what his team accomplished against the Kings. Other players' injuries had forced Habscheid into action. That meant that no player in the Edmonton lineup that night had celebrated his 30th birthday. Stan Weir was the Oilers' senior citizen against the Kings, and he was 29 years old.

"We had the youngest team in the NHL on the ice tonight and yet we played like we've been together for years," Gretzky said.

"That's because the team believes in itself. It doesn't believe in losing. That kind of winning attitude alone is worth a couple of goals a game. I'm really enjoying this season. It's a pleasure playing with a team that has this kind of spirit."

Years later, Gretzky admitted that it was this game on November 25 that made the possibility of scoring 50 goals in 50 games really come into focus for him. "I hadn't been thinking about it up until then. I truly wasn't," Gretzky said recently. "After I had that four-goal game, it got me to 28 goals in 24 games. That's when I started to think to myself that I had a really good opportunity here. I needed 22 more goals in 25 games if I wanted to break the record."

Game 25 | November 27, 1981

Vs. Chicago Black Hawks

Northlands Coliseum, Edmonton, Alberta

It's often been remarked that youth is wasted on the young. It's also often been said in hockey circles that the Stanley Cup has never been won in the regular season. With the 1981–82 season nearly a third completed, the young Edmonton Oilers were having the time of their lives. Ask any kid and they'll tell you there is nothing in hockey that can compare to scoring a goal—and the Oilers were scoring in spades.

In their last three games, all within the comfortable confines of their home arena, Edmonton had defeated the Vancouver Canucks, 8–3, the Detroit Red Wings, 8–4, and the Los Angeles Kings, 11–4, for an average of nine goals per game.

Needless to say, guarding the net against the Oilers was not a task to look forward to. But on the evening of November 27, 1981, the Chicago Black Hawks' Murray Bannerman was given the unenviable task. At least he held the Oilers under their recent average in this match, an 8–1 Edmonton victory.

At the other end of the rink, Oilers goalie Ron Low had probably slept well the night before the game, knowing that even if he allowed a mittful of goals, the Oilers would likely still come out with the win. Such was the life of an Edmonton Oilers goalie in those heady days. But he could sympathize with his goaltending cousins getting lit up like Christmas trees at the other end of the ice. "There are so many goals," Low said at the time. "The goalies we have been playing haven't had a prayer on most of them, either."

If the opposition spent a lot of time worrying about the mental state of their stoppers, the Oilers had only one thought on their minds. "It was interesting because as a group we really didn't worry too much about goaltending," Gretzky said recently, looking back at the season. "We knew that our goalies were going to be good, but if we really had to, we'd win 7–6. Unfortunately, you weren't going to win a Stanley Cup thinking that way. We had a great deal of confidence in our goalies. We never looked at them in terms of their age or who was the starter and who was the backup. We looked at them as being in a healthy competition. We just knew we had good goalies who were making each other better."

Even with a lineup missing injured regulars Jari Kurri, Matti Hagman, Pat Hughes, and Garry Unger, the Oilers seemed invincible on this night. Just as they had done in the game two nights before against Los Angeles, the Oilers treated the home crowd to a 3–0 lead in the first period, with goals by the unlikely trio of Dave Semenko, Risto Siltanen, and Doug Hicks. And just for fun, they added two more early in the second period—one by Paul Coffey, just 33 seconds in, the other by Mark Messier at the 2:51 mark. These ratcheted to score up to 5–0.

Defenceman Kevin Lowe left the game in the second period when he began experiencing symptoms of the flu. After Messier's goal, Lowe decided the lead was safe and headed for the showers. With the greatest player in the game still in the lineup and rolling a seven with each toss of the dice, it helped to make Lowe's decision that much easier. A bunch of players on the Black Hawks bench likely wished they could have followed him to the dressing room.

Fresh off the four-goal, five point game against the Kings 48 hours earlier, Gretzky engineered his third five-point game of the season (with two goals and three assists this time) at the expense of Bannerman and the Black Hawks. If that weren't impressive enough, consider the fact that Gretzky had 10 of Edmonton's 37 shots on goal—two in the first period, four in the second, and four more in the third. By comparison, Chicago defenceman Bob Murray led his team with four shots on goal—none of which beat Low.

At the time of Messier's goal, there still remained a shade over 17 minutes remaining—in the second period! And even after Rich Preston scored to make the score 5–1, the game was still out of reach for the outclassed Black Hawks. Gretzky stepped up his game with back-to-back goals in the third period. With help from Lumley and Hicks, Gretzky scored his 29th goal of the season just 29 seconds into the period, and at the 15-minute mark he bagged number 30 with help from Siltanen and Semenko, before closing out the scoring by setting up Lumley at the 17:26 mark, for the former doghouse dweller's fifth goal in the past four games.

A second straight five-point game had Gretzky looking at the heavens in thanks. "I can't believe it," he said, shaking his head in wonder. Just 25 games into the 1981–82 season, he had 30 goals and 60 points.

Following the game, Low felt quite bubbly. "Not a bad home stand," he said, grinning.

Indeed, Edmonton's four-game home stand had resulted in four straight victories, during which the Oilers had outscored the opposition by a combined score of 35–12. They were undefeated in their past seven games—the longest unbeaten streak in their NHL history (which was a mere 184 games old).

But even when the Oilers sat atop the world, their boss didn't allow them to keep their heads in the clouds. For as much as Glen Sather enjoyed seeing a smile on the faces of his players, he always reminded them that playing in the NHL was both a privilege and a job.

"I'll tell you this, he was a big believer in the notion that you skated and practised every day," Gretzky said. "We didn't get days off. That wasn't part of our repertoire. We didn't practise long, but we practised pretty much every day except Christmas day. He had a rule that if we had an optional practice, which was maybe once a month, if you weren't 23 years old or older you had to go on the ice, whether it was for five minutes or 30 minutes. His theory was that if Mark Messier and Wayne Gretzky and Paul Coffey did it, he could preach to the new young guys who would come along in later years. Secondly, he treated us like men. If we went to New York, he would base us in Manhattan, and we would bus out to Long Island and back and bus to New Jersey and back, and he treated us like men. He had one rule: don't embarrass the organization. Other than that, there were no team rules. There was no rule about being in bed at nine o'clock or anything like that. If you didn't understand what your commitment was to the team, well, those guys got weeded out. He made us grow up a lot quicker than we would have with a lot of other coaches."

Game 26 | November 29, 1981

Vs. Winnipeg Jets

Winnipeg Arena, Winnipeg, Manitoba

S hould we really be surprised at Wayne Gretzky scoring like no NHLer had done before?

Gretzky had been nothing less than a scoring machine from virtually the first time he played organized hockey. Frankly, it would be worrisome if he weren't scoring at a record-breaking pace. At the same time, few teams gave a hoot about playing defensive hockey in those heady days of the early 1980s. Scoring goals was all the rage. In time, that changed, and stars like Gretzky—among others—came back to earth. For now, though, the NHL was pretty much an all-out offence league—at least during the regular season. Defence tightened up significantly once the playoffs came around.

The Edmonton Oilers still held the league's top spot and were averaging a record-breaking 5.56 goals per game while allowing 3.64 goals per game—which was good enough to put them in top half of the league defensively. Yet rarely, if at all, could one find a story that focused on the Oilers' defensive play. Their offensive prowess almost always gobbled up the headlines, and the team was happy to oblige, scoring goals at a pace that no other team in NHL history could match.

Those in the Edmonton media had been warned by their Boston brethren—who had had Bobby Orr to rave about for a decade—that they would eventually grow tired of having to write something "new" and "fresh" about Wayne Gretzky. According to the *Edmonton Journal*'s Terry Jones, eventually it felt as though "there would be nothing left to write that hadn't been written before."

And maybe that partly explains why the chase for "50 in 50" became such a story so quickly, and particularly in Edmonton, where the papers had begun running daily thermometer-type charts to track the progress of Gretzky's attempt at making history. The chase was a new angle.

That's not to say that there weren't other stories surrounding the Oilers to be found, not the least of which was 20-year-old defenceman Paul Coffey, who now hovered on the cusp of NHL stardom.

After a spectacular junior career with the Ontario Hockey League's Sault Ste. Marie Greyhounds and Kitchener Rangers, Coffey broke into the NHL in 1980–81, scoring nine goals and 32 points with 130 penalty minutes in 74 games. The Toronto native didn't have a great start to the 1981–82 season—he didn't get a single point in Edmonton's first three games. But he kicked it into gear with an assist in the Oilers' fourth game, and from there he embarked on a 10-game points streak. Coffey hit another lull, going without a point in the four straight games preceding the one on November 23 against the Red Wings, when he took eight shots on goal. By the time this night came about, he'd heated up once again and had scored four goals and six points in the team's last three outings.

Coffey was a gifted skater who wore skates two sizes too small and bare feet inside the boot. His method allowed him to get a stronger push-off and better control over his skating, and in a stride or two he could glide through the neutral and offensive zones with startling ease. And he did so faster than anyone in the unfortunate position of having to chase him. With such a unique skill set, Coffey's mission was to produce offence. His all-out offensive style often caused Glen Sather to complain about the miscues that gave scoring opportunities to the opposition, but a stubborn Coffey only had eyes for the other team's net.

"I think Slats believed in order for us to win, Paul had to change," said Oilers defenceman Kevin Lowe recently. "Nobody on the New York Islanders played like Paul played. Denis Potvin, as great as an offensive player as he was, he was also a great defender. He didn't sacrifice defence for offence. I think Slats was always pushing Paul to be a better two-way defender for the good of his game, but also for us to win."

Against the Jets in Winnipeg on November 29, Coffey stole some of Gretzky's thunder, scoring two goals and adding three assists. His five-point performance gave him 33 points on the season—one more than he managed in the entire 1980–81 campaign. Gretzky, too, had yet another big night, with a goal and three assists to raise his season totals to 31 goals and 64 points.

To the Jets' credit, they held the rampaging Oilers offence at bay for almost the first 10 minutes of the game, but after Gretzky opened the scoring with a breakaway goal, the floodgates opened. Edmonton soon extended their lead to three when, late in the first, Matti Hagman (at 17:19) and Glenn Anderson (at 17:53) scored goals 44 seconds apart. It was the fourth time in the last five games that the Oilers had opened with a 3–0 lead, and this time they did it with just five shots on goal.

If, at the end of the first, anyone questioned who had the game in the bag, they stopped wondering when Edmonton came out flying in the second period. The visiting team scored three more goals by the 6:18 mark. Having assisted on the first two Edmonton goals of the night, Coffey added a third assist when, after only 18 seconds had ticked off the clock, Dave Lumley extended his scoring streak to five games, making the score 4–0. Just 46 seconds later, Gretzky set up Dave Hunter for his seventh goal of the season. Living it up on Gretzky's line, Hunter led the Oilers in shots on goal in this game. At the end of the night, he had five.

Marc Habscheid then made it 6–0 Oilers, netting his first NHL goal at the 6:18 mark of the second period by beating a besieged Ed Staniowski with a long shot that surprised the Winnipeg goaltender.

Norm Dupont, at 11:27 of the second period, and Dave Christian at 14:06 beat Grant Fuhr to put the Jets on the scoreboard, but Edmonton responded with four more goals—one in the second period and three in the third—to effect the rout. On the first of the four, Gretzky made a perfect drop pass to Pat Hughes, who slapped a shot past Staniowski to make it 7–2. Twenty-seven seconds into the third period, Gretzky struck again, feeding the puck to Dave Semenko, who used his size and strength to power a shot home from in tight.

In a game where the final outcome had long since been decided, the only suspense left was to see whether Coffey could make it four games in a row with a goal. He came through brilliantly, first at the 10:52 mark of the third, before adding another at 15:31—both on long shots. On Coffey's second goal, Staniowski was preoccupied by watching a scuffle between Gretzky and the Jets' Morris Lukowich. Taking advantage of the distraction, Coffey delivered a shot that the Winnipeg stopper didn't even see. "I thought the play was stopped and the ref was going to give me a delay of game penalty if I shot into the net," Coffey declared after the game. "I decided the score was 9–2 anyway so what did it matter?"

Kevin Lowe, in a recent interview, said Gretzky put a lot of value in Coffey's guns-a-blazin' style. "Just as he did with Mark Messier, Wayne could see things in Paul's game that he knew would be beneficial to the Oilers, and he really appreciated what Paul brought to the table. Paul and Wayne both had the same agent [Gus Badali] and both were from the Ontario Hockey League. There are always those natural attractions to certain players. Lee Fogolin helped me out when I first broke into the league, and we shared the same agent. With Wayne and Paul, it was more than simply having the same agent. Wayne could see how Paul's offensive style was ultimately going to benefit him and the team."

Incredibly, despite the final score, which read Edmonton 10, Winnipeg 2, the Jets outshot the Oilers, 40–28, on this night, but Fuhr was nearly unbeatable, recording his eighth win of the season against only one loss and three ties. The multiple victories for Fuhr and the Oilers helped erase the memory of his NHL debut on October 14, in which the Jets had handed the rookie netminder the only loss, to this point, of his NHL career.

Jets head coach Tom Watt was delighted to see a sold-out crowd of 15,756 on hand at the Winnipeg Arena to watch his team try to win its second straight game over the NHL's number-one team, but after watching the Oilers scorch his club, he'd lost his levity. "I know the Oilers are going well," Watt said. "But we beat them 4–2 in their building before and had their fans booing them. Now, before our first sellout of the season and with the same personnel, we lay a bleeping egg. It's crazy!"

Winnipeg general manager John Ferguson complimented the visitors, who were 7–0–2 in their last nine games and had scored 45 goals in their past five. "They're playing well, extraordinarily well," Ferguson said. "Their players are maturing and they have some of the best forwards in the league."

In 1944–45, when Maurice "Rocket" Richard became the first player ever to score 50 goals in 50 games, he didn't score his 31st goal until Game 31. In 1980–81, when Mike Bossy matched Richard's accomplishment, he didn't get his 31st goal until Game 33. Against Winnipeg, Gretzky had scored his 31st goal in his 26th game.

Game 27 | December 1, 1981

Vs. Montreal Canadiens

Montreal Forum, Montreal, Quebec

When the NHL absorbed four World Hockey Association teams in 1979, thereby ending an escalating salary war that had rewarded good-to-average players with star-like salaries, the merger also served to dilute the product. The quality of NHL play went down, and that was one of the main reasons why scoring went up. At the end of the day, though, to win a championship you still had to figure out how to keep the puck out of your net. So teams like the New York Islanders and Montreal Canadiens, which placed a premium on solid defensive hockey, thrived.

The Islanders and Canadiens knew other teams could play pond hockey all winter and trick themselves into believing they were moving in the right direction, but when push came to shove—and more specifically, when the playoffs rolled around—it was the teams that could defend that usually succeeded.

And so it was on December 1, 1981, when the Oilers travelled to Montreal to challenge the most successful team in the history of the NHL. The Canadiens had won four straight Stanley Cups between

1976 and 1979, but a combination of age and notable departures had sent them into a tailspin even they didn't expect. They still held to many traditional hockey values, though, and one—perhaps the most significant—was protecting their own goal.

And yet, last spring, in the opening round of the playoffs, these brash and high-spirited kids from Edmonton, with many of them, including Gretzky and Messier, only a year out of their teens, had schooled the Canadiens on the art of offensive hockey. The Oilers, playing in only their second-ever NHL playoff series, skunked the Canadiens in three straight games, outscoring them, 15–6, along the way and boldly announcing their arrival as the potential "team of the future." And had apparently won over some Montreal hearts in doing so.

As the Oilers took to the famed Montreal Forum ice for a practice the day before their game against the Canadiens, the *Edmonton*

On 27 occasions, the Canadiens had won the Vezina Trophy for having the NHL's lowest goals-against average in a season—more than any other team. As well, in the 28 years since the NHL had started awarding the best defenceman the James Norris Memorial Trophy, a member of the Canadiens had taken home the silverware 10 times. In 1977–78, the league began awarding the Frank J. Selke Trophy on an annual basis to the best defensive forward in the NHL. Bob Gainey of the Canadiens had won it all four years. As history had shown, the Canadiens had long placed a premium on keeping pucks out of their net. The 1981–82 version of the team was no exception, and it would give up the fewest goals in the NHL over the course of the season.

Journal reported that "Gretzky heard squeals from his legion of pig-tailed, teenage girls. . . . He wasn't the only one to be saluted. There was a crush of fans trying to steal a peek or a peck from Mark Messier and Glenn Anderson, even from rookie goalie Grant Fuhr." But according to Claude Mouton, the longtime Canadiens announcer, there was one clear-cut favourite amongst all of the Oilers, if jersey sales at the Forum gift shop were an accurate measure. "Wayne Gretzky jerseys outsell all the players on the Canadiens put together," Mouton reported.

With the Oilers now in Montreal for their first meeting with the Canadiens since last spring's playoffs, the Habs must have been concerned about what was coming. Edmonton was unquestionably the hottest team in hockey, having won five games in a row and having scored 45 goals in the process. At the same time, Wayne Gretzky had propelled himself far to the front of the NHL scoring race, netting 10 goals and 20 points in that same five-game span. But the combination of last spring's embarrassment and the Oilers' recent rampaging over the rest of the NHL could not sway the Canadiens from their defence-first philosophy.

Leading up to the game, Glen Sather admitted that the recent scoring parade could not go on forever. How could it? When it came to playing the Habs, Sather said he'd gladly settle for a 1–0 win.

Defenceman Kevin Lowe also felt the Oilers were in for a tough game. Both he and his teammates were well aware that the Habs were out for revenge. "Let's face it," Lowe said recently, "we had humiliated them the spring before in front of all of Canada. I would imagine they hadn't forgotten that fact." And neither had the fans, packed into the Montreal Forum 18,094 strong, by far the biggest crowd that would watch a game in the hallowed building all season.

In the past five games, the Oilers had averaged slightly more than 38 shots on goals per game. Gretzky by himself had 34 shots in the last five games, an average of 6.8 per outing. But against the stingy Canadiens, he got only one shot per period. He didn't score a goal against Montreal, either, although he did set up three goals, while the two teams settled for a 3–3 tie. For the first time in six games, a team had held Gretzky goalless. But, try as they might, the Habs checking line of Bob Gainey, Doug Jarvis, and Mark Napier weren't able to keep him off the score sheet.

From the moment the puck dropped, this game felt different from the ones that had preceded it. The Oilers had been playing with early leads for so long that they had all but forgotten what it felt like to play from behind. Montreal's Pierre Larouche reminded them when he opened the scoring by beating Grant Fuhr with a back-hander at the 13:16 mark of the first period. Just three minutes and 10 seconds later, however, Dave Hunter caught a pass from Gretzky in his glove. Pitching the puck to his stick, Hunter relayed it back to Gretzky, who then carried the puck into the Montreal zone. At the last second, Gretzky passed back to Hunter, who fired a wrist shot past Montreal goaltender Richard Sévigny, tying the game at one.

The Oilers were outshot, 11–9, in the opening period, but picked it up in the second and turned the tables, outshooting Montreal, 12–11. The teams again each scored one goal apiece. Keith Acton, on a deflection, gave the Habs a 2–1 lead at 16:35. The Oilers responded. With only 53 seconds left in the period, Gretzky and Hunter set up Glenn Anderson to knot the game at two.

Fuhr, undefeated in his previous 11 games, was unquestionably the star of the third period, making 15 saves on the 16 shots that Montreal pumped his way. Only Mark Napier beat him, and that goal came 2:20 after Dave Lumley had given Edmonton its only lead of the night, landing his seventh goal in the last six games on a 30-foot blast, with Gretzky and Hunter assisting.

It was a hard-fought game for both sides, ending in a 3–3 tie, and from Montreal's perspective, merely keeping Gretzky from scoring a goal was a victory. "Our game plan was to neutralize Gretzky if we could and we actually did a good job on him," defenceman Guy Lapointe said afterward. "He only had two or three chances, but he made some unbelievable plays anyway."

The spring before, on the eve of their playoff encounter, Canadiens goaltender Richard Sévigny had boldly predicted that Montreal superstar Guy Lafleur would "put Gretzky in his back pocket." After this game, the Canadiens stopper changed his tune. "Gretzky is the best and he proved it against us," Sévigny told the reporters. As a side note, Lafleur had missed the game with the Oilers because he had the flu.

Gretzky could live with not scoring a goal in Montreal. He was impressed by and respectful of the Habs' resilience in equal measure. Montreal had shown determination to make amends for being bounced by Edmonton in last season's playoffs. "This was one of the fastest games we've been in, in a long time," Gretzky said afterward. "It was a lot of fun. No dirty play, nothing physical, just a lot of good, hard skating. People have been criticizing us for a long time for being too offensive-minded, but at the same time we've been keeping our opponents' goals down."

"It was old-time hockey," Glen Sather stated to the press, unsurprised by the battle fought by the Canadiens. "They checked us so closely we never got a chance to open up, but any time you get a point in this building, that's an achievement as far as I'm concerned."

Fuhr had now gone 12 games without a loss, and speculation was starting to mount about his candidacy for the NHL's rookie-of-the-year award. After the game, with eyes as big as pie plates, he talked about the magic of playing his first game in Montreal. "This is the first time I've played in the Montreal Forum," said the game's first star. "It was a bit of a shock for me. I was nervous at the beginning, but I calmed down after a few minutes."

The previous spring, Andy Moog had been the Edmonton goalie giving the Canadiens fits, and in this game Fuhr did much the same. "Fuhr has so much confidence in his glove," Guy Lapointe said after the game. "He gives you a big opening to shoot at because he knows he'll get over and get the puck. I think somewhere along the line he must have been a baseball player."

Informed of Lapointe's comment, Fuhr laughed and said, "I play a little baseball in the summer. I'm a catcher and third baseman."

Game 28 | December 2, 1981

Vs. Quebec Nordiques

Colisée de Québec, Quebec City, Quebec

Only one other time this season, in the Oilers' first two games, had Wayne Gretzky gone without a goal in back-to-back outings. In the first half of the season, he was running away with the NHL scoring title and was on pace to establish a new NHL points record. So when he didn't score against the Canadiens on December 1, it seemed impossible that he wouldn't score against the Nordiques on December 2. But a total of 17 goals were scored in Quebec City that night, and not a single one was credited to Gretzky.

The Nordiques, who had been blasted by the Oilers, 11–4, on October 31, turned the tables and handed the visiting Oilers a 9–8 defeat. Gretzky, shadowed all night by Nordiques Pierre Aubry and Alain Côté, recorded just one shot on goal and was a minus-2, although he garnered two assists. All this was probably not enough to send him packing for another five-night stay in Florida like the one he had spent in the days following the Canada Cup, but a sudden "mini-slump" was a source of frustration nevertheless.

"We talked strategy this morning and we checked the videos," Côté told reporters after the game. "The plan to cover Gretzky was to stay with him inch to inch. I am not surprised the scoring was so high even though Gretzky got only two assists. Edmonton is a very good team."

Despite the Oilers' impressive record and position at the very top of the NHL standings, a wagering man might have put money on the Nordiques. For starters, Quebec had plenty of firepower, they were a fast team, and they could play with an edge. They'd scored 20 goals in their last three games, in which they emerged victorious against the New York Rangers, Boston Bruins, and Hartford Whalers.

On December 2, Mark Messier and Nordiques Dale Hunter, the rugged younger brother of Edmonton left winger Dave Hunter, duked it out on the score sheet, and in this defence-starved contest, each of them would end up with three goals apiece. What could have been a great competition between the equally aggressive Hunter brothers failed to materialize, however. After colliding with Mario Marois of the Nordiques and spraining his knee in the first period, Dave left the game and did not return. Another set of brothers, the Šťastnýs—Peter, Marian, and Anton, who played for the Nordiques—combined for four goals, including one each in the second period. A family hat trick, if you will.

It was a wild night, with goals coming at a rate of one every three and a half minutes. Early on, it appeared the Oilers had shaken off the defensive shackles placed upon them the night before in Montreal. They jumped to a 3–1 lead in the first period courtesy of two goals by Messier and one by Matti Hagman. The Oilers appeared to be in complete control, even though Aubry answered Messier's opening goal a minute and 22 seconds after it occurred. The act of coming out strong was from a script the Oilers had followed numerous times already that season, but in this game the ending had changed.

Just before the first period ended, Dale Hunter scored for the Nordiques, his first of the game, to make the score 3–2 Edmonton. In the second period, the Nordiques rode that momentum, outscoring the Oilers 4–1 in the period. Peter Šťastný scored twice, and his brothers Anton and Marian each added singles. Only Risto Siltanen connected for the Oilers, and at the end of the second period the scoreboard read 6–4 for the Nordiques.

Quebec added to its lead when Dale Hunter scored his second of the game at the 1:19 mark of the final period, setting the stage for a wild finish. At the 7:15 mark of the period, Lumley got pulled down as he broke in alone on Quebec goaltender Daniel Bouchard. Awarded a penalty shot, Lumley kept his remarkable goal-scoring streak alive, making it seven games in a row with a goal and cutting the Nordiques' lead to two, 7–5. Lumley's goal sparked the Oilers, and Pat Hughes got his first of two on the night 61 seconds later, at 8:16. Suddenly, the score was 7–6 Nordiques. Game on.

At 12:16 of the third, Dale Hunter temporarily halted the Oilers' comeback attempt, completing his hat trick and making the score 8–6, only to have Messier complete his own hat trick at the 16:39 mark to make it a one-goal game. Pierre Aubry's second of the game, scored with only 63 seconds left, restored Quebec's two-goal advantage and effectively iced the game in their favour. With 17 seconds left on the clock, Edmonton's Pat Hughes notched his second of the night to make the final score 9–8.

"I knew it would be a wide-open game," said Glen Sather in the aftermath of the Oilers' first defeat since the Boston Bruins beat them 5–2 on November 12. "My team was tired. We did things tonight we haven't done all year. The game plan was to contain the Šťastnýs." In that regard, the plan was a total failure as the Šťastnýs combined for five goals and 12 points. "Let's face it, Quebec has some exceptionally skilled players," Sather said. "They are a great skating team."

Down the hall in the Nordiques dressing room, Quebec coach Michel Bergeron agreed, but suggested it had been like playing a game of shinny that night. "You had two of the best teams in hockey on the ice and there was no checking at all," Bergeron said. "What did anybody expect, a defensive struggle?"

For Oilers goalie Ron Low, it had been a great season up until that night. He wasn't pleased to be leaving town with a 7–2–0 record. "Eight goals should have been enough," a frustrated Low told reporters after the game. "We didn't have much defence or goaltending out there. It stank."

Though this one was a loss for the Oilers, with each passing game, it became more obvious to their opponents that simply to concentrate on stopping Gretzky was a foolish strategy. With the emergence of Messier and Paul Coffey, teams were discovering that the Oilers had more than one weapon they needed to worry about. Focusing on just one player wouldn't get the job done.

As for Messier, after three two-goal games, he had finally turned the trick this season with the second three-goal game of his NHL career. He entered the game with 16 goals and 28 points and exited with 19 and 31. Though he was still primarily playing left wing, and he would ultimately make his biggest mark on the game playing centre, Messier was growing into a leader and a very valued teammate of Gretzky's. They were just kids, born just eight days apart in January 1961, but Gretzky and Messier already had a solid understanding of what each could do for the other. No sibling rivalry marred their relationship. Only mutual admiration existed between them.

"We saw some teams that had internal problems, and we came together at such an early age and had to rely on each other so heavily that we had a deep respect for each other," Messier said many years later. "Also, all the players on our team had a huge respect for Wayne and what he was up against in terms of the needs and demands placed upon him. We didn't look at him in terms of getting favouritism or special treatment. We understood where he was at and actually just tried to complement him. We realized Wayne was a special player who needed special attention on and off the ice. We figured the best way to help him was to complement him and fill in the holes. What made that easy was Wayne's incredible humility and the way he treated everyone around him and made everyone feel inclusive, no matter how big or small their roles were. It was Wayne's unselfishness that allowed us to galvanize as a group of kids."

Long after he had retired, Gretzky looked back fondly on the early days when he and Messier were wet behind the ears and working together to find team success in Edmonton. "It was amazing," Gretzky recently recalled. "Mark and I often laugh when you see different sports and different teams when superstars don't get along, because we just don't understand it. We were the best of friends. If Mark scored three goals and after the game you bumped into us, you'd think I got the three goals because I was so happy for him and vice versa. We pulled for each other constantly because we wanted each other to do well as individuals, because we knew that would contribute to the team's success. We made each other better. In practice, I had to go against him in every drill and on every shift. I like to think I made him a better player, and there is no question he

made me a better player." Gretzky added: "It was a special relationship because we were both kids and loved playing in Edmonton and
in the NHL. We made each other better. It was as simple as that."

Game 29 | December 4, 1981

Vs. Vancouver Canucks

Northlands Coliseum, Edmonton, Alberta

Tough guys generally know their role and understand that deviating from it could lead to a spot in the press box . . . or worse. There's an old saying in hockey that when a crusher becomes a rusher, he soon becomes an usher.

Dave Semenko had no illusions that he might one day challenge teammate Wayne Gretzky for the Art Ross Trophy. His primary job was to protect the Great One and the other skilled players on the Oilers, and he knew it. At six feet, three inches and 215 pounds, the 24-year-old Semenko was one of the biggest and most feared enforcers in the NHL. And if an opponent dared mess with Gretzky, he knew he would have to deal with Semenko.

In the NHL of 1981–82, rules regarding fighting were either rarely enforced or nonexistent, so players were left to police themselves. With very few exceptions, even the game's most gifted players often had to fight their own battles. For example, there was a little-known rule on the books, introduced in 1937, dictating that any player starting a fight should be ejected from the game. But it wasn't until the 1992–93 season that the league got serious about enforcing it by adding the instigator rule to expel from the game those who initiated fights.

Semenko was the perfect candidate to ride shotgun for Gretzky. Feared because of his toughness, Semenko accumulated 511 penalty minutes in 152 games as a junior with the Brandon Wheat Kings of the Western Hockey League. But he could also play the game. Semenko scored 47 goals and 91 points in his time in Brandon. He went on to play two seasons with the Oilers in the WHA and actually scored the final goal ever in the league, during the 1979 Avco Cup final, which Edmonton lost to the Winnipeg Jets. Now in the NHL, Semenko continued to do what was expected of him: namely, beat people up. On occasion, though, he chipped in with a goal . . . or two.

After the perturbing loss to the Nordiques, in which the Oilers broke their winning streak, they had a tough home-and-home series scheduled against the pesky Vancouver Canucks. Entering the first game, on December 4 in Edmonton, the Canucks hovered around the .500 mark with a record of 12–10–4 and had already faced the Oilers twice in the 1981–82 season. Vancouver had held Gretzky off the score sheet at the start of the season in their 6–2 victory over Edmonton on October 9, and with 31 goals in 28 games, Gretzky had been goalless in his past two outings. Was there any chance the Canucks could push his drought to three? Gretzky did, after all, torch them for two goals and four points on November 21, when Edmonton had handed Vancouver an 8–3 loss.

Playing their 14th game in 24 days, the Oilers started the game on December 4 slowly. Ivan Boldirev beat Edmonton goalie Grant Fuhr at 1:54 of the first to give Vancouver the early lead, but the man who was suddenly money in the bank, Dave Lumley, extended his goal-scoring streak to eight straight games—with an assist from Gretzky—at the 15:13 mark of the period. Lars Molin restored the Canucks' lead three minutes later, however, and it looked like the Oilers could be on their way to their second straight loss. After 20 minutes, they trailed the visitors from Vancouver by a score of 2–1.

But then, moving up to play on a line with Gretzky and Lumley, Semenko notched his fourth goal of the season, beating Vancouver goalie Richard Brodeur at the 2:30 mark of the second period. Less than a minute later, a goal by Matti Hagman shot the Oilers into the lead, and then Semenko took a pass from Gretzky and scored from close range at the 9:01 mark, giving the Oilers a 4–2 lead, one that they wouldn't relinquish.

Despite his two goals, the crusher was not entirely a rusher on this night. When Semenko believed Canucks tough guy Tiger Williams had taken liberties with Gretzky, he engaged Williams in a fight and came out ahead. It turned out that Williams had actually hit Glenn Anderson, but Semenko didn't let a guy mess with any of his teammates.

Edmonton scored three more goals (by Mark Messier, Pat Hughes, and Paul Coffey) in the first eight minutes of the third period, and the Canucks' Ron Delorme concluded the scoring with an otherwise meaningless goal at 19:03 in the 7–3 Oilers' win. Gretzky finished the game with three assists and Glenn Anderson, Marc Habscheid, and defenceman Lee Fogolin each registered two assists for the Oilers, but the night belonged to Semenko.

"Semenko was the one that got us going," said Oilers assistant coach Ted Green after the game. "He set up our first goal with his hitting, scored two of his own and took care of Tiger in a fight. After that, the Canucks weren't the same team."

Even though his team lost, Vancouver head coach Harry Neale had kind words for Semenko, the game's first star. "He's a very valuable guy," Neale said. "He gets enough goals to keep him happy and he's a physical threat that every team needs."

For Semenko, having his coach show faith in him by playing him with Gretzky was a big boost, but he knew the onus was on him if he wanted to keep getting playing time. "The only way to stay in the lineup is to play consistently," Semenko told the reporters after the game. "It's amazing what happens when you get confidence."

In the end, the Canucks were successful in keeping Gretzky from putting the puck in the net. But Gretzky made an impact against the Canucks with an assist in each period, giving him eight helpers in the past three games.

Twenty-nine games into the season, and having now gone a season-high three games without scoring a goal, Gretzky was stuck on 31 goals. Overall, he was still on pace to score 86 goals, and the 50 in 50 still looked like a real possibility, so nobody panicked, least of all Gretzky. "As long as I'm helping the team and other guys are scoring, then I'm satisfied," Gretzky said after the game. "A centre is paid to be a playmaker and that's what I've been doing. And we're not losing."

Game 30 | December 5, 1981

Vs. Vancouver Canucks

Pacific Coliseum, Vancouver, British Columbia

One game without scoring a goal was a blip on the screen for superstar Wayne Gretzky. Two games without a goal raised a few eyebrows. Three games without goals was officially a slump for the NHL's leading scorer, who had a mind-blowing 72 points in 29 games and eight assists in the past three games. Four games without a goal was almost unthinkable, especially while he was making a serious run at becoming the third NHLer to score 50 goals in 50 games. And yet, when the Oilers tied the Canucks, 3–3, in Vancouver on December 5, one day after spanking them, 7–3, in Edmonton, Gretzky was shut out once again. For the third time this season, the Canucks prevented Gretzky from scoring a goal.

Left winger Dave Lumley, on the other hand, kept his scoring streak alive, getting two of Edmonton's three goals, which brought his total to 12 on the season and meant that he had now scored goals in nine consecutive games.

In the previous three games, Gretzky had taken a total of seven shots on goal: three against Montreal, one against Quebec, and three against Vancouver. Since shooting more often was Gretzky's stated aim at the start of the season, on this night he stepped in the right direction, getting five shots in the rematch against Vancouver: two in the first period, three in the second, and then they skunked him, but at least he made it up to five. And while Gretzky could not find the back of the net, he did keep providing assists.

Each team took nine shots in a scoreless opening period, with Grant Fuhr in goal for the Oilers and Glen Hanlon (who had surrendered Gretzky's first NHL goal two seasons earlier) in the nets for the Canucks. Little by little, the Oilers were showing more faith in Fuhr, and why not? Since losing his NHL debut on October 14 to the Winnipeg Jets, he had gone 9–0–4.

Rugged, low-scoring defenceman Harold Snepsts of the Canucks got the first goal of the game at the 1:01 mark of the second period when his 50-foot shot found its way through a crowd and past a startled Fuhr. "I was looking the other way and only saw the puck at the last instant," Fuhr said afterward. "I thought the shot was going to be deflected."

The goal woke up the Oilers, who responded with two of their own in the second period: with assists from Gretzky and Dave Semenko, Lumley connected at the 4:40 mark with a nifty deke that fooled Hanlon; and Mike Forbes, with assists from Gretzky and Doug Hicks, cashed in with his first NHL goal at the 13:57 mark.

Forbes was not known for his offensive contributions, and he poked a little fun at himself afterward. "The goalie must have read that I never scored and he felt sorry for me," Forbes said to reporters. "Actually I was just shooting for a deflection, trying to hit Glenn Anderson. He missed and the puck went in."

And while no one could have known it at the time, for the

little-used Forbes, the goal against Vancouver would represent the only one of his brief 50-game NHL career.

Even though they were outscored, 2–1, in the second period, the Canucks had decisively outshot the Oilers, 18–9, laying the groundwork for an interesting final frame.

At the 5:56 mark of the third period, Lumley beat Hanlon with a 30-footer for his second of the game to give Edmonton what appeared to be a comfortable 3–1 lead. On many nights, a two-goal lead with less than 15 minutes to go would be safe for the NHL's top team. But the Oilers were a tired bunch, and that fatigue started to show. Since their back-to-back game nights on November 14 and 15, the Oilers had averaged a game almost every second night. It was only the fifth of December, and this was already their fourth game of the month.

The Canucks tied the game with goals scored 126 seconds apart, by Thomas Gradin at 14:20 and by Randy Rota at 16:26. Gradin was starting to earn himself something of a reputation as a homer, as 15 of his 16 goals of the season had been scored at Vancouver's Pacific Coliseum.

After the game, Fuhr admitted that Gradin fooled him on Vancouver's second goal. "I thought he would shoot it along the ice so I went down on my stomach," explained the Edmonton goalie. "Trouble is he waited and flipped a shot that looked like a butterfly as it fluttered over me."

Rota's tying goal was taken on a shot that even he figured Fuhr would stop, but the puck somehow found its way into the net and the game concluded 3–3. The Oilers had been looking for a different result, but took some consolation in their young goalie's running his undefeated streak to 14 games.

Hanlon, who made 24 saves of his own, also played a strong game. When the Oilers led by two, he stopped Gretzky twice and Glenn Anderson once, all on breakaways. "I just guessed that Gretzky was going to shoot so I came out and challenged him," Hanlon says. "He was low on his stick with his head was down. On Anderson's breakaway my skate or stick hit his stick. I don't even know where the puck went." Luckily for Hanlon and the Canucks, it flew over the net.

Gretzky may be the greatest goal scorer of all time, but breaking in alone was never his strong suit. "I have been having trouble scoring by deking so I thought I'd shoot when I saw him come out on both of my breakaways," Gretzky told reporters after the game.

Upon retiring, Gretzky insisted scoring droughts such as the four-gamer he went through in 1981–82 were nothing to sweat about (in the second half of the season, he had a stretch of six straight games without scoring a goal). "It's a long season and you know there will be spurts when you don't get any goals to add to your total, but in my mind, I was more conscious of how I was playing," Gretzky said recently. "If I was playing well, it didn't even faze me that I wasn't scoring. To me, scoring goals was a bonus as long as I felt I was playing well."

As for Lumley, his dream run had him downright giddy and feeling like never before. "I keep telling people I'm not a goal-scorer," Lumley said after the game against Vancouver. "But I'm dreading the day when I stop and people start asking me what's gone wrong."

Long after Lumley retired, he fondly recalled what it felt like to be holding such a hot hand. "You hear athletes talk about being in the zone," Lumley said. "Basketball players say the hoop is nine feet wide and baseball players say the ball looks so huge. That's what it was like for me. It was so magical. Jari Kurri gave me the best advice.

He said, 'Even if Gretz isn't looking at you, always have your stick on the ice and be ready because he'll put it right on your tape.' There was one game where Wayne was going into the corner, and I watched him. He never looked at me. I swear he looked into the glass and saw my reflection and backhanded the puck onto my stick and I put it in the net. It was just unreal."

At the end of the night, the Canucks were proud to have forged a comeback against the top team in the league. That said, they also acknowledged how good the Oilers were. "They had lots of reasons to lose, being tired and hurt," said Harry Neale. "But they played well enough to get a point. That looked like it was enough for them."

Added veteran defenceman Colin Campbell: "The Oilers are just eating up teams. Against some teams you can't give them the blue line. Against Edmonton—especially against Gretzky—you can't give them centre ice. With the Oilers reputation preceding them, teams don't want to get embarrassed."

After only one win in the team's last four games, Sather told the press that results on December 5 were almost predictable. "We just got tired and made some mental mistakes. I looked over at our bench late in the game and some of the guys weren't sweating anymore. They just didn't have anything left."

After the tie with Vancouver, the Oilers got their much-needed time off. There were no games scheduled for the team for the next three days.

Game 31 | December 9, 1981

Vs. Los Angeles Kings

The Forum, Inglewood, California

With 30 games in the books and Wayne Gretzky on a scoring pace that has him on track to achieve 83 goals and 197 points—both of which would be NHL records—the Edmonton Oilers departed for Los Angeles and their third meeting of the season with the Kings.

When the teams had last played, on November 25, Gretzky had been in the midst of a scoring tear during which he had accumulated 10 goals and 20 points in a five-game span. On that particular night, he had torched the Kings for four goals and five points in an 11–4 victory for the Oilers. It had been his second four-goal, five-point game of the season and brought him to 28 goals in 24 games.

In the last several games, though, Gretzky had fired blanks. He had 31 goals in 30 games, and the 50 in 50 wasn't out of reach, but all of a sudden it didn't look like the sure thing that it had appeared to be a couple of weeks before.

The Kings were in the midst of yet another poor season. Since being crushed by the Oilers in late November, they had gone 1–3–0, and with a 10–16–0 record on the season they desperately needed a win, especially against a divisional opponent. The Oilers, on the other hand, were still the NHL's top team, with an 18–7–5 record, and despite having just one win in their past four games, they only had one loss in their last 13. After the tie against the Canucks on December 5, Glen Sather thought his team looked tired, so he rewarded them on their three days off with a trip to La Costa resort in picturesque Carlsbad, California, about 87 miles south of Los Angeles. In the mind of the Edmonton coach, there was nothing like a little golf and sunshine to break up the madness of an 80-game hockey season.

"Three days off might not seem like much, but when you are used to the grind every day, it seems like longer," said defenceman Paul Coffey. "My stick felt like it weighed 1,000 pounds."

A little rest, however, can also cause a little rust, and the Kings took advantage of this by scoring three straight goals before the game was 12 minutes old. Rookie Steve Bozek opened the scoring just 68 seconds into the game on a 15-foot shot through a crowd of bodies in front of the Edmonton net. Dave Taylor, the NHL's second-leading scorer, behind only Gretzky, added a power-play goal at the 3:18 mark, and then Bozek potted his second of the game at 11:34. Staring at a quick 3–0 deficit, Grant Fuhr was in a position to lose for the first time since October 14, which would give him his second loss of the season and break a personal 14-game unbeaten streak.

Then again, Edmonton was a scoring factory, and plenty of time, almost 49 minutes, remained on the clock. The Oilers were averaging 5.7 goals per game, so technically they could still surrender one more before they really had to start worrying. With a little less than five minutes remaining in the opening period, Pat Hughes put the Oilers on the board with his 12th goal of the season and fourth in the past four games.

Between periods, the Oilers seemed to shake off the cobwebs. At the 6:17 mark of the second period, Lumley took a swipe at a bouncing puck and the shot eluded Los Angeles goalie Doug Keans as it flew over his shoulder. This gave Lumley his 12th goal in his last 10 games and the 100th point of his NHL career. It also brought the Oilers to within one goal as the Kings held on to an increasingly tenuous 3–2 lead. With at least one goal in 10 consecutive games, Lumley put himself in some pretty exclusive company, tying the career bests of such great scorers as Andy Bathgate, Mike Bossy, and Bobby Hull. Suddenly, and almost inexplicably, Lumley was only six games shy of the NHL record, achieved 60 years before. In 1921–22, Harry "Punch" Broadbent set the record for the most consecutive games with at least a goal, getting to 16 when he played for the Ottawa Senators in 1921–22, a year in which, not surprisingly, he led the NHL in scoring with 32 goals and 46 points in 24 games.

Having enjoyed a little golf on the Oilers' recent days off, Lumley joked after the game, "I always said I was good at those soft pitch shots."

With Lumley having reached his record, it was time for the focus to switch to Gretzky. At the 8:06 mark of the second period, with the Oilers on the power play, the Great One finally got the monkey off his back with his 32nd goal of the season. Just like that, the 50 in 50 seemed possible once again—and the Oilers had tied the game at three. Edmonton's momentum was short-lived, though; Bozek completed the first hat trick of his young NHL career eight minutes later with a power-play goal of his own, thereby restoring the Kings' lead.

In the third period, the Oilers dug deep with Mark Messier tying the game at four apiece just 61 seconds into the period and Hughes getting his second of the game at the 5:40 mark to give the Oilers a 5–4 edge.

Then all hell broke loose. Offensively challenged Los Angeles defenceman Mark Hardy, who earlier in the day had joked with a Kings executive that he would score as many goals as Gretzky that evening, fielded a high pass with his glove and tossed the puck down to his stick before blasting a long shot past Fuhr for the tying goal at the 10:51 mark. The Oilers strenuously argued that the goal shouldn't have counted because Hardy had closed his hand on the puck before dropping it to the ice, and then contacted the puck with his stick, but referee Dave Newell didn't see it that way and no penalty was called. The Oilers also insisted that Hardy was a few feet offside. Television replays supported their argument, but this was long before the era of goal reviews. "[Hardy] was two feet outside the [blue] line," said an exasperated Ron Low, who was backup goalie that night. "It was offside. We all stopped and hesitated because the puck went out of our zone. We were waiting for the whistle."

Los Angeles coach Parker MacDonald came to Newell's defence after the game, suggesting that while Hardy's skate might have been outside the blue line when he made contact with the puck, his glove was inside the Oilers' defensive zone. "But, hell," MacDonald said, "I was on the bench and didn't see it as well as other people."

Fuhr, who ultimately kept his unbeaten streak alive at 15 games in what ended as a 5–5 tie, had another beef with the officials. "All I know is somebody hooked my legs out from under me as Hardy was shooting," Fuhr told reporters after the game. "They did it all night. I don't know what Newell was watching!"

Perhaps the most annoyed Oiler was Gretzky. He scored what appeared to be his team's sixth goal of the game midway through the third period, when Edmonton was ahead by a score of 5–4. At first, the referee indicated it was a good goal, but then waved it off, saying that the puck had hit the post. "You don't see a ref change his mind like that too often," Gretzky said afterward.

On a night when the Oilers were down 3–0 early in the game, they earned a tie, and even though they felt ripped off by the on-ice officials, they quickly put things in perspective. "It took a while to forget about the fairways at La Costa," said Kevin Lowe after the game, in a pretty honest assessment of the Oilers' play. "But we came back strong after being down 3–0. We had them beat. The difference between this year and last is we would have lost a game like this in the past. Now at least we get a point."

Game 32 | December 13, 1981

Vs. New York Islanders

Northlands Coliseum, Edmonton, Alberta

O n the road to the Stanley Cup, the best gauge of a team's progress is the current Cup champions. For a team on the rise, beating one that has already climbed to the top of the mountain does wonders for its confidence. And though the Calgary Flames would eventually become the Oilers' ultimate rival—the Battle of Alberta took on a life of its own—the New York Islanders of the early 1980s were still the NHL's kings of the castle and the team that held what the kids from Edmonton so desperately wanted.

Lucky for the Oilers, on the evening of December 13 the exhausted Islanders limped into town to play the seventh and final game of a seven-game road trip—one that had them riding a three-game winless streak. At the other end of the spectrum, the Oilers had suffered just one defeat in their previous 14 games and it looked, at least before the game, as though they could get the upper hand in the match against their foes, the Islanders.

And yet it was the Islanders who struck first when defenceman Mike McEwen scored just 94 seconds into the first period, beating

Grant Fuhr. On a different occasion, this early goal against might have rattled the young Oilers and led them to second-guess themselves against the two-time Stanley Cup champions, but they were a first-place team now, one with confidence growing by leaps and bounds.

It also helped that the Oilers had in their possession two of the hottest players in the NHL: Gretzky, who was the runaway leader in the race for the Art Ross Trophy as the NHL's highest scorer, and Dave Lumley, who continued to play remarkably well for the Oilers, with goals in 10 straight games. Gretzky helped him on the line, but Lumley was proving himself to be worthy of the opportunity to skate with the Great One. And when the Oilers were down in the first, Lumley tapped his own rebound past Islanders goalie Billy Smith at the 11:29 mark to make it 11 straight games with a goal. Lumley's goal tied the game and gave the Edmonton forward his 13th goal in 11 games, with Gretzky drawing an assist on the play. "It was just a little bunt," Lumley said later. "Nothing like that has ever happened to me before, but then I've never played with Wayne Gretzky before."

The never-say-quit Islanders might have been tired, but there was a reason why they were the defending champions: they didn't bow to adversity. Bob Nystrom scored to catapult the Islanders back into the lead at 2:31 of the second period, but the advantage did not last for long, as a game within a game began to unfold before the eyes of everyone in the arena.

Back on October 11, during Edmonton's 11th game of the season, when Billy Smith used his goal stick to bash Gretzky in the knee, forcing the young centre to the dressing room, the goalie started something Gretzky would not soon forget. Using that incident as inspiration, the young Edmonton player took over the game, setting up back-to-back second-period goals by Dave Semenko at

3:18 and Paul Coffey at 9:55 to give the Oilers their first lead of the night, 3–2.

John Tonelli tied the score at three for the Islanders just 37 seconds after Coffey's goal. For a team at the end of a gruelling road trip, the Islanders hung in nicely, and with time running out in the third period, it seemed the Oilers would have to settle for their third straight tie.

But Wayne Gretzky was about to work his magic. He had taken three shots in the first 40 minutes and took two in the third period—the second of which decided the contest.

With only a little over a minute remaining in the game, Gretzky zipped past Islanders defenceman Denis Potvin and, all alone, skated in on his nemesis, Smith. The Islanders goaltender stopped Gretzky's first shot, but could not handle the rebound and Gretzky put the game-winner in the back of the Islanders net at the 18:58 mark. For Gretzky it was his 33rd goal of the season, and a deeply satisfying one at that.

To put things in context, in 1980–81, he hadn't scored his 33rd goal until Edmonton's 55th game of the season, on February 13, a full two months later in the year than this game. "It's probably the happiest I've been after scoring a goal," Gretzky said with delight after the game. "I don't think I've ever had one this late to win a game. I know I scored with 39 seconds left to tie the Islanders the last time we played."

Gretzky admitted that he misjudged the situation on his initial shot on Smith and was fortunate to get a second opportunity. He took his first attempt—a wrist shot—from about 30 feet out. "I could have gone in further, but I remembered that [Smith] stopped Lumley earlier when he tried to deke him," Gretzky said. "I was hoping to catch him off-guard. Luckily the rebound came back to me."

For his part, Potvin also admitted after the game that he had misjudged Gretzky on the play that led to the winning goal, specifically when Gretzky froze him with a fake slap shot. "I was always taught to play the man," Potvin said. "But he jumped in front of me and he had the momentum to go the other way."

Gretzky almost let up on the play. "I thought I was offside," he said. "I thought I heard the whistle and I was going to stop. Denis may have thought it was offside also."

There was no love lost between the Oilers and Islanders, but, even if begrudgingly, there was a mutual respect. Islanders centre Bryan Trottier marvelled at Gretzky's ability to lift his team when the game was on the line. Gretzky had a goal and three assists at the end of the game, and for the ninth time that season, he produced at least four points in a game.

"He's fun to watch," Trottier said after the game. "Maybe not so much fun to play against, but he sure does some great things out there. Wayne made a dynamite play and he finished it off."

Gretzky's late goal gave the Oilers the lead, but the Islanders did not surrender easily. In the closing seconds, Mike Bossy of the Islanders drilled a long slap shot that hit Fuhr in the shoulder and headed into the net before Kevin Lowe lunged and knocked it away. The heroic effort by Lowe kept the Oilers three points ahead of the Buffalo Sabres in the overall NHL standings and also allowed Fuhr's undefeated streak to run to 16 games (10 wins, six ties). "Part of the puck was over the line," Lowe exclaimed. "The good thing is it was spinning like a top."

As one might expect, Billy Smith was grumpy after the game. "I played like horse-crap and let in a couple of questionable goals," Smith fumed. "I had no chance on [Gretzky's] rebound. It went under my arm. What are you going to do? I made the first save and it was about the only good goal they scored."

If Gretzky's chase for 50 goals in 50 games wasn't hard enough on its own, doing it with a couple of plumbers, Lumley and Semenko, on his wings was making the feat even more challenging, at least according to those who followed the Oilers. *Edmonton Journal* columnist Terry Jones wrote, "If Gretzky has to go 18 more games with Dave Semenko on one wing and still scores 50 goals, I say it'll be his (not to mention Semenko's) greatest accomplishment."

To his credit, Gretzky wasn't seeking new linemates and was particularly thrilled by Lumley's play. Lumley was now five games shy of tying Punch Broadbent's record of 16 consecutive games with a goal. "I'd really like Lummer to break the record," Gretzky told the press.

For his part, Lumley made no secret of his belief that Gretzky was passing on his own scoring opportunities to try to set him up for goals. For that matter, Gretzky said when he played with Lumley and Semenko, he believed his role was to feed them scoring chances. When he played with Brett Callighen, Jari Kurri, and Pat Hughes, he expected them to get the puck to him. Nevertheless, he didn't mind assisting Lumley on his quest. "I'm going to do everything I can to give him the opportunity to do so," Gretzky said at the time. "This kind of thing has changed Lummer's whole life. Everyone knows now about the attitude problem he used to have. What he has accomplished has given him a great new attitude and he has a new confidence in himself on and off the ice that I think he's going to keep for a long time to come."

Lumley was quite aware of the opportunity he had been afforded, playing on a line with the sport's best player. "I can't help but wonder what the other players in the league are thinking," Lumley said. "The other players have watched me play. I know they are all thinking, 'How in hell can he score in 11 straight games?' They must be scratching their heads." Lumley smiled as he talked about his fortunate situation. "It's fun playing with [Gretzky]," he said. "Everybody on the other team is dazzled by him. I just sneak in while they're watching him and he puts the puck on my stick."

Game 33 | December 16, 1981

Vs. Colorado Rockies

McNichols Sports Arena, Denver, Colorado

After an emotional encounter with the New York Islanders three nights earlier, the Edmonton Oilers could be forgiven for suffering a letdown when they travelled to Denver to face their next opponent. The Colorado Rockies were an awful team, in the middle of their sixth and final year in Colorado before relocating to New Jersey. But the NHL had not been ill advised to put a franchise in the Colorado market, even though Denver hadn't traditionally shown a strong hockey following. When the Quebec Nordiques later set up shop in Colorado, in 1995–96, and won the Stanley Cup that same season and again in 2000–01, hockey became all the rage. But that was far in the future.

When the Oilers pulled into town on December 16, the Rockies had lost 12 of their past 16 games. To the Oilers, the Rockies had already dropped two out of three. It had been a 7–4 decision for Edmonton on the Oilers' opening night on October 7, a score of 3–1 for the Oilers on October 24, and then the Rockies had stunned Edmonton with a 5–4 win on the evening of November 7. Not that the last win mattered to Rockies fans, who had begun staying away from their games in droves.

For the game against the Oilers on this night, only 6,168 people showed up. Apparently, Gretzky's run for 50 in 50 was not big news in Denver, and neither was Dave Lumley's string of 11 straight games with a goal. Nevertheless, the show must go on.

Having defeated the Oilers on November 7, in a game during which he made 46 saves, and after having played spectacularly in the 3–1 loss on October 24, during which Edmonton outshot Colorado, 53–19, Chico Resch, not surprisingly, got the start in the Colorado goal. But on this night, he didn't do as well.

At the 59-second mark of the opening period, Gretzky scored his 34th goal of the season, beating Resch with a backhand shot. Gretzky's goal kicked off an onslaught as the Oilers proceeded to score three more goals in the next two minutes and 40 seconds. Garry Unger made the score 2–0 when he tipped home a shot by Kevin Lowe at the 2:46 mark, and then Mark Messier joined the party, jamming a rebound past a startled Resch at the 3:25 mark to make the score 3–0 Edmonton.

This offensive outburst marked the fastest three goals the Oilers had ever achieved at the start of a game, and they weren't done yet. When defenceman Paul Coffey snapped a shot between Resch's pads at the 3:39 mark, with Gretzky drawing the assist, the Oilers were up by four after just three minutes and 39 seconds of play, setting another franchise record. Goals two, three, and four had been scored in the grand total of 53 seconds.

Ron Low had been given his first start in the Edmonton net in five games. Surely, half of the people who had bothered to go to the game at McNichols Sports Arena wondered where it was heading

Coffey's goal was his 17th of the season, tying Risto Siltanen's club record for most goals in a season by a defenceman. With 47 games remaining in 1981-82, there was a good chance Coffey would have the team record all to himself sooner rather than later.

when Bob Miller beat Low at the 13:45 mark of the first period to make the score 4–1. Temporarily, the home side had a little hope. Very little, it turns out, since two minutes and 46 seconds later, Dave Lumley scored to stretch his consecutive-games-with-a-goal streak to 12 and reestablish Edmonton's four-goal lead. Resch had no chance on Lumley's 20-foot blast. Getting an assist on the goal, Gretzky was already up to three points for the game. Almost amazingly, although the Oilers had built a 5–1 lead by the end of the opening period, the Rockies had registered 18 shots on goal, just two shy of Edmonton's 20.

Brent Ashton made the score 5–2 when he scored for the Rockies seven minutes into the second period, but Lumley's amazing run continued when he scored his second of the game at 12:26, followed by Lowe's second goal of the season at 13:20, bringing it to 7–2 in the Oilers' favour.

Resch enjoyed many great nights in his wonderful career, and there were more highlights to come. This game, however, was not one of them. Mercifully, Colorado head coach Marshall Johnston took pity on the stopper at the onset of the third period and allowed him to watch the rest of the slaughter from the bench.

Luckily for Resch's replacement in the Colorado net, Phil Myre, by now the Oilers had put it on automatic pilot and were content to coast the rest of the way. The Rockies outshot the Oilers, 12–7, in the third period and got the only two goals of the period courtesy of Don Lever and Bob MacMillan, both of whom had recently been acquired in a trade with the Calgary Flames. By game's end, Edmonton had outshot Colorado by a count of 40–37 in securing an easy 7–4 victory.

Edmonton's triumph made them the first team in the NHL to reach the 20-win plateau. After tying two games in a row, the Oilers had now won two in a row. Such was the extent of the Oilers' dominance in the first two periods that Edmonton's goaltender was actually grateful for the Rockies' third-period outburst. After 40 minutes with precious little going on in his end of the rink, he had been growing tired of doing mental calisthenics. "Getting a 4–0 lead so early made it easier and then I got some work which helped," Low said afterward.

Meanwhile, with Glen Sather under the weather, assistant coach Billy Harris handled the bench duties. "I was hoping we'd get off to a good start," Harris said, "but I never believed we'd do it this way."

Lumley continued to be a rock star. "It's like *Fantasy Island*," he said after the game of his continued good fortune. Against the Rockies, Lumley had led the Oilers attack with two goals and four points. When asked about the game, Lumley joked that the Rockies defence must have stayed in the dressing room for the first four minutes. But he perhaps took pity on Resch, who with the Islanders had won the Stanley Cup in 1979–80 (as the backup to Billy Smith). "He must look at his Stanley Cup ring and cry, the poor guy," Lumley said.

A lot of teams expressed sympathy for the opposition if they fell so far behind so early in the game. Not the Oilers. They were young, cocky, and a whole lot of enthusiastic. Gretzky liked his team's start to the game and he saw the direction things were going: "When it was 4–0, I looked over at Lummer and said, 'Let's fill the net.'"

Game 34 | December 17, 1981

Vs. Calgary Flames

Stampede Corral, Calgary, Alberta

Well, it was fun while it lasted. In his nine-year professional hockey career, Dave Lumley scored a total of 98 goals and 258 points. He had his name engraved on the Stanley Cup twice, the ultimate testament to his value as a hockey player. At five feet, 11 inches and 185 pounds, Lumley was a scrappy player who ground it out as a plumber surrounded by surgeons. Having 33 fights in 437 games proved the lengths he would go to to make an impact and help his team. To walk comfortably and proudly among some of the best players in NHL history, Dave Lumley was willing to pay a price.

So it was with great pleasure that the hockey gods looked down on this lunch-bucket player and rewarded him with a run for the ages: 26 days of sheer glory.

Years later, Lumley still got giddy when he recalled his magical 12-game scoring streak. "The guys really got behind me, and the reporters suddenly were interested in me," he said recently, with a chuckle. "As I got closer to the record, around the 10-game mark,

I started thinking about the players I was chasing—guys like Rocket Richard, Phil Esposito, and Gordie Howe. It was crazy!"

Lumley would never be mistaken for Wayne Gretzky, but for 12 games he outscored the Great One, 15 goals to 13. In fact, Lumley and Gretzky each recorded 28 points during that 12-game run. Clearly, Lumley could not have done it all without Gretzky, and the accompanying good fortune of skating alongside the best player in the world, but Lumley also deserves, at the very least, some credit for his amazing streak of scoring goals in 12 consecutive games. "As for Wayne, what you see is what you get," Lumley said recently. "He was one of the hardest workers ever. I sat beside him in the dressing room for almost eight years. I was always first in the shower because the press was all around my stall and nobody wanted to talk to me. Wayne was a funny guy . . . just one of the guys."

Yes, Lumley fell short of Punch Broadbent's record of scoring in 16 straight games, but even being in the conversation was something most other players only dreamed about.

And despite dropping a 5–4 decision to their provincial rivals on the evening of December 17th, the Calgary Flames put a halt to Lumley's career-highlight goal-scoring streak. "I wasn't sour when the streak ended," Lumley said years later. "I played with Gretz a few more games, but you know what, as quickly as I felt the magic of being in the zone, I felt it go away just as quickly. I could just feel the difference, and Sather noticed it, too. Then I had to go and play on a line with Mark Messier and Glenn Anderson. Bummer.

"My favourite part of the story is, after the game against Calgary when I didn't score, we come back to Edmonton to face the Minnesota North Stars and we win, 9–6. I score three goals and add three assists and I am chosen the second star of the game. Second star! That little weasel [Gretzky] had seven points and is the first star of the game."

There was much for Gretzky to remember in his outstanding 1981–82 season, but years later he revealed Lumley's hot streak still brought a smile to his face. "We were all excited for him," Gretzky said. "We were all pulling for him. We wanted him to go 20 games in a row scoring goals. That was the thing about that group; it didn't matter who was enjoying success; we all kind of pulled for each other and everybody felt a part of it. Each and every guy that got the chance to play with Lummer, especially when he got to about eight games, there was a conscious effort that we had to get him a goal. Each player to a man felt the same way: that this was kind of cool and what he was doing was pretty amazing."

Stopping Lumley was one thing. Keeping Wayne Gretzky off the score sheet? Well, that was quite a different matter. With a goal against the Flames, Gretzky carved out a nice little four-game goal-scoring streak of his own, and his quest for 50 goals in 50 games gained momentum and remained the biggest news story of the 1981–82 NHL season. So much was made of Mike Bossy becoming the second player in decades of NHL history to get 50 in 50, and yet there they were, just a year later, and Gretzky was poised to become the third.

The game against Calgary was a tough one for the Oilers. The Flames were still a long way off from winning their first and only Stanley Cup, but a few weeks earlier they had acquired Lanny McDonald and a fourth-round draft choice from the Colorado Rockies. Calgary general manager Cliff Fletcher sent 28-year-old veterans Don Lever and Bob MacMillan to Colorado in exchange for McDonald, who at the same age was just entering the prime of his career.

Looking back on the deal that brought him to Calgary, Lanny McDonald said it was nothing short of a life-altering experience. The Rockies were going nowhere and the Flames, with Cliff Fletcher driving the bus, were inching toward respectability and ultimately a Stanley Cup in 1989. "When a trade happens, you are first feeling rejection, but after you think about it for a bit, you start to look at the other side, the positive side, which is that somebody wants you," McDonald said recently. "I remember first being down about that trade, and I was going through the Rockies team bus, saying goodbye to the guys, and pretty soon they were all kicking me off. Rob Ramage and Mike Kitchen were jokingly yelling at me to 'Get out of here!' They were happy for me because I was getting out of Colorado."

McDonald quickly discovered that the Oilers were the Flames' most hated opponents. "Even before the Oilers and the Flames were in the NHL, anything Edmonton-and-Calgary-related was always a rivalry based on bragging rights," McDonald said recently. "But when the Oilers and Flames got going, that took things to a whole other level and it quickly became one of the greatest hockey rivalries of all time, and there was nothing that either one of us wouldn't do to get the upper hand."

McDonald said the problem the Flames faced when playing the Oilers in the early '80s was that Edmonton had Gretzky, Mark Messier, Jari Kurri, Glenn Anderson, Paul Coffey, and Grant Fuhr: "Six of the best players in the league.

"The other thing that team had—that is often overlooked today—was toughness," McDonald says. "Despite all the offence, all the flash and skill, they were at their core a very tough team. Our team, the Flames, was built specifically to beat the Oilers. And really, Cliff had no choice; we had to beat the Oilers to win the Stanley Cup. They were the ones in the way."

On this particular night, December 17, 1981, the Flames delighted their hometown fans—a standing-room crowd of 7,226 filled the tiny Stampede Corral (which had a seating capacity of 6,450, plus the aforementioned patrons who were forced to watch the game while standing)—by taking a 2–0 first-period lead thanks to goals by Jamie Hislop at 2:31 and Denis Cyr at 8:32. The Oilers answered back in the second frame with back-to-back power-play goals by defencemen Risto Siltanen (at 2:54) and Paul Coffey (at 6:25), both on blasts from the point that eluded Calgary goaltender Pat Riggin. This night was shaping up to be one in which both goaltenders would have to battle, and in the case of one goalie, not just against the puck. While Lumley's goal-scoring streak was being snuffed out, rookie goaltender Fuhr was looking to extend his own personal 16-game unbeaten streak. He hadn't lost a start in the more than two months since he made his NHL debut in a 4–2 loss to Winnipeg on October 14.

First, Fuhr was victimized by a fluke goal at the 8:37 mark of the second period, when Calgary's Willi Plett sent a shot toward the Edmonton net that bounced off the skate of Oilers defenceman Doug Hicks and proceeded directly into the net to give the Flames a 3–2 lead. The goal hurt, but not nearly as much as what happened next. In a goalmouth collision in front of the Edmonton net, while Fuhr was making a leg save, he slammed into Calgary forward Jamie Hislop and dislocated his right shoulder, the same shoulder he had also dislocated the season before while playing junior with the Victoria Cougars. He'd also banged it up a week earlier in the game against the New York Islanders, so it was already tender. "I didn't even see Hislop coming," Fuhr said later. "It was a complete surprise to me and I landed on my shoulder the wrong way."

When it became obvious that he could not continue in the game, Fuhr was carted off the ice on a stretcher and Ron Low replaced him in the Edmonton net. With Calgary ahead 3–2, Fuhr's undefeated streak seemed as though it would end with him icing his shoulder in the dressing room. Now the game was Low's to win, lose, or tie.

In the confines of Edmonton's dressing room, Flames doctor Nick Kastelan popped Fuhr's dislocated shoulder back into place, and the game went on. At the 11:53 mark of the third period, a goal by Calgary's Mel Bridgman put the Flames up 4–2 and the win appeared to be theirs, but with a little over eight minutes left on the clock, the Oilers kicked it into high gear. Pat Hughes connected on a rebound at the 12:43 mark to make it a 4–3 game, and a little less than two minutes later, Gretzky scored on a breakaway after taking a pass from Mark Messier. In addition to tying the game at four, the goal kept Gretzky's points streak alive at 13 games. "When I got the puck, I looked up and I knew Gretz was going to be clear," Messier said after the game. "All I had to do was pass it to him."

"That was one of the finest plays I've seen him make," said Gretzky of Messier's pinpoint pass. "He recognized the situation right away and he didn't hesitate."

Gretzky was grateful for the pass from Messier and even more pleased to see Riggin making a move to try to stop him. "As soon as I saw that Riggin had stuck his stick out I knew I was going to deke him," Gretzky told the reporters after the game. "I saw his stick slide out and I put the puck under him."

The game was now tied. And so it came down to the final minute. With 51 seconds remaining, in an almost eerie replay of what had happened on Willi Plett's earlier goal, Edmonton defence-man Kevin Lowe directed a long shot toward the Calgary net that hit Flames defenceman Phil Russell and eluded Riggin. For the Oilers, now celebrating a 5–4 win, turnabout was fair play. Jari Kurri got an assist on the goal, and with it the 100th point of his NHL career. "I just lobbed the puck at the net," said Lowe, after the fact.

The Oilers had snatched a victory from the hands of defeat. It was Edmonton's third win in a row, and the Oilers were now unde-feated in six. But the victory itself was not the only news of the day. For the second year in a row, Gretzky had been named Canada's male athlete of the year in a Canadian Press year-end poll of sports-writers and broadcasters, and as a result was awarded the Lionel Conacher Trophy. Gretzky had received 54 first-place votes, 17 second-place votes, and three third-place votes. Skier Steve Podborski was the runner-up and swimmer Alex Baumann took third. Mike Bossy of the New York Islanders placed fourth in the voting.

As always, the ever-humble Gretzky put things in perspective. "Any time you can win an individual award, it is something special; especially that [Conacher Trophy] with so many great athletes in Canada now," Gretzky said before adding. "I think my parents will be proud. . . . I think everyone who has an opportunity to win an individual award surely would like to win it," Gretzky stated. "Whether you win it once or you win it five times, it's still always a pleasure to be able to win." Then came the obvious: "I think if there is one award I'd like to win it would be the Stanley Cup."

But with his goal against the Flames, Gretzky had now carved out a nice little four-game goal-scoring streak of his own, one that put him at 35 goals on the season after 34 games as his quest for 50 goals in 50 games continued.

Game 35 | December 19, 1981

Vs. Minnesota North Stars

Northlands Coliseum, Edmonton, Alberta

In his first 34 games of the 1981–82 NHL season, Wayne Gretzky had scored at a pace other NHLers—past, present, and future—could only dream about. With 35 goals and 83 points, Gretzky was now on pace for 82 goals and 195 points, which would establish new NHL records for goals and points in a single season.

Of the 34 games, there were only four games in which the opposition had prevented Gretzky from registering a point. Generally, he was the model of consistency, and his Edmonton Oilers, though extremely young and inexperienced by NHL standards, had established themselves as a franchise of note, a team with championship potential. With Gretzky scoring at such a record pace, it seemed impossible he could ramp it up any more. And yet he did exactly that as 1981 drew to a close.

Against the Minnesota North Stars on December 19, Gretzky had his best game yet of the season, with three goals and four assists—the third seven-point game of his young NHL career. Although he had been on an unparalleled offensive tear, even Gretzky was dazzled by his big game against the North Stars. "I really haven't had any big nights until this game," Gretzky said afterward, though his six four-point games and three five-point games could hardly be considered unremarkable.

At 13–9–9, the North Stars were enjoying a decent season of their own, although they were riding a two-game losing streak and had gone 1–5–1 in their past seven games. For a team that had made it to the Stanley Cup final the previous spring and lost only four of its first 24 games in 1981–82, the month-long slump was quite concerning. Just two wins in 15 games, and now they were facing the mighty Oilers.

The red-hot Oilers, on the other hand, had three consecutive wins in and were in the midst of a six-game unbeaten streak. And they'd lost just once in their past 17 games.

One thing was certain: both teams could score goals. The North Stars were averaging 4.2 goals per game in their 31 games. Seven times, the North Stars had scored six goals in a game, and in an offensive outburst rarely seen at any level of hockey, on November 11 they had beaten the Winnipeg Jets, 15–2. In contrast, with 191 goals through their first 34 games, the Oilers were averaging 5.6 goals per game.

All this pointed toward defence being a very low priority when the North Stars and Oilers hooked up for their second meeting of the season, and even though the first game produced a fast-paced, exciting 2–2 draw, on this night, the goals came fast and furious. By the end of the first period, both teams had a combined nine goals.

Because of other players' injuries, Gretzky had skated with a variety of wingers thus far in the 1981–82 season. From Pat Hughes to Dave Semenko, from Dave Lumley to Dave Hunter, none were considered elite offensive players. Even Lumley, whose remarkable 12-game goal-scoring streak had just come to an end, fared better at mucking and grinding than at dangling with the puck.

For this game, Jari Kurri joined Gretzky and Lumley on a line. In time, Gretzky and Kurri formed a dynamic duo in Edmonton, and later in Los Angeles. But after 34 games, Kurri wasn't enjoying a great season in 1981–82. As a rookie the previous year, he'd scored 32 goals and had 75 points in 75 games, but thus far Kurri had only seven goals and 26 points in 26 games. His output hadn't been helped when he missed eight games after pulling a groin muscle in practice on November 24. But, in the same way Lumley had got his break with the Great One, Kurri's season took a turn for the better thanks to being put alongside Number 99.

On December 19, the North Stars showed they meant business from the get-go. Steve Christoff opened the scoring on Edmonton starter Ron Low just 2:46 into the game. Perhaps the Oilers were in sleep mode at the beginning of the game, but if so, Christoff's goal jolted them awake. Within 20 seconds, Hughes tied the contest with his 15th goal of the season and his second in back-to-back games. Not to be deterred, the North Stars struck back with two goals, one from Steve Payne at 3:20 and one from Brad Palmer at 5:38. The ice at Northlands Coliseum was barely dry and the scoreboard already showed four goals scored, 3–1 for the North Stars.

Then, as if he had been waiting for a cue, Gretzky sprung into action. Carrying the puck at top speed, he made a shift that fooled Minnesota defenceman Ron Meighan, taking him out of the play. Left on his own, North Stars goalie Gilles Meloche rolled the dice and charged out of his net toward Gretzky. Gretzky sidestepped Meloche and deposited the puck into the vacated goal to make the score 3–2 after close to seven minutes of play. Again, though, the North Stars stormed back, with Bobby Smith beating Low at the 9:40 mark and restoring Minnesota's two-goal lead.

Gretzky responded with his second of the game, connecting from a scramble in front of the Minnesota goal at the 14:31 mark. "More than ever before I am getting more goals like that on pileups and scrambles," Gretzky said after the game.

With 71 seconds left in a wild opening period, Gretzky set up Kurri to tie the game at four. And then, just 33 seconds after that, Lumley scored his 17th of the season, and the period ended with the Oilers out in front by a score of 5–4.

Edmonton goalie Ron Low, pressed into action by Fuhr's injury, had played some wonderful games with the Oilers this season, but this was definitely not one of them. The second period was a much calmer affair than the opening frame, but Minnesota scored two goals on seven shots and the Oilers responded with one goal on 15 shots. Brad Palmer at 3:44 and Ron Meighan at 13:38 got one each for the visiting North Stars while Jari Kurri at 17:30 netted his second of the game, with help from Gretzky and Lumley. And after 40 minutes, the scoreboard at the Northlands Coliseum read 6–6.

Having allowed six goals on just 16 shots, Low took a spot at the end of the bench for the third period, while Andy Moog replaced him. Moog had been recalled from the minors as a result of Fuhr's injury. The switch paid off, as the Oilers outscored the North Stars 3–0 in the third period. Lumley got two of the goals—with Gretzky drawing assists on both—giving him his first career hat trick and his first six-point game in the NHL. Gretzky scored the other Edmonton goal of the period, his third of the night, resulting in the ninth three-goal game of his NHL career. The final score was 9–6 for the Oilers, who had won their fourth game in a row and reached the 200-goal plateau after playing only 35 of the 80 games on their regular-season schedule.

All told, the Gretzky-Lumley-Kurri trio produced eight goals and 16 points. Not bad for a night's work. Gretzky's goals on the season now totalled 38 and his points 90.

Almost as impressive as Gretzky's performance was Lumley's run. With this game, he moved into fourth place in team scoring at 19 goals and 39 points. His hat-trick goal was scored with goalie Meloche pulled in favour of an extra skater. "I could hear the fans yelling at me to get the hat trick," Lumley said after the game. "I really feel like they're my friends up there." Lumley pointed out that all of his goals at home had come in the first and third periods. "I haven't scored once in the second period yet."

Playing on a line with Gretzky caused Lumley to change his style. An abrasive winger known for his physical play, Lumley said of himself, "I can't remember the last time I hit a guy. On Gretzky's line you have to score."

Lumley, Gretzky, and Minnesota head coach Glen Sonmor agreed that the North Stars' strategy on this day—which was to try to match the Oilers goal for goal—was not a sound one. The game involved very little that could be mistaken for defensive play and virtually no hitting. "Wayne thrives on games like this," Lumley said. "When there is no hitting, that's his game. I could see his eyes light up. They jumped into an early lead and we had to open it up and they thought, 'Fine, we'll play a wide-open game.' Anybody who comes into our building and wants to do that is just going to get blown out."

Gretzky added, "When you get that much room, you're bound to be able to make plays. The North Stars are a pretty good skating and shooting team, but I think they realize they made a mistake trying to outgun us."

Sonmor spat nails at the game's conclusion. "Of all the teams to get into a shootout with, this is the worst," the coach told the media. "We haven't been getting goals lately and now we finally get some and we want to get in a shooting derby. We've got a lot of selfish hockey players who think the way to play this game is to fish for the puck continually. Their thinking is, 'If I come up with the puck I'll get a few points.' And they aren't all forwards, either.

"They see what Gretzky can do and they all think they'll try to do it. But they don't understand how great he is and that there's no one around who can do what he does. If it's one or two players, it's pretty easy to do something about it. But when the disease affects the whole team, it's pretty tough." Sonmor's rant didn't stop there. "We're apparently unwilling to pay the price it takes to battle our way through these things. If you continually try to come up with the puck and don't run into anybody, you're going to get beaten. The easy way to play this game is to poke the puck. You never get hit with a stick on the side of the head and never get an elbow in the mouth when you do that. It's nice and easy."

The game against the North Stars was number 194 of Wayne Gretzky's NHL career. Thanks to his seven-point outburst, he now had collected 391 in his career.

On the same day that Gretzky produced this seven-point game against the North Stars, the *Toronto Star* proclaimed him "The No. 1 Player Right in Toronto." How did the paper come to this conclusion? Simple. Longtime sports reporter Jim Proudfoot paid a visit to Doug Laurie Sports at 62 Carlton Street, situated right between the main entrance of Maple Leaf Gardens at 60 Carlton and Alton's

Barber Shop at 66 Carlton, and asked the store's proprietor, Tommy Smythe, a simple question: Out of all the jerseys sold, which NHL player's is the most popular?

"Darryl Sittler has always been the leader for us, closely followed by Börje Salming, and it has been that way for a good many years," Smythe revealed. "But Gretzky has become our single best seller." Smythe told Proudfoot that he expected to sell about 1,000 Gretzky jerseys, the adult size priced at $52.99, over the course of the season.

And the merchandising trend was not limited to Toronto. "I've never seen a demand for one team close to the call for the Oilers," Jerry Sabourin told Proudfoot. Sabourin's Montreal-based firm produced the official NHL crest that went on all the uniforms, the ones worn by the players and those purchased by the fans. Sabourin estimated that, on the whole, merchandise related to the Oilers was outselling those of the Toronto Maple Leafs and Montreal Canadiens combined, by a margin of two to one. "It's pretty clear, then, that the Oilers have taken over as the outfit most Canadians cherish," Proudfoot concluded, "and in just their third year of NHL membership."

Game 36 | December 20, 1981

Vs. Calgary Flames

Northlands Coliseum, Edmonton, Alberta

Upstaging the Great One during his greatest hockey season ever was a difficult task, but not an impossible one. Just ask Lanny McDonald.

Being traded by the Colorado Rockies to the Calgary Flames on November 25 had been McDonald's get-out-of-jail-free card. In Canada, where people gave a hoot about hockey, McDonald had been an NHL star with the Toronto Maple Leafs during his first six years in the league. Colorado, to whom he had been traded on December 29, 1979 wasn't hell, but you could see it from the bleachers. The 1981–82 season was the Flames' second in Calgary, after they relocated from Atlanta, and while they were still playing out of the Stampede Corral, which held just 6,500 seats (plus standing room), the franchise was quickly developing fan interest.

Beating the Oilers didn't happen often, but sometimes the key to winning against them wasn't to shut Gretzky down, but to match his output and pray everything else fell into place. So even on a night when Gretzky produced yet another three-point game, with two goals and an assist—the 18th time this season he got three or more points—the Flames had a three-goal effort from their newest weapon, the mustachioed McDonald.

McDonald opened the scoring for the visiting Flames at the 7:45 mark of the first period. Andy Moog got the start for the Oilers after spelling Ron Low in the third period the night before and blanking the Minnesota North Stars in a 9–6 Edmonton victory. There would be no blanking on this night. McDonald beat Moog on a breakaway.

Mark Messier evened the score at 13:00, beating Flames goalie Reggie Lemelin, but Mel Bridgman restored Calgary's lead with a power-play goal three minutes and 47 seconds later. After 20 minutes, the Oilers trailed by a goal and were down two men. First, defence-man Garry Lariviere was carried off the ice on a stretcher and sent to the hospital with severe back spasms, and then fellow defender Kevin Lowe was ejected from the game by referee Bob Myers. Calgary's Jim Peplinski had tagged Lowe, knocking him to the ice after the pair engaged in verbal warfare. Seeing his teammate in trouble, Mark Messier attacked Peplinski. When Lowe stood up, he joined the fray and Myers dubbed him the third man in an altercation—warranting an automatic ejection—much to Glen Sather's chagrin. "Last week I sent a telex to the league asking for the definition of an altercation," Sather exclaimed, "and they couldn't give me one."

On this night, Sather had plenty more grief to come.

McDonald made it 3–1 for Calgary with his second goal of the game at 3:41 of the second period, but Edmonton's Paul Coffey drew his team back to within a goal with his 19th of the season at the 5:29 mark.

You might think a pair of goals, scored back to back by Gretzky, which brought him to 40 goals for the season, would be enough to sooth Sather. Gretzky deftly tipped home a Risto Siltanen blast from the point, 11 seconds into an Edmonton power play at 10:25, to tie the game at three, and then converted a feed from Brett Callighen a little less than five minutes later to give the Oilers a 4–3 lead. But in between the two Gretzky goals, it was a goal that didn't count that incensed Sather and the Oilers. On a seemingly innocent play, a pass in the corner from Glenn Anderson found its way into the back of the Calgary net after deflecting off Mark Messier's skate. Confusion reigned as linesman Ryan Bozak contended that Messier had intentionally kicked the puck in with his skate, even though referee Bob Myers actually signalled it as a good goal. Bozak's insistence wore Myers down, and in the end the ref deemed there would be no goal.

Messier was mystified. "I went to stop so I didn't run into the net, and the puck hit my foot." And while televison replays seemed to back up Messier's explanation, the call on the ice stood. No goal.

After 40 minutes, Sather might have been going nuts, but what he'd seen in the second period was merely a prelude to an even more infuriating third period. Pekka Rautakallio scored at the 3:57 mark to knot the score at four. A little over two minutes later, Ken Houston put the Flames back on top a little with yet another contentious goal.

Willi Plett of the Flames attempted a pass and, in similar fashion to the disputed Messier goal, the puck hit Houston in the leg and eluded Moog. The Oilers expected this one to be waved off, too, but were shocked and disappointed when Myers judged it to be a good goal. "Both teams head to the blue line for a faceoff and [Myers] carries the puck to centre ice and says, 'Goal!'" Sather ranted afterward. "The Flames didn't even think it was good. They were as shocked as we were."

The puck seemed to have a mind of its own this night. So perhaps it was fitting that the man who scored the game's decisive goal called a "fluke." The play started when Calgary's Mel Bridgman beat Edmonton defender Lee Fogolin to the corner of the rink to negate an icing call, passed the puck from behind the net, and inadvertently hit Fogolin's skate, which deflected it past a startled Moog. Afterward, Bridgman admitted he had been trying to pass to Denis Cyr, who had been in front of the goal.

McDonald completed his hat trick for the Flames at the 19:16 mark, and then Fogolin made up for the goal that helped the Flames win by scoring one of his own—his first of the season—with 11 seconds left on the clock. But the goal came much too late for the Oilers. The final score was 7–5 for Calgary.

As a player, Glen Sather may be best described as a journeyman. Over the course of a 10-year NHL career that saw stops in Boston, Pittsburgh, New York, St. Louis, Montreal, and Minnesota, Sather scored a total of 80 goals and 193 points. Offensively lacking, instead Sather carved out a reputation as a third- or fourth-line grinder who made up for his shortcomings with his mind for the game and his strong work ethic.

In a 1968 interview with the *Hockey News*, Boston head coach Harry Sinden described Sather as "a handy guy to have around. If anyone gets hurt he can play either wing and he's always hustling. He's a good man on the ice killing penalties. It's true you can't call him a goal scorer but he is strong on defence." And as his 724 career NHL penalty minutes attest, he was tough, with a reputation as a player who wouldn't back down from anybody, whether an opponent or a referee.

In the fall of 1976, Sather jumped from the NHL to the rival WHA and played the final season of his professional career with the Edmonton Oilers. With 18 games remaining in the 1976–77 season, he was named the team's new player/coach. When the 1977–78 season began, he decided to hang up his skates for good and served exclusively as the Oilers head coach.

With the change in job, Sather appeared to those who followed the Oilers to be noticeably "tamer," less belligerent, and to some in the know was thought to have mellowed. But on the night of December 20, in the postgame media scrum after the loss to the Flames, the old "Slats" reappeared, angry, full of venom, and with a toxic tongue at the ready. With the reporters' tape recorders running, Sather railed against the officials in a way that in today's NHL would have earned him a hefty fine and suspension. First, Sather referenced a recent incident in which Paul Holmgren of the Philadelphia Flyers slugged referee Andy Van Hellemond while trying to get at Paul Baxter of the Pittsburgh Penguins in a fight. "I can understand why a guy like [Holmgren] can punch a referee if the officials are as incompetent as the ones we saw tonight," Sather screamed. "[Tonight] wasn't a game against the Flames; it was a game against Myers, Bozak, and [Jim] Christison."

It was but Edmonton's second loss in 19 games, but Sather didn't care. He was enraged. "Why is it we get the same three guys two games in a row?" Sather defiantly continued. "What is the league trying to do . . . save some money by not bringing anybody else in? They can fine me if they want, but I won't pay it.

"I'm going to keep yelling and they'll have to have an inquiry. That's what I want. I'm going to have some film to prove my point. Instead of isolating on a player with our cameras, I told them to just watch Myers for the last two periods."

Sather claimed that when he yelled at Myers during the game, the referee responded by saying, "We'll see who has the last laugh." To the Edmonton head coach, it all meant one thing: "It looks like [Myers] is deciding the game."

While Sather foamed at the mouth, Oilers captain Fogolin kept a more level head, though he agreed with his boss. "It seems everybody is mad at officials . . . and it's tough to be one," Fogolin said. "But how can they say Messier's and Houston's are two different things? They say Mark kicked his in and Houston's bounced off his leg."

The mood was quite different in the Calgary dressing room, where Lanny McDonald was all smiles. Only a few weeks ago, McDonald had been swimming upstream with the Colorado Rockies, wondering if he'd ever be happy in the NHL again. Now, with a three-goal effort, he helped the Flames upset the number-one team in the league. "We wanted to beat them so badly we could taste it," McDonald told the media. "It is the best Christmas gift the team could have received."

Amidst the chaos of the loss that the Oilers blamed on the officials, Gretzky had quietly scored two more goals, which gave him 40 on the season and left him only 10 shy of the 50 he was gunning for. Fourteen games remained between him and the 50-game mark. "I think I can break [the record] if all goes well," Gretzky predicted. "The odds are in my favour as long as I don't get hurt and the team continues playing aggressively. I am not feeling any added pressure. I just go out and play my game and I'm not going to let anybody interfere with that."

Looking ahead, Flames head coach Al MacNeil noted Calgary and Edmonton had another game scheduled for January 10, 1982. That was eight games away for the Oilers, and it would be their 44th game of the season. "I just don't want him to break it against us," MacNeil admitted. "There's no way he's going to be stopped unless he is injured. He's a magician with the puck and if you relax for a minute he'll kill you."

With 10 goals to go, people began predicting when Gretzky would hit the 50-goal mark. Most, including someone in the know, anticipated that he would do it during the Oilers' 47th game, which would be at Toronto's Maple Leaf Gardens on January 16. Gretzky's family still lived in his hometown, Brantford, slightly more than an hour west of Toronto, and the reasoning went that Gretzky would want to break the record with his mom, Phyllis, and dad, Walter, in attendance. "That's the game he wants to do it," said Gus Badali, Gretzky's agent. "He would love to be able to get his 50th with his parents watching."

Clearly, Badali wasn't the only one circling the Oilers' upcoming visit to Toronto on his calendar. In addition to the usual sellout crowd of 16,182 expected at Maple Leaf Gardens that evening, it was estimated that at least 4,000 additional requests for tickets had been denied. "It's really wild," said Maple Leafs director of public relations Stan Obodiac. "I'm getting the kind of desperate pleas for tickets to the Maple Leafs game January 16 that I usually only get for big rock stars."

Obodiac added that he hadn't seen so many requests for tickets since the second game of the 1972 Summit Series was played at Maple Leaf Gardens. "I had a call from a fellow in Sydney, Australia, and another from a Canadian who works for Bell in Saudi Arabia," Obodiac said. "The fellow from Saudi has already arrived. He came home for Christmas and says he'll wait for the game."

One fan even tried to bribe Obodiac with two tickets to see Luciano Pavarotti in exchange for two tickets to see Gretzky and the

Oilers. Gold seats—the best in the house—normally sold for $15 apiece, but Obodiac estimated scalpers would be asking upwards of $200 for a pair to the January 16 game.

And the requests weren't limited to the game, either. "Suddenly there are a lot of girls working for school newspapers who say they absolutely must see Wayne at practice," said Obodiac. "I've also been hearing from a lot of reporters I've never heard from before. One fellow wants to come from a radio station in Grande Prairie, Alberta, and there've been request from three senators in Ottawa."

Wayne Gretzky had suddenly morphed into something even more popular than a rock star.

Game 37 | December 23, 1981

Vs. Vancouver Canucks

Northlands Coliseum, Edmonton, Alberta

Three nights after their bitter loss to the Calgary Flames, a defeat that snapped a seven-game unbeaten streak, the first-place Edmonton Oilers hosted the Vancouver Canucks. This was the third game of a five-game home stand for the Oilers, and Christmas came early in Edmonton in the form of Grant Fuhr's return to health, his bum shoulder having kept him out of the lineup since December 13. Still, goaltending had not been a major issue in his absence, as the Oilers had averaged 6.5 goals per game in their previous four outings. With Fuhr's reappearance, Andy Moog went back down to the minors, where he remained for the rest of the season.

Fuhr was now indisputably the team's number-one goaltender and was riding a 16-game unbeaten streak that dated back to his NHL debut. The Oilers hadn't expected Fuhr to be back this quickly, but they certainly didn't complain when he was declared fit to play. On the other hand, the visiting Canucks entered the game against Edmonton with a winless streak that had stretched to six, with four defeats and two ties.

Wayne Gretzky had been feasting on his opponents in the month of December, but even so the Canucks had held him goalless in back-to-back games earlier in the month. Though he did manage five assists on those two nights, the Canucks had caught Gretzky in a rare funk. Entering the game on December 23, Gretzky had scored in every game he'd played since the 3–3 tie in Vancouver on December 5, which made it six straight games with a goal and nine goals in all. Those goals went in tandem with 10 assists for a total of 19 points in six games. On December 23, his greatest impact on the outcome of the contest was as a playmaker, and he saved his best for last.

It was a tight first period, with each team directing 11 shots on goal. With a little help from Vancouver defenceman Kevin McCarthy, who accidentally relayed a pass behind his team's goalie, Glen Hanlon, Mark Messier gave the Oilers an early lead at the 3:15 mark of the period, and former Oiler Blair MacDonald tied it for the Canucks at 9:55. Gretzky then set up Jari Kurri, who was quickly becoming one of the Great One's favorite targets, to shoot the Oilers back into the lead at the 15:11 mark of the period. Kurri's goal was his third in the past five games. He had also produced five assists in that time.

The Canucks threatened to take over the game in the middle period, but Fuhr made his presence felt, stopping all 16 shots that came his way. The Oilers, meanwhile, managed just four shots on Hanlon, who also didn't let one past. Fuhr's heroics in the Edmonton goal left Canucks coach Harry Neale shaking his head. "Young Fuhr looked like old Fuhr," Neale said after the game. "We had a pretty good period and it's discouraging when you outshoot a team and they have a bad period and you get zip. Especially against a team as explosive as the Oilers."

In the third period, which opened with Edmonton still holding a 2–1 lead, the Oilers turned the tables on the Canucks, outscoring them 4–0 on route to a 6–1 victory. Gretzky set up Dave Semenko at 2:58 and then did likewise with Dave Lumley at 6:17. Semenko's goal came on the power play from in tight, while Lumley struck when the Oilers were a man short, connecting on a breakaway. It was Lumley's 20th goal of the season and tied his single-season high from 1979–80.

Defenceman Paul Coffey got in on the act, scoring his 20th of the season at the 16:46 mark. Gretzky iced the cake with his 41st goal of the season at 18:46, giving him at least one goal in seven straight games and points in 16 straight. Gretzky had notched six goals and 14 points in Edmonton's last three games. He also was making a mockery of the NHL scoring race, leading all players with 96 points.

Even with the spotlight blazing upon him and his miraculous season, Gretzky gladly shifted the attention to the team's young goaltender. "Grant was fabulous," Gretzky declared after the game. "If he's not considered for the rookie-of-the-year award, there's something wrong. He's one of the main reasons why we have gone from 14th to first place."

A year ago, in his rookie campaign, Coffey quietly scored nine goals and 32 points in 74 games. He took his game to the next level in the 1981 playoffs, when he struck for four goals and seven points in nine games. His strong play had continued through his sophomore season. He reached the 20-goal mark before Christmas, an extremely rare achievement for any NHL defenceman.

Glen Sather also credited Fuhr for holding down the fort while the rest of the team found its game. "The team was flat and wasn't going anywhere. Grant made the difference. To come back after missing three days of practice, well, he just gave us an outstanding effort."

The Oilers' victory extended Fuhr's personal undefeated streak to 17 games, with 11 wins and six ties. During the game, Fuhr wore a protective brace to protect his tender shoulder and admitted afterward to being a little tired early on during the contest. "All the work in the second period helped me get my edge back quickly," Fuhr remarked to reporters.

The Oilers paid a price for their victory, though. Veteran centre Garry Unger suffered two fractured ribs and winger Pat Hughes hurt his rear end when he slammed into the goalpost in the first period. Unger was enduring a streak of bad fortune, as he had already gone down with a broken cheekbone twice this season. The Oilers summoned centre Lance Nethery from Wichita to replace him. Nethery's timing was impeccable. He had been called up to the Oilers just in time, and as a result he would have a front-row seat to hockey history.

Game 38 | December 27, 1981

Vs. Los Angeles Kings

Northlands Coliseum, Edmonton, Alberta

The leap to superstardom rarely occurs in one defining moment. In the case of hockey players, the gifted ones usually enjoy many exceptional games in their careers. That's what separates the stars from the superstars.

Defenceman Tom Bladon, for example, had a four-goal, four-assist game for the Philadelphia Flyers on the night of December 11, 1977, but this magical eight-point performance did not vault him into the superstar stratosphere. He was a good player who on one occasion had a great game. Likewise, Red Berenson had a memorable six-goal, seven-point game for the St. Louis Blues on November 7, 1968, and yet he remained a solid, but not extraordinary two-way performer who made his most significant impact on the sport later on as a coach with the University of Michigan. The results of one special game did not an overnight sensation make of Bladon or Berenson. Likewise, no single game made Rocket Richard an instant superstar, nor Gordie Howe or Bobby Orr. Their status grew over time.

The first time Wayne Gretzky skated on the backyard rink his dad, Walter, had built for him, he was on the path to NHL superstardom. At 18 years old, Gretzky burst onto the NHL scene with 51 goals and 137 points in his first season. Although Gretzky had played professional hockey in the World Hockey Association the year before he joined the NHL, it was clear that the skinny kid from Brantford had found his natural home in the best league in the world. Though some were skeptical, suggesting that he had neither the size nor the grit to be successful in the league, with each passing game he proved the NHL was his for the taking.

By the time Gretzky was in his third NHL season, some were already calling him the greatest player ever. If he were to become just the third player in NHL history to score 50 goals in 50 games, Gretzky would put an exclamation point on that assessment. With 12 games to go before his Edmonton Oilers hit the 50-game mark, and having already scored 41 goals, Gretzky seemed poised to join the legendary Richard and Mike Bossy in the exclusive 50-in-50 club.

No one in the NHL scoring race was coming close to Gretzky's 41 goals and 97 points in 37 games. Despite a few low moments when he couldn't get the puck in the net, his exemplary play had hockey fans and fellow NHL players alike marvelling at his skill. In each contest, even when he didn't score himself, he played a game that lifted the level of his teammates. Gretzky's journey to superstardom was almost complete. And in two games, played over a three-day period, the Great One fully arrived.

"Right then, all heaven broke loose," Gretzky would later say, referring to his December 27 game against the Los Angeles Kings. "Pucks just started going into the net on their own. I'd tip them in, bounce them in, wobble them in, elbow them in, wish them in. No matter what I tried, they kept finding their way past goaltenders."

Gretzky's race toward 50 goals in 50 games had taken on a life of its own, perhaps because Bossy had accomplished the feat just one season ago amidst so much hype, or perhaps because it seemed entirely possible Gretzky would do it in fewer than 50 games. Whatever the reason, Gretzky's season had come alive, and the game against the Kings constituted the penultimate event in perhaps the most spectacular odyssey in hockey history.

For 21-year-old Oilers forward Ken Berry, the December 27 game will always be memorable because it was the night he scored his first-ever goal in the NHL. Just called up to the team, 24-year-old Lance Nethery cherished the night because it marked his first game with the Oilers, one in which he registered two assists. These also turned out to be the last two points of his brief, 38-game NHL career.

The rest of the hockey world remembered the December 27 game against Los Angeles Kings as the game in which Gretzky took one giant step toward an unheard-of record by having a four-goal outburst in Edmonton's 10–3 thrashing of Los Angeles. It was the third time in the 1981–82 season that Gretzky had scored four goals in a game, and the second time he had scorched the Kings for four goals.

Gretzky wasted no time putting the Oilers on the board with goal number 42 of the season at the 1:39 mark of the first period, scooting out from behind the Kings net to beat goalie Mario Lessard. It was the eighth consecutive game in which Gretzky had scored a goal—a personal best for him in the NHL—and he had now registered at least one point in 17 consecutive games. After Paul Coffey made it 2–0 at the 16:13 mark of the period with his 21st goal of the season and his third in as many games, Gretzky struck again with only 17 seconds remaining in the period when he stuffed a rebound past Lessard.

In the second period, Los Angeles rookie Steve Bozek scored back-to-back goals at 9:25 and 13:08 to give the Kings new life and make the score 3–2, but Gretzky got the Oilers back on the right track with a shorthanded goal at 15:11. With teammate Dave Semenko in the penalty box, Gretzky scooped the puck at centre ice and headed toward the Kings' zone. After deking out sophomore defenceman Jay Wells, Gretzky zoomed toward the Los Angeles net. As he got close, Lessard dived out in an attempt to knock the puck off his stick, but Gretzky slid it under him for his third goal of the game and his 10th hat trick of the season.

In the third, Glenn Anderson, with his first goal in 11 games just 21 seconds in, and Ken Berry, at the 3:52 mark, made the score 7–2 for Edmonton. Gretzky scored his fourth goal of the game at 7:26 by connecting on a breakaway, once again while a teammate was in the penalty box. For good measure, he set up Doug Hicks at 11:27 to bring the score to 9–2.

The only thing for the Kings to smile about was Bozek's performance. The 20-year-old native of Kelowna, British Columbia, was in the midst of his rookie campaign, during which he scored 33 goals. It was the best season he'd enjoy in the NHL, as he never scored more than 21 goals in an NHL season again. Twenty-three seconds after Hicks scored, Bozek completed his own hat trick, making it the second straight game in which he'd scored three against the Oilers. Just over a minute after Bozek's third goal, Jari Kurri netted Edmonton's 10th and final goal of the game.

Gretzky's four goals brought his season total to 45 in just 38 games, which almost assured that he would become the third player in NHL history to score 50 goals in 50 games. It was starting to look as though he could do it in 40.

Gretzky's five-point night also pushed him over the 400-point plateau (403) for his career in just 189 games. No other player in NHL history had made it to 400 points so soon. Gretzky had taken his game—and the sport—to greater heights. How high he could go remained to be seen, but he was on a breakneck scoring pace never before witnessed at this level of hockey. The season was not even half over yet, and he had a staggering 102 points. He had openly talked about wanting to be the first player to hit the 200-point plateau and was currently on pace for 215. He also had Phil Esposito's single-season record of 76 goals in his sights—he was on pace for 95.

Kings coach Parker MacDonald said of Gretzky, "It's like trying to throw a blanket over a ghost. I know our defence backs off him because they're scared he's going to beat them. Then he'll make a heck of a play and let someone else score." When commenting on what Gretzky meant to the Oilers, MacDonald said, "When Gretzky gets going the way he was going tonight he gets the whole lot of them going. They're a bunch of kids who really can skate and when he goes, they just follow behind."

Regarding the Kings defenders—and anyone else with the tough assignment of stopping Gretzky—Oilers assistant coach Bruce MacGregor said, "Hockey is a game of where people should be and where people are going to be. Gretz anticipates those things so well he is two or three steps ahead of everybody."

The Oilers defencemen knew how lucky they were not to have to face Gretzky in games. Going up against him in practice was tough enough. "I think all defencemen in the league should come to a hockey school to learn how to defend Gretzky," said Doug Hicks.

Kevin Lowe was not quite as lighthearted and generous as his teammate. "He's a great player," he said. "But you would think the

Kings would be able to get him once in a while. You can't miss him 100 per cent of the time."

After this game, the Great One assumed he'd have a target on his back in the near future. He had 12 games in which to score five goals for the 50-in-50 feat. That in itself could make his task more difficult. "No team likes to be the one that gives up the record, so I expect I'll be looking at much tougher coverage in the next 10 to 12 games," Gretzky said that night. "The odds are definitely in my favour, but I don't expect it to be easy."

Years later, Gretzky looked back on the game against the Kings at the end of December and admitted he was feeling trepidation at the time. "I recall a game before that in Minnesota, when I had three goals and seven points [the game on December 19], and that was about the time I really started to think, 'Here's a great opportunity for me,' and all I kept thinking was, 'Richard and Bossy did it and I don't want to be known as the guy who got close and didn't do it,'" Gretzky said. "I had a fear of not accomplishing it in those last four or five games."

Game 39 | December 30, 1981

Vs. Philadelphia Flyers

Northlands Coliseum, Edmonton, Alberta

M any athletes believe in jinxes, and professional hockey players are certainly no exception. The most superstitious of the lot have been known to always take the same route to the arena on game days, eat the same pregame meal over and over again, put their equipment on in the same order, and tape their sticks exactly the same way for every game.

If Wayne Gretzky worried about jinxing himself after scoring four goals in a 10–3 win over the Los Angeles Kings, he certainly didn't let on. Looking ahead to the Edmonton Oilers' next game, three nights later against the Philadelphia Flyers, a fast, aggressive, and defensive-minded team, Gretzky spoke of how tough it might be to continue his hot scoring streak. But the fact was that if he continued on the same track, he would be the first player to score 50 goals in *under* 50 games.

"I hope I didn't use up all my goals against the Flyers the last time we played," Gretzky joked, recalling a game between the two teams in March 1981, when he scored four goals. He needed to score five times in this night's contest to reach 50. Such a feat was not unprecedented. Gretzky had scored five goals in a game once before, against the St. Louis Blues in February 1981.

The day before the Oilers played their 39th game of the 1981–82 season, Gretzky was announced as the 1981 Man of the Year by the *Sporting News*, becoming the first hockey player to capture the award. For many sports enthusiasts south of the border, hockey was considered a niche sport, so for Gretzky to be recognized in such a fashion by a U.S.-based publication was significant.

Leading up to the Flyers game, Gretzky's goal-scoring binge made it obvious that Richard and Bossy's dual record of 50 goals in 50 games would be broken. The only question that remained was when. "Gretzky isn't just anybody and this isn't the first record he'll break," said Bossy, who seemed resigned to what was ahead. "He seems on a course for a 100-goal season and I think he can do it."

Meanwhile Bobby Orr, the greatest defenceman ever to play in the NHL, scoffed at the notion put forward by some that Gretzky was a one-dimensional player, great on offence but a defensive liability. "What I have noticed is that Gretzky has the puck all the time," Orr observed. "To me that's the finest defence.

"Gretzky has such great hockey sense—and such exceptional vision that he seems to know where his teammates are all the time. He can adjust to almost any situation. Look, it's almost unthinkable that anyone should score 200 points in a season but Gretzky makes it look possible. He scores in any rink against any team."

Gretzky led the NHL scoring race by 39 points as the game against the Flyers approached. But on December 30, he was feeling lousy. In the game against the Kings three nights earlier, he'd banged up his right knee and it ached. And then there was the pressure of chasing the 50 in 50. Gretzky told Glen Sather about his knee, and before he knew it the Edmonton head coach had returned holding a couple of Aspirins and a piece of tape. "Put those on your knee," he told Gretzky, and then walked away. Gretzky sat there laughing, and then carefully taped the Aspirins to his knee, inside the kneepad, and headed out the dressing room door and walked into history.

Like the Oilers, the Flyers had also been very hot through the month of December 1981, winning 10 games and losing just two leading up to their game in Edmonton, though at times during the season, it had also looked as though the Flyers were a team in real trouble. They lacked an experienced defenceman, one with the mobility to get the puck up to the forwards, and they employed a three-goalie rotation—with a trio that would fail to record a single shutout in 1981–82, a first in the team's 15-year history.

The Flyers had won their share of games lately, but had also laid a few eggs, including being hammered by the Canadiens, 11–2, in Montreal on October 27. That defeat sent the Flyers spiralling downward, and they found themselves surrendering 42 goals over a six-game span. Philadelphia had then suffered a 10–4 loss to the struggling Washington Capitals on November 21, and, entering the game against the Oilers, had allowed 14 goals in their past three games. While they won more often than they lost in December 1981, the Flyers were vulnerable.

The 1981–82 Flyers were coached by Pat Quinn, who'd been behind the bench with the club the previous three years and had found success, most notably in 1979–80, when the Flyers enjoyed an NHL-record 35-game unbeaten streak and made it all the way to the

Stanley Cup final, only to lose to the New York Islanders in six games. Quinn had been a rough-and-tumble NHL defenceman for nine seasons, and his teams never shied away from physical engagement, but as a coach he placed a heavy emphasis on speed and skill. Both were on display on the night they played the Oilers.

In Edmonton, the Flyers did their best to skate with the young Oilers, but in the end, they were no match. In many ways, this particular game epitomized both Gretzky's and the Oilers' tremendous regular-season prowess and success. Even though, in the big picture, the Oilers were still developing as a team, this singular contest indicated their glory days to come.

The game was played at breakneck speed with a minimum of stoppages and numerous end-to-end rushes from both teams, as the Flyers tried their utmost to keep up with the kids from Edmonton. The first major play came when Paul Holmgren flipped the puck off the boards and past Paul Coffey, which allowed Philadelphia's Ken Linseman, one of the fastest players in the NHL and nicknamed "The Rat" because of his nasty, scrappy style, to scoop it up and break in alone on Grant Fuhr. Making one quick deke to his left as Fuhr slid across the net in an attempt to make the save, Linseman took advantage of an exposed five-hole, drawing first blood and scoring his ninth goal of the season. This put the Flyers in the lead at the 4:11 mark of the first period.

With Philadelphia's Brian Propp sitting in the penalty box, the next big play of the game occurred. While the Oilers applied lots of pressure on the shorthanded Flyers, Edmonton defenceman Paul Coffey took a pass at the left point and drilled a shot just inches wide of the Philadelphia goal. Luckily for Edmonton, the puck bounced off the boards and ended up on the other side of the goal, where Gretzky waited, unguarded. The Great One simply tapped the waiting puck through the legs of Flyers goaltender Pete Peeters at 7:47 to tie the score, 1–1. Coffey garnered an assist on the goal, making it nine straight games in which he had registered a point. For Gretzky, it was now 18 consecutive games with at least one point, and goal number 46 set the tone for one of the most memorable games of his career.

"After Wayne scored that first goal, [backup goaltender] Ron Low looked at me on the [Oilers] bench and said, 'I'll bet you he'll do it tonight,'" Sather said later.

And sure enough, just two minutes and 25 seconds later, Gretzky struck again. Playing with a purpose, Gretzky seemed to be skating in overdrive. In another magnificent play, while in the Flyers zone he took a drop pass from linemate Dave Lumley, cut to the middle of the ice, and smoked a slap shot high to Peeters's glove side. The Philadelphia goalie appeared to think that Gretzky was going for the other side of the net and leaned toward the stick side. He was too far committed when Gretzky shot to the short side of the net. The puck hit the post and went in for Gretzky's second of the night.

Now up by a score of 2–1, the Oilers continued to roll. Coffey started the next goal-scoring play with a snap shot from the point that Peeters turned aside. The rebound went directly to Gretzky, who was positioned in the faceoff circle. Gretzky quickly sent the puck back to the right point, on to the stick of defenceman Risto Siltanen, who spotted Coffey creeping in close to the Philadelphia net from his left-point position. The two then played give-and-go until Coffey blasted a slap shot low to the short side of the goal. Peeters couldn't see it coming thanks to a perfectly timed screen courtesy of Glenn Anderson, and so, at 13:49 of the first period, Coffey scored his 22nd goal of the season. The Oilers outshot the visitors, 16–6, in the first period and took a 3–1 lead to the dressing room.

With a little more dedication and off-ice commitment, Philadelphia's Reggie Leach could have been one of the greatest NHL scorers of all time. In his prime, the Riverton, Manitoba, native was a sharpshooter who cut an inch or so off the end of the blade of his stick to generate more speed on his powerful slap shot.

In his best season, 1975–76, Leach reached career highs with 61 goals and 91 points, and then established an NHL record by scoring 19 goals in 16 playoff games. By 1981–82, however, it was clear that Leach was slowing down, but he was still capable of the occasional display of brilliance.

Early in the second period, Linseman was booted out of the faceoff circle, and Reggie Leach moved in to take the draw. He won the faceoff to the left of Fuhr and, after a scramble, retrieved the puck, snapping a quick shot that Fuhr saved, only to have it drop behind him just inches from the goal line. Linseman dived toward the puck, but inadvertently knocked it out of the crease with his skate. Leach was there to slap at the loose puck, and it bounced off Fuhr's trapper and into the net.

After the Leach goal, it took just 10 seconds for Gretzky to complete a hat trick. The play started when Gretzky flipped the puck ahead on a faceoff, but the Flyers got it and pushed it toward the Edmonton blue line. Lumley raced back hard toward his team's goal, making a wild swipe at the puck, chopping it in the direction of the centre-ice area and somehow getting it to Gretzky, who was standing way up the ice, near the Philadelphia blue line. Taking the puck at full speed when it landed on his stick, Gretzky split the Flyers defence pair of Bob Hoffmeyer and Mark Botell before firing a slap shot that seemed to startle the Philadelphia goaltender. Gretzky's

48th goal of the season was scored high on Peeters's stick side from the top of the faceoff circle.

Up in the broadcast booth, Tim Dancy handled the television play-by-play, and Don Cherry gave the colour commentary. The loud and boisterous Cherry, one of hockey's greatest-ever characters, had spent five years as the Boston Bruins head coach in the mid-to-late '70s, leading them to two Stanley Cup finals, before spending the 1979–80 season with the Colorado Rockies, where he was relieved of his duties at the end of the year. Now, Cherry, who would one day become one of Canada's most famous sports celebrities, was getting his feet wet in the broadcasting business. His stint as a colour commentator would be brief, however, mainly because of his tendency to openly "cheer" for either a specific player or team that he was covering.

"Well, we might see the 50 yet, Tim," Cherry bellowed, in an effort to be heard over the crowd, mere seconds after Gretzky had scored his hat-trick goal, before adding what most observers had also been thinking: "I tell you, this guy, what more can you say. . . . God gave him that gift, the puck follows him."

With the Oilers leading 4–2, the never-say-die Flyers pushed back with a goal by Ron Flockhart at 6:11 to cut the deficit to one. Flockhart, whose speed and reckless style came to be known as "Flocky hockey," took a pass and split the Oilers defense pair of Risto Siltanen and Doug Hicks before overpowering Fuhr with a high shot to his glove side. Three minutes later, Mark Messier restored the Oilers' two-goal advantage by scoring his third goal in four games and 26th of the season. The play began when Edmonton forecheckers Matti Hagman and Glenn Anderson worked diligently along the boards in the corner to the right of the Flyers net and eventually freed the puck. Anderson corralled it and sent it toward the net, where it bounced off Peeters and directly to Messier, who was poised in front of the net and easily nudged it past the unprepared Philadelphia goaltender to make the score 5–3 Edmonton after two periods.

The play that would lead to Gretzky's 49th goal began innocently enough a little over five minutes into the third period, when Philadelphia's Reggie Leach carried the puck up the ice along the right boards. Coffey checked him at the Edmonton blue line. Spotting Gretzky way up the ice on the other side of the rink, Coffey made a spectacular pass, drilling the puck off the boards behind Gretzky so that it caromed right onto Gretzky's stick. Gretzky cut to the middle of the ice, scooted past Flyers defenceman Bob Hoffmeyer, and drilled a slap shot that knuckleballed its way past Peeters and high into the goal.

"What a goal, what a goal," said Cherry to images of the Northlands crowd standing, wildly cheering, an image and ovation that continued as Dancy informed the viewing audience that Gretzky had not only scored his 49th goal of the season, but had set a modern-day NHL record by scoring four goals in one game, four times in one season. As Dancy rhymed off the four teams that had surrendered the four-goal nights, the cheering continued without letting up, leaving Cherry to remark that all of the four goals had "been earned, not a cheap one in the whole thing and a standing ovation and he should be, I'll tell ya."

Hoffmeyer, who played 198 career NHL games with Philadelphia, Chicago, and New Jersey, did not immediately relish playing a part in this extraordinary game. "It's not so special at the time when you get victimized by a player like that," Hoffmeyer recalled recently.

"You're kind of set back by it. You don't like it, and you're unhappy about it. At the same time, the whole hockey world is buzzing about it and it's such an historic thing. We felt we had a good club and were a solid team and he just seemed to dismantle us. That said, you looked around and he was doing it to everybody."

Hoffmeyer said that Gretzky's 49th goal brought him more notoriety than anything else he ever did in his career. "People will say, 'I saw you on TV the other day,'" Hoffmeyer said. "That goal gets replayed all the time. The 50th goal was into an empty net, so it seems to always be the 49th goal that gets shown because the goalie is still in. You can see my name going across the screen just before he shoots and scores. Some people tease me that he beat me pretty bad, but I tell them I wasn't the only one."

Shortly after scoring his fourth goal of the game, Gretzky attempted to record number 50 when he broke in alone on Peeters. At the last second, he tried to deke the Philadelphia goaltender by tapping the puck in between his legs, but Peeters was equal to the task and made the save.

The Flyers may have been impressed with Gretzky's individual exploits, but they were still in the game as the third period wore on, and even more so after scoring back-to-back goals at 11:31 and 11:48. Paul Holmgren made it a 6–4 game when he picked the puck out of a scramble in front of the Edmonton goal, and then, just 17 seconds later, Philadelphia defencemen Fred Arthur gained the Oilers zone unabated and scored his lone goal of the season on a long slap shot from just inside the blue line that beat Fuhr to the top corner of the net to make the score 6–5.

Give the Flyers credit: with all the commotion created by Gretzky's march toward 50 goals in less than half a season, they stayed focused.

Oilers fans were going berserk as it grew obvious they were witnessing history, and yet the Philadelphia players disregarded most of the noise and distractions and focused on winning the game. Territorially speaking, the Flyers were even the better team over the final 40 minutes.

It didn't matter, though. The hockey gods would not be denied. In the final few moments of the game, down 6–5, the Flyers pulled Peeters out of their goal in favour of an extra skater. It was not a move made without some debate, particularly on the Philadelphia bench. "A frustrated Pete Peeters was begging Pat Quinn to keep him in goal so Gretzky wouldn't get his 50th into an empty net," remembers Jim Matheson, who covered the game for the *Edmonton Journal*. "He really argued with Pat Quinn to not pull him when they were down by a goal. He wanted the 50th goal to be on him and not into the empty net." Not surprisingly, the Philadelphia head coach won out and Peeters took a seat amidst his teammates, as the Flyers took to the ice with an extra attacker.

With 1:04 remaining, Bobby Clarke beat Mark Messier on a faceoff to the right of the Oilers net and passed the puck back to Bill Barber, but the play was whistled to a stop by referee Kerry Fraser. Apparently somebody had moved too early, thereby giving the Flyers an advantage on the draw. That was a no-no, and the faceoff had to be taken again.

The two teams lined up for a do-over, with Clarke and Messier again at the dot. Gretzky usually played centre, but on these critical faceoffs he deferred to Messier and lined up at left wing.

Once again, Clarke won the draw, sending the puck back to Leach, who whipped it around the boards behind the Oilers net. Edmonton retrieved the puck, fired it down the ice, and were charged with icing.

Tension built as another faceoff took place in Edmonton's zone. The Flyers gained control of the puck following the faceoff and played a little tic-tac-toe, with Leach feeding Brian Propp, who relayed it to Ken Linseman, who then got it back to Leach for a shot that Fuhr knocked down with his trapper but failed to catch. The puck scuttled to Lumley at the faceoff circle, and he spotted Gretzky leaving the defensive zone along the right side boards. Gretzky took a pass and cut to the middle in an effort to avoid a check by the Flyers' Bill Barber. But Gretzky lost the puck. The Flyers snagged it and moved forward, but were offside entering the Edmonton zone.

As the two teams prepared for the faceoff, just inside the centre-ice red line on the Oilers' side, 21 seconds remained on the clock. As the camera focused on Number 99, Tim Dancy reminded television viewers, "Gretzky's looking for the 50th. If he gets it now, it would be the 50th into an open net."

Cherry interrupted: "Listen, he'd love to get it any way he can— he's . . . he's a tiger, he's got that killer instinct."

The Flyers once again won the draw and dumped the puck into the Edmonton zone. Fuhr left his goal crease and, when he recovered the puck, relayed it to Coffey, who swept it around the boards. Coffey's intention was to get the puck out of the zone— out of danger—but the Flyers crushed that attempt. Then, when puck jumped free, Glenn Anderson recovered it at the top of the faceoff circle. Spying Gretzky once again heading up ice, Anderson passed and the Great One took it, first out of the Edmonton end of the ice, and then through the neutral zone, cutting past Barber—a forward and the last man back—in the neutral zone. Gretzky shot from the blue line toward the empty net.

Those who think that setting a record by scoring an empty-net goal is a little cheesy fail to fully appreciate the unparalleled greatness of scoring 49 goals in the first 39 games of an NHL season, let alone of scoring four of those goals in the 38th game. Gretzky's feat was beyond compare. It still is. So let us not judge that, after Gretzky eluded the Flyers' last man back, he took steady aim and, with three seconds remaining in the game, shot the puck that scored his 50th goal.

Once again, the fans went nuts. In fact, fans chanted Gretzky's name for quite some time. Much later, as the Great One left the rink, they were still going.

As soon as he scored, Gretzky's teammates poured onto the ice to congratulate their hero. Up in the broadcast booth, Cherry attempted to say something, managed the phrase, "Isn't that something . . . ," and then the roar of the crowd drowned him out. The Oilers buried their teammate in the corner, revelling in the fans' jubilant celebration.

Pictures of the delirious crowd filled the screen before the camera settled on the goal light behind the Philadelphia net. In front of it, the glass literally shook from the noise.

"Fifty goals in 39 games," Dancy announced.

Cherry added, "He's got 50 goals before anyone else has got 30. Life is great, eh?" The scoreboard simply flashed: *50 . . . 50 . . . 50*. Glen Sather, left alone behind the Edmonton bench while his team swarmed Gretzky on the ice, had a smile that said it all.

But three seconds of play remained in the game. After a rush to clear the ice of hats, programs, and various other pieces of debris, the play resumed and the last three seconds ticked off the clock. As the cheering began to subside, there was a sense that something had just happened, something so unbelievable, so out of the realm of the possible. Something that needed the benefit of time to sink in.

Cherry tried to put what happened into some sort of context. "I'm not even going to say anything about him now. He can do anything. Imagine that. You just watched history here. I'll tell ya, I don't know if anyone is ever going to break that one. Fifty in 39. I don't care how many guys . . . unbelievable."

"Maybe Gretzky himself," Dancy speculated.

But Cherry didn't think so. "Everything fell in place, everything's going beautiful . . . no injuries or anything like that."

Because the Oilers jumped over the bench to celebrate with Gretzky, they were assessed a minor penalty by referee Kerry Fraser. Sather couldn't have cared less. Who gave a damn if his team had drawn a two-minute penalty for delay of game because they left the bench to celebrate one of sport's all-time unbreakable records? The 17,490 fans standing and cheering wildly certainly didn't. "This is an incredible thing that nobody will ever surpass," Sather said afterward. "Everybody on this team should be proud of his accomplishment because they are all a part of it."

Years later, Gretzky reflected on the moments leading up to the 50th. "With a minute left in the game . . . I was going to do anything and everything to get to that puck. I could have outskated Paul Coffey! Bill Barber once told me a funny story, that right before I shot the puck, he was going to throw his stick at it—and he almost did! With an open net, the goal would have automatically counted. It would have been a great trivia question: Who scored 50 goals without ever getting his 50th goal?"

When asked by a reporter about Gretzky scoring the 50th goal into an empty net, Sather replied, "Wayne and empty nets . . . it's like a dog in heat." Over the course of his NHL career, Wayne Gretzky scored 55 empty-net goals.

The Flyers may have been stunned, but they were equally impressed. Quinn was as surprised as anybody that his team had allowed Gretzky to set the record. He admitted afterward that, earlier in the day, he thought to himself that at least he didn't have to worry about Gretzky getting the record against the Flyers. "If anybody had told me before the game he'd get five goals against us tonight, well, I'd have bet a lot of money," Quinn told the reporters after the game. "Any superlatives that I might suggest would be inadequate after a performance like that."

Gretzky's teammates were suitably blown away. They skated with him, sat on the bench with him, and watched him, just like the fans. They observed him every day as he worked on the intricacies of his game in practice. Gretzky's work ethic was legendary, and his teammates got to the see the fruits of his labour. And yet they were still in awe. "Things like this aren't supposed to happen," Coffey said. "He's had nine goals in two straight games. Yet when he sets a goal for himself, he gets it; it's that simple. He wanted to do it before the 40th game. You could have bet one million dollars against him doing it, but I knew he would."

"He just keeps going and going," Kevin Lowe told reporters. "Wayne doesn't really talk much about his goals but when I talked to him today he said there was no reason why he couldn't score five against the Flyers. He'll probably want to get 65 in 50 now. He just wants to score and win."

Coffey recently commented, "I drove with him to those last two games, and this is just the way Wayne was: I'd pick him up, and after the game [in which] he got four goals, which was pretty exciting, I picked him up for the Philly game and he says, 'I think I'm going to get five tonight.' Honest to God, he says, 'I'm going to get five tonight.' I looked at him and say, 'Well, if you get five, we're going to win; I know that for sure.'"

Peeters didn't do somersaults about allowing four of Gretzky's five goals this evening, but he didn't throw himself under a bus for his performance, either. The Flyers goalie believed Gretzky's big night was destiny. "I wouldn't have done anything on his goals," Peters said. "What he did is absolutely amazing."

In other words, Gretzky was unstoppable. Flyers defenceman Jimmy Watson agreed. "We take a lot of pride in that we can force other teams to play our game; that we can control a big guy like that with zone defence. But I don't think anybody is going to stop him."

Peeters did think, however, that the Flyers could have played Gretzky a little differently. "We backed off him all night," the goalie said. "We were letting him fly."

The Flyers playing assistant coach, Bobby Clarke, wasn't so certain. Stopping Gretzky was much harder than it sounded. "This is absolutely crazy," Clarke said in the dressing room. "At least with Bobby Orr you'd see him wind up in his own end and you could try to set up some kind of defence to stop him. Gretzky just comes out of nowhere. It's scary."

"Last year I would have passed on three of the goals I scored on tonight," Gretzky admitted after the game. Gretzky didn't just shoot more often, as he had vowed to do at the beginning of the season, but he shot more effectively. His final 15 goals were scored on just 32 shots. That kind of accuracy wins a lot of stuffed animals at county fairs.

In the dressing room immediately after the game, when asked about his five-goal night, Gretzky remained ever so humble. "It's the second-best feeling I've had," Gretzky admitted. "It's not quite as thrilling as beating Montreal in the playoffs last year."

Gretzky had done the impossible, and he had done it more quickly than anyone expected, scoring a total of nine goals in games 38 and 39 to reach the 50. Because no one expected the record to be broken that night, the game was not broadcast on television outside the Edmonton area, and in the days before the Internet and 24-hour sports channels, and with cable television still in its infancy, word didn't start to spread until the next day, when people picked up their morning newspapers, and later, when they saw the highlights on the evening news.

Still, word of Gretzky's feat soon reached Maurice "Rocket" Richard and Mike Bossy—the only others up until then who had scored 50 goals in 50 games. Happy for Gretzky, Bossy sent him a message that said, "I was proud of getting the record and I hope you are as proud."

Richard, who was 60 years old at the time, felt the league's talent base was watered down compared to when he played. "I knew the record could be broken when they extended the National Hockey League to 12 or 15 teams," Richard said. "The calibre of hockey is not the same as it was in my day. And the last couple of years, with all the scoring . . . it seems that every team that falls behind by two or three goals seems to be quitting. That's why they get so many high-scoring games."

If Richard sounded a little crusty and jaded, that was not the case when he spoke directly of the man who had scored 50 goals in 39 games. "Gretzky's a natural-born scorer like I was," Richard declared.

"He's moving all the time and it seems that players trying to check him can't catch him. There's no doubt he would have scored—not as many goals—in my day, but he would have been the best scorer in the league."

Figuring Gretzky out in an effort to shut him down was the ultimate task for the opposition. It was not easy, especially when there were conflicting views on Gretzky's strengths and weaknesses. "The guy was not the fastest skater in the world by far," Hoffmeyer declared. "On the 48th goal he had a breakaway and I almost caught him—but I didn't. He knew how much space and time he had. If it was the fastest guy on our team chasing him they would have 'almost' caught him, too. He had that sense that he knew how much time he had."

Bobby Clarke, Hoffmeyer's teammate, saw it differently. He thought people underestimated aspects of Gretzky's game. "You hear Gretzky's not a great skater," Clarke said. "Hell, I bet there aren't a handful of players in the league who are faster than he is. And the shot; it's hard and anyone who says it isn't is kidding themselves. Again, there might only a few guys around today who shoot harder."

The Flyers prided themselves on being able to physically punish their opponents, but when it came to corralling Gretzky, it was a no-go. "Pat Quinn used to say, 'You've got to hit him; you've got to hit the guy,'" Hoffmeyer said recently. "Quinn didn't want us to run him through the end of the building, but he would ask, 'Why don't you guys hit him?' We're all sitting there thinking we'd *like* to hit him, but we can never catch him. He never put himself in a position to be hit. A lot of times you would think you had him lined up, but he would turn his skates so that if you did hit him, he'd go away from you instead of toward you. You were actually pushing him away and he'd escape with the puck. Also, it was always in the back of your mind if you did nail him, there were a lot of guys who were going to be climbing over the boards on the next shift, coming in your direction."

Despite Coffey's declaration that Gretzky felt he was primed to score five goals on the morning ride to the rink, when Number 99 explained what had unfolded, it was obvious his father's advice that modesty is the way to go prevailed. "I don't ever go into a game thinking I'll get five goals," Gretzky said, "but I never go in thinking I can't."

Gretzky went on the record many times over the years about his 50 goals in 39 games being his most cherished record. It continues to be a huge source of pride for the Great One. "The thing I remember a lot about that game was the fact I had some really good chances that I missed," he said recently, with a laugh. "I missed a one-on-one chance against Peeters, when I had an opportunity to score with the goalie in, and again, you start thinking, 'Gosh, you've got 49 goals; don't blow this now!'

"Philadelphia was known as a pretty tough competitor and was also known to be a very good defensive-minded team," Gretzky said. "By no means did I ever expect or think that I was going to get five goals that game. I think the first goal I scored was kind of a fluky goal. Paul Coffey shot it and it went off the end boards and out the other side, and I kind of banked it off the goalie's pads and in. I came back to the bench and Coffey—who always said if I got a goal or a point early, watch out because I could get four, five, six, or seven—he looked at me, and I'll never forget him saying, 'All right, tonight is going to be the night.' From there I just rode the wave of momentum from the excitement of the game.

"It was a Christmas crowd at Northlands and it was really vocal and exciting because there were still a lot of Flyers fans at the game who grew up watching and cheering for Philadelphia before we joined the NHL. The energy level in the building was high and I just rode that wave and went with it. Consequently, I ended up with the five goals."

Gretzky still lights up when he thinks about his big night against the Philadelphia Flyers. "I don't think anybody anticipated me scoring five goals that night," Gretzky said. "I was probably more surprised than anybody else. It was just one of those nights when everything went my way. Glen Sather just basically threw me out after the second period whenever I was ready, so I played a lot of hockey in that third period. He gave me every opportunity to get the five goals."

For many in attendance that night, watching Gretzky connect for five goals to hit the 50-goal mark in just 39 games is a memory that will last forever. For Gretzky, what happened long after most people had departed Northlands Coliseum stays with him today.

"I was last guy in the locker room and I was sitting with one of the trainers and Joey Moss, our locker-room attendant," Gretzky says. "It was one of the coolest things in my career. Bobby Clarke and Paul Holmgren of the Flyers had waited after things had died down to come in and congratulate me. I was one or two years removed from watching Bobby Clarke playing on TV, and I thought that was so cool. That was one of the highlights of the entire night. He said, 'Playing against Bobby Orr, I kind of knew exactly what was going to happen. Playing against you, I don't know where you are or where you are coming from.'"

"I know everything's that's been written about you," Clarke told Gretzky. "I think none of it is adequate."

His Only Competition is Himself

Halfway across Canada, late on the evening of December 30, 1981, Walter Gretzky sat in his home in Brantford, Ontario, the same one in which he'd built the backyard rink for his famous son, and turned the dial on his radio, searching for any station that might broadcast an update about that night's game in Edmonton between the Oilers and the visiting Philadelphia Flyers.

An installer and repairman for Bell Canada, Walter had to go to work the next morning, and with the two-hour time difference between Edmonton and Brantford, the hour was getting late. Finally, at 11:30 P.M., a bulletin came over the radio stating that Wayne had scored four goals in the first two periods, leaving him only one goal shy of the magical 50. A little less than an hour later, the news flashed that Wayne had scored his 50th goal in 39 games.

Minutes later, the phone rang. The call came from inside the Oilers dressing room.

"Did you hear?"

"Yeah," Walter replied, before teasing his son. "How come it took you so long?"

"Aw, I didn't want to do it too quickly."

"You excited?"

"Yeah, but I have to go now. The place is full of reporters. I just wanted to make sure you knew. Bye."

Years later, Walter Gretzky would reminisce about that phone call. "You know, people are always asking what it's like to have Wayne in the family. I could have answered them so easily that night. There he was, surrounded by TV cameras, microphones, magazine and newspapermen, and he'd excused himself for a minute so he could phone home. It might sound corny, but the record seemed small compared to that call. A moment like that stays with you forever. Not the moment he got the goal; the moment I got the call."

"Sanity, on the wane for more than a year now, officially took its leave of the National Hockey League at 12:16 EST this morning," proclaimed the *Toronto Star* in the lead story on the paper's front page. "It was chased into extinction by a 20-year-old man-child who put on one of the most remarkable individual achievements in the history of hockey."

"Make no mistake. It wasn't just another Great Gretzky game last night," wrote Terry Jones in the pages of the *Edmonton Journal*. "It was the greatest hockey game ever played by the greatest player in the history of the game—to break the greatest record ever set in the game. Nothing less than that."

"Gretzky has overwhelmed the records so completely as to render them irrelevant," declared *Newsweek* magazine. "His only point of reference now is himself."

Unlike a year before, when the momentum had time to build in the days leading up to Mike Bossy scoring 50 goals in 50 games, Gretzky's 50 in 39 had caught everyone unprepared, not because he had accomplished the feat, but because he had done it so quickly, by scoring nine goals in his last two games. As a result, the media was playing catch-up to a story that the public couldn't get enough of. For many reporters based in Toronto, this necessitated a 90-minute drive southwest to Brantford, where Walter Gretzky, Phyllis, and their children Kim and Keith were posed for photographers with copies of the newspapers trumpeting Wayne's stunning achievement. The newsmen also discovered that they weren't the only ones caught off guard by the suddenness of the 50 in 39.

"Well, I knew he would do it," Walter told the reporters that had camped out at his home. "It was just a matter of time. But I never in my wildest imagination thought he'd do it in 39 games." Such was their own sense of surprise that the family revealed that Phyllis had made plans to fly to Edmonton for the Oilers' upcoming Saturday night game against the Boston Bruins, game number 41 on the schedule, on the assumption that it might be the night that the 50th goal would be scored. For Phyllis, it would have been the capper to a week during which she had driven her three younger sons to three different tournaments.

And now, with the standard of 50 goals in 39 games set, attention shifted to the next potential record to fall: Phil Esposito's 1970–71 record of 76 goals in a single season. Somewhat surprisingly, talk about that had begun with Wayne Gretzky himself, in the Oilers dressing room after he had scored the 50th. "As long as the rest of the guys on the team keep playing the way they are, I think I'm capable of doubling what I've done so far."

His father didn't disagree. "It's just something else. I sometimes look on [Wayne] as a runaway locomotive: you wonder what's going to happen in the end."

———

That "runaway locomotive" didn't have much time to rest after his 50 in 39. The NHL schedule makers had pencilled in the Oilers for a road game in Vancouver the very next night. Gretzky was held pointless in a 3–1 loss to the Canucks in that game. But, after all, the pressures, both internal and external, were a lot for anyone to absorb. "There are times when I get frustrated," he admitted to one of the reporters that followed the Oilers, "times when I want to be alone, to live my private life. But I have to realize I can't, that's just the way it is for a professional athlete."

After the game against the Canucks, however, Gretzky and the rest of the Oilers were given a rare opportunity to cut loose a bit. "The entire team went out for one of those nights that you never forget," he later recalled. "It was one of those nights when it just felt great to be young, healthy, and getting paid to play hockey. It was New Year's Eve, after all, so we all went to a restaurant and celebrated. We had about as many champagne bottles opened as we did players. . . . When the hangover lifted, I knew I was gonna beat Esposito." But first, he would have to endure an East Coast road trip quite unlike anything anyone had seen before.

When the plane containing the Edmonton Oilers touched down in Washington on Tuesday morning, January 12, 1982, a day in advance of their game against the Capitals, Wayne Gretzky's season totals to date stood at 54 goals and 119 points after 44 games. And yet, for a change, those weren't the numbers that stood out for the team's public relations director, Bill Tuele. On his mind were the 132 media requests for one-on-one interviews with Gretzky during the Oilers' four-game tour of the East Coast, which included games in Washington (January 13), Philadelphia (January 14), Toronto (January 16), and Detroit (January 17).

Dubbed by those surrounding the Oilers as "The Road to Toronto," where the Oilers would be making their only visit of the 1981–82 season, the tour was descended upon by an advance party of sportswriters from Toronto to meet Gretzky as soon as he got off the plane in Washington, just to fill their newspapers with announcements of his impending arrival in Hogtown Friday morning, three days hence. The appearance was being referred to by non-Toronto journalists as "The Second Coming."

When he arrived in Washington, Gretzky engaged all of the waiting reporters, answering their questions, many of which had become quite familiar, without complaint. He was then whisked into a waiting limousine, which he shared with NHL president John Ziegler, and the pair toured D.C. television and radio stations, in between stops doing interviews in the limousine, promoting the NHL All-Star Game being held in Washington in a little less than a month. A film crew also shadowed him. They were recording his every move for an upcoming film to be titled *A Day in the Life of Wayne Gretzky*.

Such was the level of his celebrity at this time that on one occasion, as the Oilers were travelling in their team bus from the airport, they passed a roadside sign advertising the hotel they would be staying in. In large, black, bold capital letters, the sign said STAY AT WAYNE GRETZKY'S PLACE.

———

Amidst the media deluge, some wondered if all of the attention and demands would affect his on-ice performance. The next night against the Capitals, Gretzky temporarily squashed those doubts, scoring two goals and adding three assists, for a five-point performance in the Oilers' 6–6 tie with Washington. In Philadelphia, Gretzky faced the same kind of media attention and demands, but his one goal and one assist didn't much help his team as the Flyers steamrolled the Oilers by a score of 8–2.

And then Toronto beckoned. With so many outstanding media requests in Toronto, a press conference was organized to accommodate the unprecedented demand. "We decided to have a two-hour press conference on Friday so we could handle everyone at once," said Gretzky a couple of days beforehand. If not, he said, "I would have been interviewed in Toronto from just about the moment we landed until we took to the ice."

No one in the city could remember a similar event for any athlete having taken place before. Peter Smith, the manager of the Westin Harbour Castle, bowing to demand, moved the location of the press conference into the Governor General's suite and stated that the only comparable press event he could remember having to accommodate was during a visit by the Queen.

"There have been heroes before, summoned from the ice ponds and hockey rinks across the country," opined *Maclean's*, the Canadian weekly news magazine. "The names of Joliat, Morenz, Richard, Howe, Hull, and Orr still conjure 'greatness.' But Wayne Gretzky transcends them all."

"Away from the arena, he had moved far ahead of his hockey colleagues in celebrity," commented Peter Gzowski, a prominent Canadian media personality. "He was lionized beyond any of the heroes who had preceded him. His popularity transcended that of hockey itself. . . . By the middle of the 1981–82 season, no Canadian who read newspapers or magazines could be unaware of who Wayne was or what he looked like. His image adorned billboards and posters everywhere."

Just a few minutes past one o'clock on the afternoon of January 15, 1982, Wayne Gretzky passed through the swinging glass doors of the Westin, suitcase in hand, clad in a trench coat that covered his beige suit, white shirt, and striped tie. As he strode across the lobby, he was followed by an entourage of photographers and fans, many of the screaming teenaged variety, creating a scene that recalled those surrounding rock stars. For two hours, the media throng had waited for his arrival, steadily growing impatient as they milled around, drinking coffee and asking Peter Pocklington, the Oilers owner who had specifically flown in for the occasion, a series of questions, in effect making him the opening act for the headliner.

At the front of the room, a podium had 19 microphones strapped to it and was surrounded by a series of camera tripods. To some observers, as he entered the suite, Gretzky looked tired and preoccupied, but as he stepped up to the podium, that all-too-familiar smile crossed his lips. A 20-minute question-and-answer session followed, and then a half-hour of one-on-one interviews with both the radio and the television media.

Those closest to Gretzky were generally awed by his dealings with the media crush and his ability to make time for everyone. "This scene is absolutely unbelievable," remarked Peter Pocklington. "If you weren't convinced before, you have to be convinced now that Wayne has done more to put Edmonton on the map than all of the other 650,000 citizens of Edmonton combined."

"It's just like when he's on the ice," added Gretzky's agent, Gus Badali. "He doesn't get tired. He has some inner quality."

"He's the most patient guy I've ever seen," remarked Glen Sather. "I know I don't have the patience. I had five interview requests for Tuesday when we arrived in Washington. One guy from Pittsburgh wanted to have dinner with me. I just don't have the time or patience to go along with that. And the stupid questions . . . I just don't have the patience to deal with them. But Wayne still answers everyone. How can I complain? Wayne deserves this. He just proved again what a classy young gentleman he is. The kids today need somebody to idolize. I think it's better that they choose to idolize Wayne Gretzky than Mick Jagger."

Following the press conference, Gretzky made a secret trip to Brantford to spend a small portion of time with his family in his hometown. Praised in public for how he was handling the attention, privately there were some concerns. "It was wearing him down," Walter Gretzky later admitted. "We could see it that night when he slipped home to spend the night with the family. Wayne calls it the year he lost the last of his privacy. There'd been media attention since he was six or seven, but it was mostly with hockey people. Now, every time he passed a magazine stand, he saw his picture on the cover—not just on sports magazines, on all kinds. He was recognized on the street now. Sitting down in a restaurant meant signing between bites. In chasing Richard and Esposito, he'd caught the imagination of the whole country."

That Friday night in Brantford, surrounded by a select group of family and friends, Gretzky relaxed in the comfortable confines of the house that he had grown up in. Gathered around the television, they watched a videotape that Walter Gretzky had prepared that highlighted some of Wayne's goals and contained a debate from the CBC current-affairs show *The Journal*, in which Wayne's achievements were disputed by longtime Gretzky critic Dick Beddoes. Shortly afterward, Gretzky retreated to the bedroom that had been his for the first 14 years of his life, and went to sleep.

The next morning, he arrived at Maple Leaf Gardens for the Oilers morning skate, then made his way over to the Hot Stove Lounge, located inside the Gardens, where he received a presentation from Daoust skates, a company that he endorsed. Just before the ceremony started, 78-year-old Francis "King" Clancy, a legendary figure who had been an integral part of the Toronto Maple Leafs' first Stanley Cup–winning team half a century before, approached Gretzky to get his autograph for his grandchildren. Bobby Hull and renowned Toronto sportswriter Milt Dunnell also asked Gretzky for his John Hancock.

As for the game itself, it was a night to forget for Gretzky and the Oilers. The Great One did score a goal, the only one in the Oilers' 7–1 loss to the Maple Leafs. He also missed an open-net opportunity and was stopped on a penalty shot by Toronto netminder Michel "Bunny" Larocque. The loss also put an end to Grant Fuhr's personal 23-game unbeaten streak.

In light of the recent media frenzy, and with the game being broadcast live on coast-to-coast television by *Hockey Night in Canada* (and with a viewing audience of close to four million viewers, which represented a 46 per cent share of that night's television audience), the embarrassing loss to the Maple Leafs was a 1981–82 regular-season low point. Understandably, Gretzky and his teammates wanted nothing more after the game than to get showered, get dressed, make their way to the airport, and get out of Toronto. In an effort to safely escort Gretzky from the dressing room to the waiting team bus, the Oilers brain trust located a little-used side door, by which they thought they could avoid the waiting hordes outside. It didn't take long to realize how wrong they had been.

"Somehow this mob of girls figured it out and came charging at us. I thought, 'We're going to die,'" Bill Tuele said. Pressed into action, hulking Oilers forward Dave Semenko, accompanied by several other team officials, huddled and formed a protective circle around Gretzky, in what would ultimately be a successful effort to get Number 99 past a multitude of high-pitched, squealing teenaged girls who screamed at the top of their lungs at the mere sight of him and tried their best to touch him. Upon entering the bus and walking down the aisle, a sheepish Gretzky muttered, "I feel like the Beatles."

The next night, in Detroit, the Oilers and Red Wings skated to a 4–4 tie before a crowd of 20,628, which set a record for the largest crowd to witness an NHL regular-season game. Afterward, Gretzky walked along the police barricade set up at the Joe Louis Arena. "There had to be 5,000 of them," said a visibly harried Tuele, who by this point must have counting down the moments till the end of this eastern excursion. "They could reach within about two feet of a wall, so Gretz and I just put our heads down and ran for it. It would be fun to live his life for a day, maybe a weekend, knowing that it would end. It's only going to get worse."

———

On Wayne Gretzky's 21st birthday, January 26, 1982, he played with his team in in St. Louis. The Oilers defeated the hometown Blues by a score of 6–4, with the birthday boy nabbing a goal and an assist.

The goal was his 62nd of the season, and the two points gave him 138. The game against the Blues marked the 52nd of Edmonton's season. Glen Sather had been attempting to keep the media at bay after the Oilers' humiliating four-game losing streak on their East Coast swing. The strategy appeared to be paying off, as that night's win over the Blues was the team's fourth in a row.

Despite Sather's no-media edict, Terry Jones from the *Edmonton Journal* got into Gretzky's room the night of his birthday and secured an interview, one in which Gretzky gave a glimpse of how his life and the demands being put on him by others were in a state of constant flux.

"The change I've seen in the past year, heck in the past month, is a bigger change than I've seen in the last 20 years. I can't go to a ball game and have a beer and a hot dog and be just like everybody else anymore. I can't be myself now. I can go to all sorts of private boxes, but I can't go sit in the stands and have a hot dog and a beer."

He relayed to Jones that he knew that the situation was only going to get more extreme, that the demands would only increase. As a result, he found himself pushing back against the relentless attention. "I still enjoy being recognized and having people ask for my auto-graph," he admitted. "But there's so much of it. It's also frustrating."

———

On February 8, 1982, Gretzky was back in Washington for the NHL's annual All-Star Game festivities. The game would take place the next night, but first there was a luncheon hosted by President Ronald Reagan at the White House, in honour of the two NHL All-Star teams that would be competing. "I'm most certainly not going to forget this experience," Gretzky later recalled. "Meeting Ronald Reagan, the President of the United States, and Bob Hope . . . I was in a fog all day. I couldn't believe it was me sitting there at the White House with them. Even just being able to go inside the White House was a big thrill." For the normally unflappable Gretzky, surrounded by his fellow All-Stars and various other NHL dignitaries, there was a sense of unease that he couldn't quite escape from. "I kept looking at Gordie Howe and doing exactly what he was doing."

In the president's speech, he took the time to single out Gretzky. "One of the latest sports heroes in this country is a modest young man from Ontario named Wayne Gretzky. Rumour has it, Wayne, that Washington has been trying to trade and get you here for the team. And I asked what Edmonton was getting in return, and they said two first-round picks and the state of Texas," the president said. The next night Gretzky scored a goal for the Campbell Conference All-Stars, but it wasn't enough as the Wales Conference All-Stars skated off with a 4–2 win.

————

A little over a week later, the second "Gretzky Watch" of the 1981–82 season began. On the night of February 17, at the Northlands Coliseum, the Oilers defeated the Minnesota North Stars by a score of 7–4. With the win, Edmonton improved its record in its last 13 games to 10 wins, one loss, and two ties. And yet, despite the hot streak, whispers that Gretzky appeared tired surrounded the team. Never mind that he had extended his personal points-scoring streak to 17 games with five points against the North Stars. "People expect me to get four goals every game," he said after the game. "I'm not tired. I'm frustrated. I just don't think I've played up to my abilities in the last couple of weeks, that's all."

The five points brought his season total to 161, just three shy of the NHL record that he himself had set a season before, with 19 games still remaining on the schedule. And yet, this achievement received precious little coverage. The two goals against Minnesota, numbers 71 and 72 on the season, drew all of the attention and put Gretzky just four shy of Phil Esposito's mark.

Concluding a nine-game home stand two nights later, the Oilers hosted the Hartford Whalers. With the team set to embark on a nine-game road trip, Gretzky, who that week had graced the cover of *Sports Illustrated* for the second time in 1981–82, had a burning desire to at least tie Esposito's record in front of the home crowd. He would have to score four goals in order to do that, and nobody needed to be reminded, especially after the spectacular fashion in which he had reached the 50-goal mark, that he needed only five goals to break the record.

When the game ended and Gretzky had "only" managed three goals and two assists in the 7–4 Edmonton win, the regret in his voice was audible. "We play our last two games at home this year," a remorseful Gretzky told the media after the game. "If I score in either of those two games, that's the one the fans will remember. That will be the real record."

The media—and the NHL, for that matter—had been caught off guard when Gretzky scored the 50 in 39, but they were determined not to make the same mistake again. When Gretzky and the Oilers arrived in Detroit for their February 21 game against the Red Wings at the Joe Louis Arena, they were greeted by NHL president John Ziegler and the record holder himself, Phil Esposito. Each would be travelling with the team until Gretzky scored the historic 77th goal.

"Wayne was particularly pleased that Esposito had come," Walter Gretzky later recalled. "Mr. Ziegler was there on behalf of the league. Esposito was there because he wanted to be. He'd come on his own. . . . He knew better than anyone the feeling Wayne would have when it fell. He'd had it himself."

Detroit seemed a more than likely spot for Gretzky to score both the record-tying and record-breaking goals. The Red Wings were one of the worst teams in the NHL, would employ five different goalies over the course of the season and ended up with the league's second-worst record (the Colorado Rockies occupied the basement that year). Things were so bad for Detroit that before the game, a local sportswriter predicted that Gretzky wouldn't score a goal against the Red Wings, saying, "I think he'd prefer to wait and score it against a real NHL team."

The sportswriter turned out to be wrong. Gretzky tied the record in Detroit, scoring his 76th goal of the season when he took a pass from Glenn Anderson and beat Red Wings goaltender Bob Sauvé at the 16:34 mark of the third period, in what ended up being a 7–3 Edmonton win.

Gretzky had scored his 76th goal on his 293rd shot of the season. By contrast, when Esposito set the record in 1970–71, he had taken a massive 550 shots. Now that he shared the record, Esposito couldn't have been happier.

"I wanted to be here and I wanted to be wherever it is that he breaks it," he told reporters after the game. "I wanted to be here. When I broke Bobby Hull's record (58 goals), I wished he could have been there to see it. I was coming here whether the NHL said or not. It's great what Wayne is doing for the game."

Esposito also recalled for the reporters that the first time he had heard about Wayne Gretzky was in 1975, when Esposito's father had called from Sault Ste. Marie, Ontario. "Phil," his father told him, "there's a boy who will break all your records one day. He's 14 years old and he's playing junior in the Soo. His name is Gretzky . . . Wayne Gretzky."

Esposito, who was in the midst of leading the NHL in goals for a sixth consecutive season at the time of the call, replied, "Well, that's great, Dad, but he's only 14. Let's wait and see." Seven years later, the day foreseen by the senior Esposito had arrived.

———

After Detroit, the Oilers' next game was three days later in Buffalo, and while the team, along with Esposito and Ziegler, made their way to a media circus (made up of 160 accredited reporters) in Western New York, Gretzky once again quietly went home to Brantford in an effort to get away from it all.

Out of sight and out of mind for two whole days, he reappeared in Buffalo on the morning of February 24, 1982, and was bombarded by media clamouring for every last detail of his brief sojourn in Brantford. Gretzky, looking refreshed and relaxed, obliged them as always. He had gone to visit his grandmother, who had prepared him a meal of cabbage rolls and borscht while he sat in front of the television, watching the soap opera *One Life to Live*. He also went back to his old elementary school, where he sat in on his younger brother Brent's Grade 5 class, with the same teacher who had taught Wayne in the fifth grade a decade before, Mrs. Chiu. And then he went to the local arena and, for the first time in three years, watched his younger brother Keith in action. Keith didn't disappoint, scoring two shorthanded goals and adding four assists as Brantford beat Brampton, 7–5, in a minor-midget hockey game.

Some of the media noticed that Phyllis Gretzky didn't join Walter and Wayne on the 60-mile drive from Brantford to Buffalo, finding it odd that on the day when her son was about to break one of hockey's greatest records—and so close to home, no less—she wasn't there. When asked, Walter Gretzky nonchalantly answered, "Oh, she's had to go to Quebec for a pee wee tournament. Brent's playing."

"Nobody could believe it, but that's the way it was in my family," Wayne later recalled. "One of our parents tried to be at every game. My mom always tells people—'Wayne isn't the only hockey player in the family.'"

Knowing for a long time that he would break this record, Gretzky later admitted that he felt very little nervousness before the game with Buffalo. "The only thing I felt anxious about was that Phil was here and I wanted to do it so he could get back to work."

On the night in Buffalo, Sabres goalie Don Edwards did his best throughout the game's first two periods to thwart destiny. In the first period, Gretzky set up two Edmonton goals as the Oilers jumped out to a 3–1 lead after 20 minutes. The second period saw Buffalo score the only goal of the period, but it was Gretzky—and, by association, Edwards—who provided all the excitement. On three separate occasions, Gretzky appeared to have the record-breaking goal in his grasp, only to have the Sabres goalie get the better of him each time. Early in the third period, the Sabres tied the score at three. And then, at the 6:42 mark of the period, with Buffalo caught up ice, Gretzky, with his teammate Glenn Anderson, broke free on a two-on-one. After a give-and-go between the two, there stood Gretzky to the right of the slot, with a wide-open net in front of him. Gretzky unloaded a quick wrist shot, only to see a desperate Edwards dive headfirst and somehow manage to deflect the puck with his glove. That was now *four* glorious opportunities on the night for Gretzky, and he had no goals to show for it. A few more shifts followed, but Gretzky didn't come close to the Buffalo net, and with time running out, it appeared that the record-breaking goal would have to wait for another night.

Gretzky would later admit to looking up at Esposito, seated just above centre ice, and claim that the look on the old record-holder's face spoke to him, suggesting, "C'mon Wayne. I didn't pack enough clothes for this trip."

And then, trying to control a loose puck at centre ice, Buffalo right winger Steve Patrick started skating in the wrong direction (toward his own net) and was unable to corral the puck, which was bouncing in his feet. Taking advantage, Gretzky picked the Sabre's pocket and turned toward the Buffalo net. Skating side by side with the Sabres Richie Dunn, Gretzky used his body to shield the puck from the Buffalo defender. A desperate Dunn hooked Gretzky with his stick, trying to get a piece of him, but Gretzky warded him off and swept the puck between Edwards's pads for his record-breaking 77th goal of the season.

"My first thought was that it put us ahead 4–3," Gretzky told reporters afterward. "Then, as I turned to stride to the corner, I felt relief and satisfaction; it's a lot of pressure off me."

As his teammates stormed off the bench to mob him once again, Gretzky received a standing ovation from the sold-out crowd of 16,433 at the Buffalo Memorial Auditorium. The song "Celebration" by Kool and the Gang was blasted through the arena's loudspeakers. As the song and the cheering in the arena continued, on screen the camera panned to the penalty box, where Phil Esposito stood, intermittently clapping along and joyfully pumping his own arm. After an introduction by the Buffalo public-address announcer, Esposito was handed the 77th-goal puck and the microphone by one of the officials.

"Thank you," he addressed the crowd as Gretzky skated over, and then repeated his thanks. "Wayne, I want to congratulate you, man, and I want to thank you for allowing me to be part of this. I mean it. Thanks a lot, Wayne." Shaking the younger man's hand, Esposito presented Gretzky with the puck, and the two men embraced.

There remained six minutes and 36 seconds in the game, and Gretzky, now unburdened by the chase for Esposito's record, proceeded to put on a clinic, scoring goal number 78 at the 18:16 mark of the third period and his 79th at the 19:43 mark, to give him a hat trick—his eighth of the 1981–82 season—and ice the game for the Oilers, who won by a score of 6–3.

After the game, Gretzky, who had just recorded five points for the fourth consecutive game, was escorted to an interview room that was bursting with print, television, and radio reporters, cameramen, and an assortment of NHL officials. First on the agenda was the reading of a congratulatory telegram from President Reagan.

"Congratulations on your extraordinary achievement. The record for most goals in a season is one that many people thought would never be broken. Your brief National Hockey League career has already produced many record-breaking performances. But I know that this record is of special significance." Of all the press conferences Gretzky endured in 1981–82, he appeared happiest during this one.

The next day, newspapers across North America carried photos of Gretzky on their front pages. Some chose a photo of him scoring the record-breaking goal; others used photos of him with Esposito; a few used postgame photos, taken in the dressing room, of him alongside Hollywood stars Burt Reynolds and Goldie Hawn, who happened to be in Buffalo shooting the movie *Best Friends.*

In the Oilers' final 16 games of the 1981–82 NHL season, Gretzky broke a few more NHL records. On March 17, in a game against the Pittsburgh Penguins, he scored three goals for his 10th hat trick of the season, a new NHL record, and added two assists. The pair of assists gave him 110 on the season, breaking the record that he himself had set a year before. On March 25, in Calgary, he became the first player to crack the 200-point barrier, assisting on a goal by Pat Hughes. Three days later, in Los Angeles, in the Oilers' third-to-last game of the season, Gretzky scored his final goal of the year, his 92nd, to establish a new mark that has yet to be bettered. And against Winnipeg, in the Oilers' last game of the season, Gretzky registered an assist that gave him 212 points for the year.

And then there was all of the stuff away from the ice, where Gretzky had become an even hotter commodity. Inundated with offers, Gretzky's agent Gus Badali added Michael Barnett to Number 99's off-ice team to help with the load. Almost immediately, Gretzky's endorsements, which included a life insurance company, a men's cologne, a sportswear company, a video game, a doll, a cereal brand, wallpaper, and lunch boxes, began bringing in around two million dollars a year. To gauge Gretzky's impact on a brand, one needed to look no further than Titan hockey sticks. The company ranked 13th in sales amongst all manufacturers when he signed an endorsement deal; it promptly went to the top of the heap. Together, Badali and

Barnett crafted a strategy that saw Gretzky enter into long-term deals with blue-chip national and international corporations, each one containing a charitable aspect. They wouldn't cut deals with cigarette or alcohol companies, in an effort, as Badali said, to "project an image of a guy who cares about people, whom success hasn't changed."

There were some media critics who openly questioned whether this was all too much for a 21-year-old, something that Gretzky himself, at times, didn't dispute. "Sometimes I feel like Gus and Michael rush some things by me," Gretzky admitted at the time. "But that's what I hire them to do. I don't have time to worry about all those things that come as a result of what happens on the ice. My number-one priority has to be playing hockey."

As it was, the offers continued to pour in. After setting the goal mark in 1981–82, Gretzky was set to appear on *The Tonight Show* with Johnny Carson in early March, but had to cancel when he couldn't get a plane out of Quebec City. He did squeeze a few appearances into his busy schedule, though, including one on a Paul Anka television special. Meanwhile, during a trip to Los Angeles, the Oilers and Gretzky took time to visit the set of the popular television show *M*A*S*H*, resulting in a series of photos that ran in newspapers across North America.

The Oilers ended the 1981–82 NHL season with the league's second-best record, behind only the New York Islanders, with 111 points—37 more than the year prior and a jump of 12 places in the overall standings. They scored an NHL-record 417 goals, while going undefeated in the last nine games of the season. Most of the attention naturally focused on Gretzky and his record-breaking achievements, which resulted in his winning the Hart Trophy as the NHL's most valuable player for a third consecutive year.

Many of his teammates also enjoyed banner seasons. Mark Messier scored 50 goals for the first and only time in his career. Glenn Anderson recorded the first of three 100-point seasons in his Hall of Fame career. Rookie goaltender Grant Fuhr established an Oilers franchise record and finished second in the NHL with 28 wins. Paul Coffey led all NHL defencemen in scoring, with 89 points.

In the process, the Oilers had emerged as Canada's Team— young, cocky, and brash, and above all, a team that appeared poised to challenge for the Stanley Cup.

And then, in the space of one week, they came crashing back down to earth.

––––––––

The Oilers' first-round opponents in the 1982 playoffs were the Los Angeles Kings, a team that had finished the season 48 points behind Edmonton in the overall standings. In their eight meetings with the Kings in the regular season, the Oilers had five wins, one loss, and two ties and had outscored Los Angeles by an aggregate score of 51–27. In two of the victories, the Oilers had scored at least 10 goals against the Kings, and in the week before their playoff series was set to begin, they had beaten the Kings twice in a home-and-home affair by scores of 6–2 and 7–3.

To say that the Oilers didn't play well against the Kings in the best-of-five playoff affair would be putting it mildly, as their collective youth, long considered a strength, now betrayed them. Against Los Angeles, the Oilers were revealed as both an inexperienced group and an undisciplined one. In fact, had Gretzky not scored an overtime winner in Game Two, the Oilers might have had their season end in three straight games.

Electing to confront the Oilers with their own offence, as opposed to relying on the well-worn and seldom-successful tactic of slowing Edmonton down, the Kings won the series' wild first game by a score of 10–8, establishing what is still a record for combined goals in an NHL playoff game. The series' second game, settled by a Gretzky overtime winner, knotted the series at one game apiece and set the stage for what would become known as the "Miracle on Manchester."

The third game saw the series switch to Los Angeles, where the home crowd's enthusiasm was quickly extinguished by the Oilers, who jumped out to a seemingly insurmountable 5–0 lead. For Bob Miller, the Kings play-by-play man since 1973, there was a sense of another opportunity squandered. "There was so much anticipation before the game, especially after winning the first game in Edmonton and coming so close in the second. The Kings always had struggled to gain a foothold in Los Angeles, and we now had everybody excited and then we go in the dumper."

Miller wasn't alone in his disgust. Below him, the crowd thinned noticeably as many made their way to the exits, including the Kings owner, Jerry Buss. "You were hoping that they could at least break the shutout," remembers Miller. The Kings did break the shutout, with two quick goals on Grant Fuhr at the start of the third. But it was their third goal, with a little over five minutes left, that marked a turning point.

"The crowd was beginning to realize that there was a chance," Miller recalls. "That's when the atmosphere in the building changed, and the momentum started to build."

The fourth goal soon followed, and, in Miller's words, "there was bedlam in the building." The pandemonium extended to the parking lot, where those who had left—prematurely, as it turned out—listened closely on the radio and had begun their own celebration.

But the score still remained 5–4 Edmonton. And as the clock clicked down, it seemed that the Oilers would survive. With 10 seconds remaining on the clock, the puck rested comfortably on the stick of Wayne Gretzky. All he had to do was clear it from his own end, and the game would end. But for one brief moment, Gretzky's soft hands deserted him. He coughed up the puck, and before anybody could react, it was in the back of the Oilers net. With five seconds left in the game, the score was deadlocked at five.

"The Forum was in an uproar," Miller remembered, the excitement in his voice still palpable over three decades later. "There was a break before overtime to flood the ice, but the people never stopped chanting. They walked around, pumping their fists in the air . . . the building was electric."

No team in playoff history had ever come back from a 5–0 deficit. Now the impossible seemed inevitable. The Kings Daryl Evans would end the game 2:35 into overtime when his one-timer went over Grant Fuhr's glove. Flailing his arms in the air, an exuberant Evans raced to the other side of the rink.

The Oilers stood in shock. "I'll never forget Grant Fuhr," says Miller. "You could almost see the pained expression on his face, even with the mask on."

Forgotten by time is that the Oilers won Game Four of the series in Los Angeles, 3–2, to set up a winner-take-all game five back in Edmonton. Feeling all of the pressure, the Oilers, who mere days ago had carried themselves with a confident swagger, played like a team afraid to lose and very quickly found themselves in a 2–0 hole, and while Gretzky made it 2–1, the Kings responded less than 10 minutes later to make the score 3–1. After a goal by Paul Coffey, the score was 3–2 heading into the first intermission. The second period saw two teams in full contrast, as the tense Oilers were unable to hold off the relaxed Kings, who scored three goals and never looked back in a 7–4 win that put an all-too-sudden end to the Oilers' season.

The headline in the next morning's *Edmonton Journal* summed it up in two words. "THEY CHOKED!"

"A great year had suddenly turned awful in the playoffs," Gretzky later recalled. "But I still think it was the best thing that could've happened to us. It was a cream pie in the face. We'd gotten too big for our hockey shorts. We'd beaten the Canadiens the year before, and we'd stomped on the rest of the NHL during the regular season. We were young and obnoxious. . . . We were 21-year-olds who were acting our age. We didn't know until then the kind of preparation and will it takes to win in the playoffs. I learned a lesson, too. All those trophies and awards and records feel great, but you learn that the tingle goes away pretty quick when you fall on your face in the playoffs. The whole season felt sort of hollow."

———

After just three seasons in the NHL, Wayne Gretzky, at 21 years old, was in sole possession of 27 individual records. The men whose records he had broken, often in spectacular fashion, represented a roll call of hockey's greatest-ever players—Maurice Richard, Bobby Orr, Phil Esposito, and Mike Bossy—and yet each of those players had on their resumé something that Gretzky, despite his numerous accomplishments, still lacked, the one prize that he wanted more than anything, the one trophy that, after three unprecedented years of dominance, had eluded his grasp: the Stanley Cup.

Epilogue

On the night of Saturday, May 19, 1984, Wayne Gretzky and the Edmonton Oilers claimed the Stanley Cup. They did so emphatically, defeating their rivals, the four-time defending champion New York Islanders, in a five-game final.

Like their longtime adversaries, the Gretzky-led Oilers went on to win four Cups of their own, adding to their 1984 championship in 1985, 1987, and 1988. In addition to those triumphs with the Oilers, Gretzky led Team Canada to victory in the 1984, 1987, and 1991 Canada Cups.

But by the time of that last Canada Cup win in 1991, Gretzky had long ceased being a member of the Edmonton Oilers, having been traded by the Oilers to the Los Angeles Kings on August 9, 1988.

The trade shocked the nation. Thanks to a combination of his on-ice accomplishments and his carefully crafted off-ice persona, Gretzky had become a national treasure in Canada. In the hearts of many of his fans, and they were legion, his trade felt like a betrayal: a part of Canada inseparable from hockey had been bargained away.

The hockey world was shocked. Even a member of the Canadian Parliament appealed to the government to block Gretzky's trade to the Kings. But while Canada mourned, Los Angeles found itself enthralled with hockey like never before. Almost overnight, the Kings became the NHL's glamour team, selling out arenas wherever they visited and playing in front of a gaggle of celebrities at home—including the former president, Ronald Reagan.

Stephen Brunt called the trade "a complete reset of the NHL in one day." And while it was characterized at the time as "Canada's loss," it came to be seen as "hockey's gain." In Gretzky's wake, hockey began to thrive in California, as franchises in San Jose and Anaheim joined the NHL in the 1990s, and perhaps more profoundly, the number of kids playing hockey in the United States has almost tripled since Gretzky arrived in Los Angeles in the summer of 1988.

And yet, Gretzky came up short of his ultimate goal of bringing the Stanley Cup to Los Angeles. He had his chance in 1993, but the Kings lost to the Montreal Canadiens in the Stanley Cup final. A brief stint with the St. Louis Blues followed his time with the Kings, and Gretzky played his last three years in the NHL with the New York Rangers.

Wayne Gretzky's final NHL game, broadcast live throughout North America, took place on the afternoon of April 18, 1999, at Madison Square Garden. The following November, the Hockey Hall of Fame waived its usual three-year post-career waiting period and inducted him. He would later be joined in the Hall by many of his former running mates in Edmonton: Jari Kurri (2001), Grant Fuhr (2003), Paul Coffey (2004), Mark Messier (2007), and Glenn Anderson (2008). The Oilers head coach/general manager, Glen Sather, had been enshrined in 1997, two years before Gretzky. At the

NHL's 2000 All-Star Game, Gretzky's number, 99, was retired league-wide—making him the only player in hockey history to enjoy such an honour.

No player has left a larger imprint on his chosen sport than Wayne Gretzky. Over the course of his 20-year career in the National Hockey League, he singlehandedly rewrote the NHL record book to an extent unseen in hockey, or any other sport. On the day of his retirement, Gretzky held or shared an astonishing 61 NHL records. To put that in perspective, the legendary Gordie Howe lays claim to 11 records in total, while Bobby Orr has five to his name.

It has been said often, and repeated ad nauseam, that records are made to be broken. But if anything, that tired axiom, like many other limitations, doesn't seem to apply to Gretzky. Today, more than a decade and a half into his retirement, he still holds 60 NHL records. Only his standing as the all-time career leader in overtime assists has been overtaken, with that record now belonging—ironically enough—to Gretzky's former Edmonton Oilers teammate Mark Messier. And while it may be a stretch to suggest that the rest of his records are unbreakable, a remarkable number of them appear to be far out of reach for any current—and, for that matter, future—NHLer.

A few examples of Wayne Gretzky's seemingly unattainable records:

Most goals in a single season: 92 (1981–82)

Most assists in a single season: 163 (1985–86)

Most points in a single season: 215 (1985–86)

Perhaps even more daunting to any potential pursuers are Gretzky's career totals—all NHL bests—in the same three categories.

Most goals: 894

Most assists: 1,963 assists

Most points: 2,857

Consider that Gretzky's career assist total is more than any other player's total points in NHL history, and the enormity of Gretzky's career numbers becomes clear.

Of course, Gretzky's record numbers aren't limited to the regular season:

Most playoff goals, career: 122

Most playoff assists, career: 260

Most playoff points, career: 382

Of course, these nine records represent a sampling of Gretzky's abundant NHL benchmarks, the vast majority of which fall into the so-called "unbreakable" category. For example, his 51 straight games with at least one point in 1983–84; his 10 NHL scoring titles (including seven in a row); his 47 points in the 1984–85 playoffs; his 15 100-point seasons (including a record 13 in a row); and his nine Hart Trophies (including eight consecutively) awarded to the league's most valuable player.

But for Gretzky himself, there is one record amongst all of the others that he has publicly said, in his opinion, will be the hardest of the 60 to break. "I think the 92 goals could be broken someday," Gretzky recently recalled. "Mario [Lemieux] and Brett [Hull] have come close, and the 215 points might fall to [Sidney] Crosby, with all the five-on-three power plays now. But somebody would have to get 50 in 38 games. Ovechkin? Stamkos? Crosby? I don't know about that.

"As the years go by, the 50 in 39 becomes more and more my favourite record. Listen, records are made to be broken, and who ever thought I'd be able to do what I did? The game changes, and who knows what is going to happen down the road, but I think there are a lot of records that are attainable for players. The one record that I always felt in my mind would be difficult for anybody to break was the 50 in 39. That was even back in the days when there were a lot more goals and a lot more offence. I just always felt of all my records, this would be the hardest to beat, so from my point of view it was always the record I was most proud of."

Sources

Interviews

Gus Badali

Paul Coffey

Wayne Gretzky

Kevin Lowe

Dave Lumley

Dennis Maruk

Jim Matheson

Lanny McDonald

Mark Messier

Bob Miller

Denis Potvin

Garry Unger

Books

Benedict, Michael, & D'Arcy Jenish, eds., *Canada on Ice: 50 Years of Great Hockey*. Toronto: Viking, 1998.

Bossy, Mike, and Barry Meisel. *Boss: The Mike Bossy Story*. Toronto: McGraw-Hill Ryerson, 1988.

Brophy, Mike. *My First Goal: 50 Players and the Goals That Marked the Beginning of Their NHL Careers*. Toronto: McClelland & Stewart, 2011.

Brunt, Stephen. *Gretzky's Tears: Hockey, Canada, and the Day Everything Changed*. Toronto: Knopf, 2009.

Carpiniello, Rick. *Messier: Steel on Ice*. Toronto: Stoddart, 1999.

Diamond, Dan, ed. *Total NHL: The Ultimate Source on the National Hockey League*. Chicago: Triumph Books, 2003.

Diamond, Dan, and James Duplacey, eds. *Total Hockey: The Official Encyclopedia of the National Hockey League*. Kingston, NY: Total Sports, 1998.

Diamond, Dan, and Lew Stubbs. *Hockey: Twenty Years*. Toronto: Doubleday, 1987.

Fischler, Stan. *The Great Gretzky*. New York: William Morrow, 1982.

Fraser, Edward, ed. *Hockey's Most Amazing Records*. Montreal: Transcontinental Books, 2011.

Fuhr, Grant, and Bruce Dowbiggin. *Grant Fuhr: The Story of a Hockey Legend*. Toronto: Random House, 2014.

Gassen, Timothy. *Red, White and Blues: A Personal History of Indianapolis Racers Hockey, 1974–1979*. Tucson: PCMP Press, 2007.

Greig, Murray. *Big Bucks and Blue Pucks: From Hull to Gretzky, an Anecdotal History of the Late, Great World Hockey Association*. Toronto: Macmillan, 1997.

Gretzky, Walter. *Walter Gretzky: On Family, Hockey and Healing*. Toronto: Random House, 2001.

Gretzky, Walter, with Jim Taylor. *Gretzky: From the Backyard Rink to the Stanley Cup*. Toronto: McClelland & Stewart, 1984.

Gretzky, Wayne, with John Davidson. *99: My Life in Pictures*. Toronto: Total Sports Canada, 1999.

Gretzky, Wayne, with Rick Reilly. *Gretzky: An Autobiography*. Toronto: Harper & Collins, 1990.

Gzowski, Peter. *The Game of Our Lives*, rev. ed. Toronto: McClelland & Stewart, 1982.

Hanks, Stephen. *Wayne Gretzky*. New York: St. Martin's Press, 1990.

The Hockey News. *Total Gretzky: The Magic, The Legend, The Numbers*. Toronto: McClelland & Stewart, 1999.

Hunter, Douglas. *Champions: The Illustrated History of Hockey's Greatest Dynasties*. Toronto: Viking, 1997.

———. *The Glory Barons: The Saga of the Edmonton Oilers*. Toronto: Viking, 1999.

Jones, Terry. *The Great Gretzky*. Toronto: General Paperbacks, 1980.

———. *The Great Gretzky Yearbook*. Toronto: General Paperbacks, 1981.

———. *The Great Gretzky Yearbook II: The Greatest Single Season in Hockey History*. Toronto: General Paperbacks, 1982.

Klein, Jeff Z. *Messier*. Toronto: Doubleday, 2003.

Lowe, Kevin, with Stan and Shirley Fischler. *Champions: The Making of the Edmonton Oilers*. Scarborough, ON: Prentice-Hall Canada, Inc., 1988.

McKinley, Michael. *Hockey: A People's History*. Toronto: McClelland & Stewart, 2006.

Messier, Mark, Brett Hull, Walter Gretzky, et al. *Wayne Gretzky: The Making of the Great One*. Bowling Green, OH: Beckett Publications, 1998.

Morrison, Scott, ed. *Wayne Gretzky: The Great Goodbye*. Toronto: Key Porter Books, 1999.

Podnieks, Andrew. *The Great One: The Life and Times of Wayne Gretzky*. Toronto: Doubleday, 1999.

Rosenthal, Bert. *Wayne Gretzky: The Great Gretzky*. Chicago: Children's Press, 1982.

Semenko, Dave, and Larry Tucker. *Looking Out for Number One*. Toronto: Stoddart, 1989.

Sports Illustrated. *The Great One: The Complete Wayne Gretzky Collection*. Toronto: Fenn/M&S, 2012.

Strachan, Al. *99: Gretzky: His Game, His Story*. Toronto: Fenn/M&S, 2013.

Taylor, Jim. *Wayne Gretzky: The Authorized Pictorial Biography*. North Vancouver: Whitecap Books, 1994.

Willes, Ed. *The Rebel League: The Short and Unruly Life of the World Hockey Association*. Toronto: McClelland & Stewart, 2004.

Wilner, Barry. *Wayne Gretzky: Countdown to Immortality*. West Point, NY: Leisure Press, 1982.

Wolff, Craig Thomas. *Wayne Gretzky: Portrait of a Hockey Player*. New York: Avon Books, 1983.

Zweig, Eric. *Twenty Greatest Hockey Goals*. Toronto: Dundurn Press, 2010.

Magazines

Action Sports Hockey	*Hockey Stars*	*Sports Illustrated*
Beckett Hockey Magazine	*Hockey Today*	*Sports Special Hockey*
Chatelaine	*Inside Sports*	*The Hockey News*
Goal Magazine	*Maclean's Magazine*	*The Sporting News*
Hockey Digest	*Newsweek*	*The Sports Journal*
Hockey Illustrated	*Reader's Digest*	*Time Magazine*
Hockey Scene	*Sport Magazine*	*Weekend Magazine*

Newspapers

Brantford Expositor	*Globe and Mail*	*St. Catharines Standard*
Buffalo Courier-Express	*Hamilton Spectator*	*St. Petersburg*
Buffalo Evening News	*Los Angeles Times*	*Independent*
Calgary Herald	*Montreal Gazette*	*Toronto Star*
Calgary Sun	*New York Times*	*Toronto Sun*
Detroit Free Press	*Ottawa Citizen*	*Vancouver Sun*
Edmonton Journal	*Pittsburgh Post-Gazette*	*Welland Evening Tribune*
Edmonton Sun	*Regina Leader-Post*	*Windsor Star*

Wire Services

Associated Press
Canadian Press
United Press International

Internet Sources

www.cbc.ca	www.nhl.com
www.espn.com	www.sihrhockey.org
www.greatesthockeylegends.com	www.sportsnet.ca
www.hhof.com	www.tsn.ca
www.hockey-reference.com	

OTHERS

Hockey Hall of Fame Resource Centre, Etobicoke, Ontario, Canada
Queens University Library, Kingston, Ontario, Canada

Acknowledgements

The authors wish to thank Arnold Gosewich, Jordan Fenn, Kendra Ward, Doug Pepper, Aoife Walsh, and Lloyd Davis for all their help, support, and expertise in bringing this book to fruition.

Mike Brophy wishes to thank Todd Denault, a wonderful friend and partner, the National Hockey League, Jason Kay, The Hockey News, Benny Ercolani, Gary Meagher, Susan Snow, John Shannon, Don Metz, Lorraine Cousineau, and Bob Waterman (Elias Sports Bureau). A special thanks to Wayne Gretzky for continuing to be so supportive in my career.

Todd Denault wishes to thank Mike Brophy for his unwavering belief in both the book and our partnership, the Hockey Hall of Fame, Craig Campbell, Frank Orr, the Society for International Hockey Research, Tim Horgan, Derek Eagleson, Matt Jones, Nate Jones, the entire gang at Kelly's Homelike Inn, especially Gord Kelly, Sr., Gord Kelly, Jr., and Kris Kelly, and above all else, my mother, whose passion, love, and encouragement are constant sources of strength for me.

Index

Acton, Keith, 164
Anderson, Glenn, 26, 30, 98, 175,
  178, 180, 198, 213, 233,
  235–36, 239, 261, 263, 268
  attitude to hockey, 140
  early career, 139–41
  goals scored by, 50, 59–60, 69,
    91, 96, 102, 111, 135, 140,
    141, 142–43, 157, 164, 226
  inducted into Hockey Hall of
    Fame, 274
  joins Oilers, 140
  skills, 60
Andersson, Kent-Erik, 131
Anka, Paul, 267
Arbour, Al, 79, 117
Arthur, Fred, 237
Art Ross Trophy, 38, 145, 173,
  188
Ashton, Brent, 195
Atlanta Flames, founding of, 78
Aubry, Pierre, 167, 169
Avco Cup, 62

Badali, Gus, 36, 37, 38, 159, 217,
  255, 266–67
Baker, Steve, 87
Ballard, Harold, 23
Bannerman, Murray, 151, 153
Barber, Bill, 238, 239, 241
Barnett, Michael, 266, 267
Baron, Marco, 111
Barrasso, Tom, 69
Baumann, Alex, 203
Baxter, Paul, 215
Beaupre, Don, 130–31, 132
Beck, Barry, 87, 122
Beddoes, Dick, 13, 256
Berenson, Red, 126, 127, 128, 223
Bergeron, Michel, 91–92, 170
Berry, Ken, 225, 226
Bladon, Tom, 223
Blake, Toe, 2
Boldirev, Ivan, 30, 174
Bossy, Mike, 117, 190, 203
  compared to Gretzky, 124
  early career, 5–6

and goal-scoring records, 7–11,
  79, 80–81, 160, 199, 224,
  225, 230, 244, 250
  goals scored, 82, 116
  on Lowe, 137
Boston Bruins
  record against Oilers, 109–10
  team additions, 110
Botell, Mark, 234
Bouchard, Dan, 49, 90, 91, 169
Bourque, Ray, 110
Boutette, Pat, 69
Bower, Johnny, 76
Bozak, Ryan, 213
Bozek, Steve, 40, 41, 148, 183,
  184, 226
Brackenbury, Curt, 41
Bridgman, Mel, 202, 212, 214
Broadbent, Harry "Punch," 184,
  191, 198
Brodeur, Martin, 69
Brodeur, Richard, 29, 135, 175
Broten, Neal, 130
Brunt, Stephen, 274
Bure, Pavel, 31
Buss, Jerry, 269

Calder Trophy, 6
Calgary Flames, makeup of
  (1981–82), 48–49
Callighen, Brett, 27, 50, 54, 90,
  98, 106, 147, 213
Campbell, Colin, 181
Canada Cup (1981), 13–15, 125
Carlyle, Randy, 69
Carson, Johnny, 267
Cashman, Wayne, 110
Cheevers, Gerry, 112
Cherneski, John, 57
Cherry, Don, 235, 236, 239, 240,
  241
Chicago Black Hawks, change of
  division, 53–54
Chouinard, Guy, 5, 48–49, 59
Christian, Dave, 158
Christoff, Steve, 131, 206
Ciccarelli, Dino, 130

Clancy, Frances "King," 256
Clarke, Bobby, 18, 73, 238, 243,
  245, 247
Cloutier, Réal, 89
Coffey, Paul, 47, 54, 107–8, 143,
  158, 170, 183, 232, 233,
  236, 239, 241, 246, 268
  early career, 44, 156–57, 221
  on Fuhr, 66, 70–71
  goals scored by, 49, 55, 59, 65,
    69, 82, 87, 102, 142, 147,
    157, 158–59, 175, 189, 194,
    195, 201, 212, 221, 225,
    271
  on Gretzky, 242–43
  inducted into Hockey Hall of
    Fame, 274
  on playing with Gretzky, 56
  record set by, 268
  on Resch, 76
  style, 156–57
Colorado Rockies
  experience in Colorado, 193
  history of, 23
  McDonald's opinion of, 24
  record against Oilers, 193
  win against Oilers, 101–3
Conacher, Charlie, 2
Conn Smythe Trophy, 81
Côté, Alain, 167, 168
Craig, Jim, 7, 8
Crosby, Sidney, 276
Cyr, Denis, 201, 214

Dancy, Tim, 235, 236, 239, 240,
  241
Dea, Billy, 142
DeBlois, Lucien, 47
defence, and goal scoring, 52
Delorme, Ron, 175
Derlago, Bill, 96, 97
Detroit Red Wings, makeup of,
  141–42
Dionne, Marcel, 6, 13, 14, 38, 39,
  48, 85, 88, 147, 149
Dunn, Richie, 264
Dunnell, Milt, 256

Dupont, André, 90
Dupont, Norm, 47, 158

Edmonton Oilers
 1980-81 record, 21
 Gretzky joins, 12
 Kings as nemesis, 268–71
 need for change in, 79–80
 popularity of, 57–58, 210
 record against Bruins, 109
 record against Canadiens, 162
 record against Rockies, 193
 scoring statistics, 145–46, 148,
  151, 154, 155, 164, 196,
  207–8
 strength of, 139
 team records, 92
 win Stanley Cup, 273
Edwards, Don, 263, 264
Esposito, Phil, 4, 5, 13, 146, 227,
  250, 260, 261–62, 264,
  265–66
Esposito, Tony, 53, 55
Evans, Daryl, 270

Fergus, Tom, 110, 111
Ferguson, John, 160
Fischler, Stan, 13
Fletcher, Cliff, 49, 60, 199, 200,
  201
Flockhart, Ron, 235
Fogolin, Lee, 22, 56, 75, 76, 102,
  111, 131, 159, 175, 214,
  216
Foligno, Mike, 141, 142
Forbes, Mike, 148, 178, 179
Fox, Jim, 40
Francis, Ron, 63
Frank J. Selke Trophy, 112, 162
Fraser, Curt, 135
Fraser, Kerry, 238, 241
Fuhr, Grant, 54, 87, 90, 115, 163,
  179, 235, 239
 assist, 69
 early career, 45
 goals against, 47, 86, 97, 107,
  116, 122, 135, 158, 164,
  174, 178, 183, 185, 188,
  190, 201, 232, 234, 237
 goals scored, 69
 injuries, 201–2, 219, 222
 and Kings rout, 269, 270

officially becomes NHL
  goaltender, 148
 Oilers' confidence in, 178
 praise for, 47, 132, 166, 220,
  221, 222
 record set by, 268
 saves, 46, 108, 119, 130, 131,
  148, 174
 statistics, 166, 222
 value of, 69, 70–71
 wins, 66, 159, 166, 201, 256,
  274

Gagné, Paul, 102
Gainey, Bob, 112, 162
Gare, Danny, 141–42
Garrett, John, 64, 65
Geoffrion, Bernard "Boom
  Boom," 3, 5
Gilbert, Gilles, 142
Giles, Curt, 130
goals
 average scored in NHL, 52, 53
 and effect of defence on, 52
Goring, Robert "Butch," 15, 79
Goulet, Michel, 89
Gradin, Thomas, 30, 31–32, 179
Grahame, Ron, 10, 11
Grant, Danny, 5
Green, Ted, 144, 175
Gregg, Randy, 42, 140
Gretzky, Brent, 262, 263
Gretzky, Keith, 37, 250, 263
Gretzky, Kim, 35–36, 250
Gretzky, Phyllis, 35–36, 217, 250,
  263
Gretzky, Walter, 248–49, 250, 251,
  255–56, 261, 263
Gretzky, Wayne
 affinity for home games, 61
 basis for superstardom, 223–24
 B. Smith opinion of, 83
 and Canada Cup (1981), 125
 critics of, 256, 267
 early career, 12–13
 endorsements, 37, 38, 266–67
 final NHL game, 274
 hockey skills, 20, 26, 28, 32,
  56, 93–94, 99, 113, 117–18,
  122, 123–24, 127–28, 138,
  180, 181, 224, 230, 245
 impact of, 275

income, 38, 85
 and increase of U.S. hockey
  popularity, 274
 inducted into Hockey Hall of
  Fame, 274
 injuries, 81–83, 84–85, 86, 231
 joins Oilers, 12
 Man of the Year (1981,
  Sporting News), 230
 media interest in, 34–35, 37,
  38, 252, 253–55, 258,
  260–61, 262, 265–66, 267
 and Messier, 72–73, 170–72,
  202
 named male athlete of the year,
  203
 Number 99, 98, 275
 popularity of, 12, 18–19,
  36–37, 163, 210, 217–18,
  257, 266–67
 praise for the Islanders, 119
 records broken by, 266, 271,
  275–77
 regard for Canadiens, 165
 scores 50th goal, 239–40, 241
 scores 77th goal, 264
 scores 92nd goal, 266
 ties record, 261
 traded to Kings, 273–74
 work ethic, 242
Gzowski, Peter, 253–54

Habscheid, Marc, 147, 149, 158,
  175
Hagman, Matti, 42, 47, 50, 54, 59,
  64–65, 67–68, 69, 70, 90,
  91, 93, 106, 111, 126, 135,
  142, 143, 157, 168, 175,
  235
Hamel, Jean, 90
Hanlon, Glen, 29, 178, 179, 180,
  220
Hardy, Mark, 185
Harris, Billy, 79, 196
Harrison, Paul, 68–69
Hartford Whalers
 abilities, 105
 overview of, 62–64
Hartsburg, Craig, 130
Hart Trophy, 13, 125, 267
Hawn, Goldie, 266
Heinz, Rick, 29

Hickey, Pat, 86
Hicks, Doug, 22, 41, 102, 178, 201, 226, 227, 235
Higgins, Tim, 54
Hislop, Jamie, 201
Hlinka, Ivan, 30–31, 136
Hoffmeyer, Bob, 234, 236–37, 245–46
Holmgren, Paul, 215, 232, 237, 247
Houston, Ken, 49, 213
Howe, Gordie, 3, 223, 259
Howe, Mark, 63
Huddy, Charlie, 42
Hughes, Pat, 30, 41, 42, 47, 69, 97, 102, 111, 116, 121, 134, 158, 169, 183–84, 185, 202, 222, 266
Hull, Bobby, 3, 4, 5, 112, 256, 261
Hull, Brett, 276
Hunter, Dale, 89, 91, 168, 169
Hunter, Dave, 40, 42, 59, 69, 87, 106, 116, 121, 126–27, 131–32, 145, 158, 164, 168

Imlach, Punch, 23–24

James Norris Memorial Trophy, 162
Jensen, Steve, 41
Johansen, Trevor, 148
Johnson, Mark, 69
Johnston, Marshall, 195
Jonathan, Stan, 110
Jones, Terry, 156, 191, 249, 258

Kasper, Steve, 110, 112, 113, 114
Kastelan, Nick, 202
Keans, Doug, 184
Keon, Dave, 63
Kitchen, Mike, 200
Kurri, Jari, 27, 40, 42, 50, 51, 68, 91, 96, 106, 121, 127, 131, 180–81, 203, 206, 207, 220, 226, 274

Labraaten, Dan, 59
Lach, Elmer, 2
Lafleur, Guy, 5, 14, 39, 165
Laidlaw, Tom, 86
Langevin, Dave, 116
Lapointe, Guy, 165, 166
Lariviere, Garry, 212

Larocque, Michel "Bunny," 96, 98, 256
Larouche, Pierre, 164
Leach, Reggie, 234, 236, 238, 239
Lemelin, Reggie, 49, 212
Lemieux, Mario, 31, 39, 276
Lessard, Mario, 41, 225
Léveillé, Normand, 110
Lever, Don, 49, 59, 196, 199
Levo, Tapio, 75, 102
Lewis, Dave, 79
Lindström, Willy, 47
Linseman, Ken, 232, 234, 239
Lionel Conacher Trophy, 203
Liut, Mike, 125–26, 127
Los Angeles Kings
    losses, 182–83
    as Oilers' nemesis, 268–71
    Simmer drafted by, 6
Low, Ron, 46, 49, 50, 54, 59, 90, 110, 151–52, 185, 196, 212, 233
    early career, 45
    goals against, 40, 127, 142, 194–95, 206, 207
    goals-against average, 39
    losses, 111, 170
    praise for, 39–40
    replaces injured Fuhr, 202
    saves, 75, 153
    sense of humour, 91–92
Lowe, Kevin, 24, 35, 41, 45, 50, 111, 148, 186, 190, 194
    on Anderson, 140
    and Canadiens, 163
    on Coffey, 157, 159
    early career, 42–43, 44, 136–37
    ejection from game, 212
    on goalie changes, 103–4
    goals scored, 54, 195, 203
    on Gretzky, 72–73, 88, 117, 227–28, 242
    illness of, 152–53
    on Kurri, 51
    on Low, 40
    on Messier, 73–74
    on Sather, 32–33
Lukowich, Morris, 47, 158
Lumley, Dave, 126, 189, 233, 234, 239
    appreciation of Gretzky, 191–92, 208

early career, 133–36
early experience with Oilers, 120–21, 122–23
    goals scored, 122, 135, 136, 142, 145, 148, 153, 158, 165, 169, 174–75, 177, 178, 179, 184, 188, 195, 207, 208, 221
    Sather's opinion of, 123, 133
    scoring statistics, 121, 136, 191, 194, 196
    scoring streak, 180–81, 197–99, 201, 206

MacDonald, Blair, 30, 220
MacDonald, Parker, 148–49, 185, 227
MacGregor, Bruce, 227
MacInnis, Al, 49
MacLean, Paul, 46
MacLeish, Rick, 63–64, 106
MacMillan, Bill, 23, 49
MacMillan, Bob, 196, 199
MacNeil, Al, 216–17
Malinowski, Merlin, 102
Malone, Joe, 2
Maloney, Dave, 123
Maris, Rober, 304
Marois, Mario, 168
Matheson, Jim, 27, 58–59, 100–101, 238
Maxner, Wayne, 142, 143
Maxwell, Brad, 132
McCarthy, Kevin, 220
McCourt, Dale, 141, 142
McDonald, Lanny, 23, 24, 27, 28, 49, 76, 102, 199–201, 211, 212, 214, 216
McEwen, Mike, 187
McGill, Bob, 96–97, 99
McIlhargey, Jack, 65
McNab, Peter, 111–12
Meagher, Rick, 64, 106
Meighan, Ron, 206, 207
Melanson, Roland, 115, 117
Meloche, Gilles, 131, 206, 208
Merrick, Wayne, 82
Messier, Doug, 72, 73
Messier, Mark, 41, 42, 51, 59, 60, 68, 140, 153, 154, 159, 198, 238
    assists record, 275

on being a young player, 43–44
controversial goal miss, 213
controversial no-goal, 213, 216
elected to Hockey Hall of
    Fame, 274
goals scored, 30, 40, 47, 49, 50,
    64, 69, 82, 116, 122, 131,
    148, 152, 168, 169, 175,
    185, 194, 212, 220, 235, 236
and Gretzky, 202
on Hagman, 65
injuries, 132, 136
maturing of, 72
regard for Gretzky, 170–72
relationship with Gretzky,
    72–73
scores 50 goals, 268
scoring statistics, 74, 75–76,
    170
strength/playing style, 73–74
value of, 170
and WHA, 73
Mikita, Stan, 55–56
Millen, Greg, 64, 107
Miller, Bob, 195, 269, 270
Minnesota North Stars
    goal scoring abilities, 205
    success of, 129–30
Mio, Eddie, 45
Molin, Lars, 175
Moller, Randy, 89
Montreal Canadiens
    status in 1981, 161–62
    trophies won, 162
Moog, Andy, 22, 29, 39, 45, 46,
    49, 50, 54, 55, 58, 82, 90,
    102, 103, 110, 166, 207,
    212, 213, 214, 219
Moore, Dickie, 2
Morganti, Al, 37
Moss, Joey, 247
Moss, Vickie, 36
Mouton, Claude, 163
Mulvey, Paul, 69
Murphy, Larry, 41, 147
Murray, Bob, 53, 153
Murray, Troy, 56
Myers, Bob, 212, 213, 215–16
Myre, Phil, 26, 27, 74, 101, 195

Napier, Mark, 164
National Hockey League

effect on of WHA absorption,
    161
fighting in, 173–74
Neale, Harry, 32, 176, 181, 220
Neilson, Roger, 95
Neiman, Leroy, 37
Nethery, Lance, 222, 225
Newell, Dave, 185
New York Islanders
    draft Bossy, 5
    early years, 78–79
    founding of, 78
    makeup of new team, 79
    reputation of, 21
    success of, 79–80, 81
New York Rangers, success of,
    84
Nilsson, Kent, 48, 49, 50
Nykoluk, Mike, 96
Nystrom, Bob, 188

Obodiac, Stan, 217–18
Ogrodnick, John, 142
O'Reilly, Terry, 110
Orr, Bobby, 13, 101, 156, 223,
    230, 243, 247

Paiment, Wilf, 89, 97, 98
Palmateer, Mike, 95
Palmer, Brad, 206, 207
Patrick, Steve, 264
Payne, Steve, 130, 206
Pederson, Barry, 110
Peeters, Pete, 233, 236, 238, 243,
    246
penalty statistics, 111
Peplinski, Jim, 212
Perreault, Gilbert, 14
Peterson, Brent, 141
Pichette, Dave, 10
Plasse, Michel, 91
Pleau, Larry, 63, 64
Plett, Willi, 49, 201, 203, 213
Pocklington, Peter, 12, 85–86, 254
Podborski, Steve, 203
Poddubny, Walt, 24
Pollock, Sam, 44
Potvin, Denis, 80–81, 115–16,
    117–18, 157, 189, 190
Preston, Rich, 54, 153
Pronovost, Jean, 5
Propp, Brian, 232, 239

Proudfoot, Jim, 209–10
Punch Line, 2

Quebec Nordiques
    makeup of team, 89–90
    success of, 90, 168
Quenneville, Joel, 27
Quinn, Pat, 231, 238, 242, 245

Ramage, Rob, 102, 200
Rautakallio, Pekka, 59, 213
Reagan, Ronald, 258–59, 265,
    274
Reinhart, Paul, 49, 59
Resch, Glenn "Chico," 27, 74–75,
    76, 101–2, 103, 115, 194,
    195, 196
Reynolds, Burt, 266
Richard, Jacques, 91
Richard, Maurice "Rocket," 2–3,
    4, 5, 7, 8, 11, 19, 160, 223,
    224, 244–45
Riggin, Pat, 49, 59, 201, 202
Roberts, Gordie, 130
Robinson, Larry, 15, 55
Rogers, Mike, 87, 122
Rota, Darcy, 135
Rota, Randy, 179
Roulston, Tom, 86–87, 97
Ruotsalainen, Reijo, 122
Russell, Phil, 50, 203
Ruth, Babe, 1, 3–4
Rutherford, Jim, 146–47

Sabourin, Jerry, 210
Salming, Börje, 95, 96, 97, 210
Sather, Glen, 22, 25, 26, 28, 49,
    55, 56, 63, 68, 71, 98, 196
    acquiring of Finnish players, 68
    anger at B. Smith, 82–83
    becomes coach, 215
    coaching skills, 123, 139
    coaching skills/philosophy,
        32–33, 39, 154
    coaching tactics, 45, 121
    criticism of Coffey, 157
    criticism of officials, 215–16
    cure for Gretzky injury, 231
    and definition of altercation,
        212
    and disputed goals, 213
    and Fuhr, 46, 47, 70

on game with Nordiques, 169–70

goaltending decisions, 39, 45, 58, 59, 70, 90, 103, 104

on Gretzky, 138–39

on Gretzky and media, 255

and Gretzky's 50th goal, 240, 241, 242, 247

inducted into Hockey Hall of Fame, 274

on Lowe, 137

and media relations, 258

on Oilers' losses, 181

opinion of Gretzky, 88

opinion of Lumley, 133

personality, 139, 215

playing abilities, 214

praise for Fuhr, 222

preparation of team, 106

pride in Oilers, 105

regard for Canadiens, 163, 165

response to tie game with Whalers, 108

support for Oilers, 132

treats Oilers, 183

use of Lumley, 121

Sather, Glen (Slats), 44

Sauvé, Bob, 261

Savard, Denis, 53

Secord, Al, 54

Selke, Frank Jr., 2

Semenko, Dave, 26, 41, 42, 102, 110, 111, 136, 158, 173, 174, 175, 176, 178, 188, 191, 221, 226, 257

Sévigny, Richard, 164, 165

Shmyr, Paul, 64, 65

shootouts, 53

Siltanen, Risto, 30, 41, 42, 47, 68, 82, 107, 108, 147, 195, 201, 213, 233, 235

Simmer, Charlie, 5, 6–8, 9

Sinden, Harry, 214

Sittler, Darryl, 23–24, 96, 210

Skalbania, Nelson, 12

Skinner, Jimmy, 142

Smith, Billy, 81–83, 84, 114–15, 188, 189, 190–91, 196

Smith, Bobby, 129–30, 207

Smith, Doug, 40

Smith, Greg, 142

Smith, Peter, 253

Smythe, Tommy, 210

Snepsts, Harold, 178

Sonmor, Glen, 208, 209

Sports Club Comrades, 67

Staniowski, Ed, 46, 47, 158

Stapleton, Pat, 73

Šťastný, Anton, 89, 91, 168, 170

Šťastný, Marián, 89, 91, 168, 170

Šťastný, Peter, 89, 168, 169, 170

St. Louis Blues, 126

Stoughton, Blaine, 63, 106, 107, 108

Strueby, Todd, 148

Sulliman, Doug, 63

Sutter, Brian, 127

Sutter, Darryl, 53, 54, 55

Swift, E.M., 35, 36

Tambellini, Steve, 27

Tardif, Marc, 90

Taylor, Dave, 6, 143, 148, 183

Tonelli, John, 10, 82, 116, 189

Toronto Maple Leafs

makeup of team, 95–96

popularity of, 95

Torrey, Bill, 78, 79

Tremblay, Vincent, 96

Tretiak, Vladislav, 14

Triple Crown Line, 6

Trottier, Bryan, 13, 79, 116, 117, 190

Trottier, John, 10–11

Trudeau, Pierre, 15

Tuele, Bill, 252, 257

Unger, Garry, 24–27, 28, 30, 32, 41, 86, 93, 97, 116–17, 194, 222

Vail, Eric, 49

Vaive, Rick, 96, 97

Vancouver Canucks, history, 29

Van Hellemond, Andy, 215

Vernon, Mike, 49

Vezina Trophy, 162

Volcan, Mickey, 63

Watson, Bryan "Bugsy," 112

Watson, Jimmy, 243

Watt, Tom, 159

Weeks, Steve, 122, 123–24

Weir, Stan, 50, 122, 131, 142, 149

Wells, Jay, 226

Williams, Dave "Tiger," 23, 175

Wilson, Doug, 53, 54

Wilson, Ron, 46

Winnipeg Jets, early years in the NHL, 45–46

World Hockey Association, 5, 62, 73, 161

Young, Tim, 130

Ziegler, John, 252, 260, 261, 262

About the Authors

MIKE BROPHY is a veteran journalist who has covered hockey for 39 years. He began with the *Peterborough Examiner* for the first 14 years and then went on to become a senior writer with *The Hockey News*, and also writes for CBC sports and nhl.com. He has won six Ontario Newswire writing awards for his coverage of

Mike Brophy

junior hockey and his book *Curtis Joseph: The Acrobat* was awarded the Benjamin Franklin Award for best new voice. Mike and his wife, Marilyn, live in Pickering, Ontario, and have three children, Chase, Blair, and Darryl.

TODD DENAULT is a freelance author, researcher, and member of the Society for International Hockey Research. His work has been published in a number of print and online publications and he is the author of *Jacques Plante: The Man Who Changed the Face of Hockey*; *The Greatest Game: The Montreal Canadiens, the Red Army,*

Kent Denault

and the Night that Saved Hockey; and *A Season in Time: Super Mario, Killer, St. Patrick, the Great One, and the Unforgettable 1992–93 NHL Season*. Todd lives in Cobourg, Ontario.